The Complete

IDIOT'S

Guide to BUYING & UPGRADING PCs

alpha
books

A Division of Prentice Hall Computer Publishing
201 W. 103rd Street, Indianapolis, IN 46290 USA

International Standard Book Number:1-56761-274-1
Library of Congress Catalog Card Number: 93-71733

95 94   9 8 7 6 5 4 3 2

Interpretation of the printing code: the rightmost number of the first series of numbers is the year of the book's printing; the rightmost number of the second series of numbers is the number of the book's printing. For example, a printing code of 94-1 shows that the first printing of the book occurred in 1994.

Screen reproductions in this book were created by means of the program Collage Plus from Inner Media, Inc., Hollis, NH.

TRADEMARKS
All terms mentioned in this book that are known to be trademarks have been appropriately capitalized. Alpha Books cannot attest to the accuracy of this information. Use of a term in this book should not be regarded as affecting the validity of any trademark or service mark.

Printed in the United States of America

Publisher
Marie Butler-Knight

Product Development Manager
Faithe Wempen

Managing Editor
Elizabeth Keaffaber

Acquisitions Manager
Barry Pruett

Manuscript Editor
Audra Gable

Cover Designer
Scott Cook

Designer
Amy Peppler-Adams

Indexer
Jeanne Clark

Production Team
*Gary Adair, Katy Bodenmiller, Brad Chinn, Kim Cofer,
Meshell Dinn, Mark Enochs, Stephanie Gregory, Jenny Kucera,
Beth Rago, Marc Shecter, Greg Simsic, Carol Stamile*

Special thanks to Michael Hanks for ensuring the technical accuracy of this book.

Contents at a Glance

Contents

Introduction

Welcome to the ranks of computer shoppers! You're about to undertake a strange journey, fraught with perils and pitfalls. You'll hear odd terms bandied about, chock-full of numbers and abbreviations. You'll see insincere salespeople in cheap suits trying to sell you the most expensive system in the store. You'll hear horror stories from your friends about their recent mail-order experiences.

But don't fear. Armed with this book, you'll survive.

Blue-Plate Special Shoppers Crave Convenience

In general, computer-shopping folks fall into two categories. The first type of shopper considers a computer system to be a whole package. It comes with this amount of memory and that size hard drive; this monitor and that chip. These shoppers compare various systems, weigh advantages and disadvantages, and finally buy the package that fits their needs and wallets.

In a restaurant, this shopper orders the blue-plate special. These blue-plate shoppers know that the dealer has made many of the computer-buying decisions for them. They trust that the overall result will be satisfactory, like a well-balanced meal. Maybe you're the blue-plate special shopper. If buying a system already configured sounds like you, keep reading.

The software chapters in this book will help you figure out what computing tasks you'd like your new system to accomplish. Then you can communicate your needs to the dealer. Scan the hardware chapters to see the big picture.

The À la Carte Shopper

The other type of shopper takes the modular approach. This shopper considers one component—the motherboard, for instance—and mentally adds other components, only after weighing their individual merits.

The new system's hard drive capacity must complement the memory architecture; both will meld with microprocessor power. The new monitor will target specific graphics needs, which also might require a graphics accelerator board. (All of these components will be explained in their own chapters in this book!) Many, many decisions await these shoppers—as do hours of fascinating study for each component they wish to buy.

It's easy to imagine this type of shopper in a restaurant, querying the waiter for details on each menu item—then ordering several dishes, à la carte. It may take more time and trouble, but à la carte shoppers feel that the final result—a computer system designed to fit their unique requirements—is worth it. If eating à la carte is your idea of fun, this book can be your guide to putting together the best PC system for your money.

Perhaps you're buying a computer for yourself or for a business. You might decide your old system needs some refurbishing, or you may be helping someone else decide on a system. Whatever your situation, you picked up this book because you sensed you needed a guide to this perplexing process.

Buying or upgrading a computer isn't easy. But this book can diminish confusion by keeping you organized, no matter how you actually shop.

How to Use This Book

Each chapter starts with a preview of the topics to be covered in the chapters. If you're jumping around the different sections, scan the chapter summaries to help find what you're looking for. Chapters conclude with a summary of what you've learned. You can quickly scan these points to get the key ideas of the chapter.

Once you get started, you can read it from front to back, or you can choose to skip some chapters and read only what concerns you at the moment.

Here are some special icons used in this book that will help you learn just what you need:

By the Way . . .

These are special hints designed to help you get your money's worth.

Put It to Work

A bit of practice for you to perfect your new skills.

However, despite all its good intentions, this book can't help you a bit unless you crack it open and use the many tools inside. So, why delay any longer? Turn to Chapter 1 and get started.

Simple little definitions help you keep up with the jargon.

Really deep techy stuff that you can skip—unless we've really motivated you.

A quick tip on what is possibly an easier way to do something.

A bit of assistance when things hit the fan.

Part I
Look Before You Leap

So, you've decided to buy a PC. Good for you! But before you rush down to the nearest bargain outlet, you need to know what your options are. For instance, what kinds of stores sell computers, and where will you find the best deals? And why exactly do you want a computer in the first place—the kind you'll need depends on what you expect it to do. This part of the book will help you start asking yourself the right questions, so that when we start talking about the techie details later, you'll know what you want.

The Least You Need to Know

Okay, sit down and relax. This chapter's an easy one. It'll give the bare bones descriptions of the 10 most important buying and upgrading tips. Each of these topics is discussed in more detail later in the book, so relevant chapters are also indicated.

1. Where Should I Buy My Computer?

For every type of shopper there's a different type of computer store, from computer superstores to mom-and-pop operations. Mail-order computer shopping is also a popular alternative. Whether shopping at a local retail store or through a mail-order catalog, follow these guidelines:

- ☞ Make notes of all your conversations and get the names of all employees you talk to.

- ☞ Get a money-back return policy of at least 30-days, no-questions-asked.

- ☞ Get at least a one-year warranty on parts and labor, two years if possible.

- ☞ The computer seller should have accessible telephone technical support.

You can get more computer store and mail-order wisdom in Chapters 2, 3, and 4.

2. Think Before You Pay

Before you buy the hardware, think software. It's important for you to define your needs and to think of what types of software will accomplish your goals. If you only want to type simple letters and keep a Christmas card list, you don't need the biggest and best PC. If you're going into the desktop publishing business and plan to create fancy documents with elaborate graphics, better plan to spend a bit more for your needs. The more capabilities your software has, the more horsepower your PC will need.

Don't forget to plan for the future. Your software needs as a novice are likely to change as you get more sophisticated. Decide what you'll be doing with your computer in two years to accomplish your goals, and plan accordingly. Chapter 3 gives you guidance on assessing your software needs.

3. Know Your Processors!

If you're buying a PC (not a Macintosh or Commodore, etc.) you'll be evaluating the computer's capabilities based on Intel's line of microprocessors. Processors are designated by numbers such as 80286, 80386, and 80486. The higher the number, the newer and faster the processor. Intel's most recent processor ditches the number scheme. It's called the Pentium. You can think of it as a 80586.

To confuse things even further, letters are added to the numbers to indicate more (or fewer) features. You'll see combinations like 80386DX and 80386SX. Just remember DX means the chip is fully functioning; SX means it's limited. Don't get an SX anything if you can help it. They work fine, but they'll slow you down.

Processors also come in different speeds, measured in things called megahertz (MHz). The higher the megahertz number, the faster your computer will compute. If your budget is limited, get at least a 25MHz 80386DX. The better bet is a 50MHz 80486DX. For information on evaluating and upgrading processors, look ahead to Chapters 5, 6, and 22.

4. Remember the Memory Needs

Whether you're using your computer to type a term paper or to reduce the national deficit, it's RAM (Random Access Memory) chips that provide memory for the computer to store stuff while you're working. As with most computer measurements, the more RAM your computer has, the better off your computer will be.

RAM is measured in Megabytes (MB). Get a computer with at least 4MB of RAM and consider going up to 8MB. If you decide on a computer that has everything you like, but it only has 4MB of RAM, don't panic: you can add more RAM chips to increase its memory capacity. RAM chips come in 1MB and 4MB sizes (16MB sizes are becoming more popular). Make sure your computer can accept additional RAM in both 1MB and 4MB sizes. Before you buy additional RAM for your computer, consult your computer's manual to see what type of RAM chips your system accepts.

If you're buying a new computer, your RAM worries are minimal. To get more details on adding more RAM to your computer, turn to Chapters 8 and 20 for details.

5. Drive a Hard (Drive) Bargain

If RAM is where your computer stores things while you're working on them, the hard disk is where things are stored when you're not. While the contents of RAM go away when you turn your PC off, things stored on a hard drive hang around until you erase them.

You can't get away from it. It's always "how big" and "how fast." Like everything else, hard drives are judged for their size and speed. Hard drive size is measured in megabytes. A typical drive size these days is 200 megabytes—a few years back 32MB was a big deal.

A hard drive's speed or *average access time* is measured in milliseconds. Faster is better, so shoot for an average access time between 15 and 20 milliseconds.

Before buying a new or additional hard drive, make sure you know what type of hard drive controller your computer has. The manuals that came with your computer should give you the specifics you need. For more fun with hard drives, spin ahead to Chapters 11 and 21.

6. Monitor Your Monitor Situation

You can't use your computer without one, so get a good one. Your computer's video display or monitor provides a way for you and the computer to communicate. You see your work and the computer's responses to your commands on the monitor. Here are monitors in a nutshell:

Buy at least an 800 x 600 resolution, 28-dot pitch, non-interlaced Super VGA color monitor with a refresh rate of 70Hz. This monitor, along with an SVGA adapter card, can keep up with anything your software can dish out—right now and for the next few years. Make sure the monitor comes with all cables and connectors.

Tied directly to your monitor is the video interface card. It tells the monitor what to display. The best video card for your money is a 16-bit Super VGA card with at least 512KB of memory and a money-back guarantee. If you get a Super VGA, make sure the video card comes with a disk of software drivers to run your planned software—or else you'll see them in plain old VGA mode. All those letters and numbers can be confusing. Look at Chapters 12 and 13 to de-confuse yourself.

7. It Ain't Real If It Ain't on Paper

All this computing business is not too great unless you can show your work to someone else. That's where printers come in.

There are basically three kinds of printers: Dot-matrix, inkjet, and laser. Dot-matrix printers are inexpensive, but they don't produce great-looking documents. Inkjet printers cost a bit more, make better-looking printouts, and are about as fast. The top dog of printers is the laser printer. More money, more quality, more speed. For more low down on printers, turn to Chapter 16.

8. No Computer Is an Island

A *modem* is a device that enables your computer to exchange information with other computers over ordinary phone lines. If you want to talk to others in the digital world, get up-to-the-minute stock reports, or snag lots of free software, a modem's for you.

Modem speeds are measured in bits per second (bps), or how fast the computer can stuff information (programs, files, stock reports) into the phone line. Buy at least a 9,600 bps modem. The 2,400 bps modems will be cheaper, but they're too slow by today's standards. For more on modems, run, don't walk, to Chapter 17.

9. Bam! Pow! It's Multimedia

Multimedia means many media, like sound, video, and animation. Multimedia is also one of the latest and greatest things you can do with your computer. Rather than reading boring text about how an internal combustion engine works, wouldn't it be better to see it operate, hear it, and read about it—all on your computer? That's what multimedia can do. Readying your PC for the multimedia is possible, but it requires several upgrades. For a full multimedia setup you'll need a sound card, a CD-ROM drive, and an SVGA card with at least a VGA monitor. Multimedia madness prevails in Chapter 24.

10. Yes, You Can Do It Yourself

You are not afraid. You can do this. How's that for encouragement? If you're gonna upgrade your computer, remember these things:

- ☞ Back up any data (you've already done that the night before, right?).
- ☞ Turn off and unplug your computer.
- ☞ Turn off and unplug all peripherals connected to your computer.
- ☞ Read the manuals—whether you like it or not.
- ☞ Ground yourself (touch something metal other than your computer) before working with any computer components.
- ☞ Open the computer's case and perform the upgrade. If it doesn't fit, don't force it.
- ☞ Test the PC to ensure that the upgrade "took."

Too quick for ya? Check out Chapter 29 for the slow version.

No, this is not a printing error. The page truly is blank.

Chapter 1
Computer Stores in Store for You

In This Chapter

- ☛ The right and wrong way to buy a computer
- ☛ How computer stores differ
- ☛ Choose your software first
- ☛ Find the best computer to run your software

Maybe you have not yet experienced the pleasure of walking into a computer store. Or maybe one day you accidentally found yourself inside one—and scrammed out of there as fast as your high-tops could take you.

This chapter documents the fate of Bob Bungle—a guy who thought he could walk right into a computer store and buy a PC without doing any research whatsoever. (You can cover your eyes during the scary parts.)

In the next chapter, things get even hairier for Bernice, Bob's sister. She's living proof that mail-order buying with no advance preparation poses just as many pitfalls to the unwary. (She lived to tell about it.)

How *Not* to Enter a Computer Store

"You know, it's really time the Bungle family entered the Computer Age," Bob Bungle announced one Saturday morning. He glanced around the breakfast table for his family's reaction.

"Huh?" replied Penny, his wife. "Pass the Pop Tarts. Besides, we don't have anywhere to put a computer." Penny looked straight at Bob. "And don't even think about taking my woodworking room," she warned, referring to the corner of the den filled with refinishing projects.

"But, Dad, what do we need a computer for, anyway?" puzzled Marsha, age 11. Marsha's idea of fun was a romp through the nearby vacant fields with Hugo, the family spaniel, hunting down new beetles for her insect collection.

"Neat! Now I can have the gang over for Arkanoid," cheered Steve. The 13-year-old was a regular at the neighborhood arcade. "Think of all the quarters I can save," he crowed.

Despite the lukewarm response from everybody but Steve (and presumably Hugo, who was too busy nuzzling the empty Pop Tarts box to fully attend to the conversation), Bob Bungle was set on buying a computer. "Never put off 'til tomorrow what you can do today" was his motto.

If only he knew of a good computer store, Bob mused, as he slopped milk on his Nutty Loops. Suddenly a name popped into his brain—Mark! Mark from work would know. Not only did Mark own a home PC, but he'd mastered it to the point that folks at work turned to him with their computer questions. Bob resolved to phone his buddy Mark pronto.

"Mark, Bob Bungle here," Bob boomed into the phone. "Say, it's time the old Bungle family took the PC plunge. Where'd you buy your computer?" Bob lost no time getting to the point.

"Uh, hi, Bob," Mark replied cautiously. Mark could sense that Bob was in another one of his slapdash moods, which usually meant trouble for all concerned. "Sure, Bob. I can tell you where I bought my system," he began. "But you still need to research the best buy based on what you're going to do with your computer. Then you've got to do some comparison shopping."

"All that's for wimps," scoffed Bob. "Just tell me what store to hit, and I'll be back setting up my new system by afternoon."

"Have you thought of where you're going to put it?" Mark queried. "Remember, to be fully used by your whole family, the computer nook needs the right lighting, a degree of privacy, and a measure of accessibility . . ."

"Oh, who cares about all that stuff!" Bob huffed, interrupting his friend. "Look, I'll talk to you later. Right now, I'm going shopping, even if I have to run over to the first place I see in today's paper." Bob hung up.

Grabbing the newspaper's business section, Bob Bungle spotted an ad for a nearby computer store. As he scanned for the store's address, he noticed the ad was packed with numbers and unfamiliar terms; it looked as if it were written in a foreign language. He buried the thought and headed for his car.

"Besides, I know a thing or two about computers from using one at work," Bob told himself reassuringly.

You Are Here

Bob Bungle circled the crowded parking lot for the second time. After fighting the urge to abandon his car on the sidewalk in front, he finally found a parking spot and dashed through the bustling doors of Can-Do Computers.

As he stood in the doorway, slack-jawed at the sheer number of electronic doodads piled up everywhere, it occurred to Bob that he had no clue what half the gizmos did. Staring as if he'd landed on a distant planet, Bob made his way down the packed aisles. Everywhere, small groups of shoppers conversed convincingly about the doodads, asking well-timed and intelligent-sounding questions of the sales staff. The only words he recognized were names of numerals . . . so Bob vowed to keep a low profile for a while and "just look."

Studied Chaos

He meandered up and down the store's aisles, all the while feeling that the sales staff were watching him from behind the inventory piled in all those cardboard boxes everywhere. (Could the blank look on his face have anything to do with the fact that no one seemed eager to help him?)

Bob decided it must be his knowledgeable appearance that kept salespeople from approaching. "Boy, this buying a computer stuff is easy!" he chortled to himself. But soon enough, the novelty wore off. After another hour of aimless wandering—reading labels and staring at gadgets—Bob lost interest. He decided to search for a computer store with a personal touch.

Ahem. Do You Have an Appointment?

The salesman watched as Bob padded across the plush carpeting of Larchmont & Ritz Computers, Esq.. Some fancy place, Bob thought, as he picked up a laptop and shook it.

"That's no Etch-a-Sketch, sir," glared the lone salesman. "Is there something we can help you with today? Hmmmm?"

"Yeah, uh, Yes. I guess I'm here to buy a computer," Bob stammered.

"Well, fill out this form, precisely stating your software's requirements, the peripherals you need, and your budgetary limitations, if you *have* any," the salesman intoned disdainfully, handing Bob a thick sheaf of papers, "and we'll make an appointment for, say, three weeks from today?"

Bob took the papers and, after a minute of examination, discovered he didn't understand one word. A prickly feeling started up his neck.

"I, I'll fill these out at home," said Bob, bounding for the door. He gave one sheepish glance backward as he opened the door, just in time to see the salesman roll his eyes.

The Aisle of the Swirling Monitors

Bob felt a surge of relief as he pulled into the now-familiar Can-Do Computers parking lot. Once inside he found himself drawn toward the bright displays flashing on a bank of computer screens.

Ah, here's something I can relate to, Bob thought. These light shows are cool. Neat! That all-black PC's saying something, almost like a TV commercial. . . . A host of images and colors soothed that uncomfortable, unprepared feeling that had plagued Bob all day.

Do They Always Talk in Numbers?

Heads up, Bob told himself as a saleswoman approached.

"I see you've found our top display," she started. "It's a 21 incher running SVGA with 2 meg of VRAM; at 1,280 by 1024 with 256 colors, refresh rates of 72 hertz, and multisync, it's state-of-the-art. The one next to it offers just as much plus an 8514 card for the low, low price of only $999."

Bob had never heard anyone in this country speak that rapidly. Then again, maybe talking fast is easy when it's all numbers. As the saleswoman blazed on, Bob looked down at his shoes. That seemed to slow her down a bit. Then she paused. He made the fatal mistake of looking her in the eyes and nodding, which set her off again, at probably double her previous rate of speech.

Uh, I'll Take That One There

Suddenly Bob hit on a brilliant idea. If he took the top-of-the-line model, the saleswoman would think he knew what he was doing. Bob and the saleswoman darted around the store, she firing descriptions at him and he motioning her to drop the items in his cart.

Home Sweet Home

Back home, with all the PC's boxes unloaded and piled up in the middle of the living room, Bob saw with mounting frustration that he might need Mark's help after all, at least to assemble the system, if not to explain what the darn thing did. If only Bob could think of a place to put it . . .

And Now, the Right Way to Buy a Computer

Despite the warning signs every step of the way, Bob Bungle went about his computer purchase all backwards. Sure, he saved a few minutes of soul-searching and the trouble of doing some research, but he spent tons of money, he still doesn't really know why he wants a computer, and he certainly doesn't know what to do with what he bought.

Determine What You Want the Computer to Do

First, the Bungle family should have brainstormed ways they could use a new computer. A computer runs programs, often called *software*. Well, software exists for almost any purpose imaginable.

With the right software, Penny could have designed woodworking projects and kept records of materials, costs, and new sources. Beetle-fan Marsha could have catalogued her entire insect collection on the family PC.

We already know that Steve welcomed the chance to play video games on a home computer, but a little discussion could have sparked even better ways Steve could put one to use. Word processing software could help both kids complete homework assignments. And even Bob Bungle might have found a valid reason to own a computer—perhaps to organize his slapdash ways with a personal information manager software program!

Find the Software That Does the Job

Once the Bungles determined what they needed the computer to do, they should have found software that accomplished these goals. They could even see how they liked the software by trying it out at computer stores, computer user groups, or perhaps, Mark's house.

Find the Best Hardware to Run the Software

Software packages list, right on the side of the box, what computer equipment, or *hardware*, they need in order to work properly. Once the Bungles decided on software they liked, one look at the box would have told them what type of hardware they should consider.

Next, the family could have visited computer stores, comparing features and weighing performance against cost. After factoring in support and warranties, the Bungles could, with confidence, buy the Bungle-perfect system.

You don't have to be a computer greenhorn like Mr. Bungle. Armed with the sage advice this book offers, you'll undergo an enriching, enjoyable computer shopping experience.

Sizing Up a Computer Store

For every type of shopper there's a different type of computer store—each with its pros and cons. Use this section to evaluate the stores you encounter.

National Retail Chains

With names like Businessland and Computerland, and locations throughout the United States, national chains compete heavily for your computer dollar. They carry name-brand, nationally recognized PCs, sometimes referred to as *IBM compatibles*.

Negotiate the price at these stores, and don't be afraid to use written quotes from other dealers as leverage. If they are reluctant to come down in price, try to get them to throw in some software and accessories to sweeten the deal.

Investigate on-site repair facilities, 30-day money-back guarantees, after-sales support, and warranties (often used to jack up prices). Shopping for a PC you saw in an ad? Be sure to specify each component you want, to guarantee it's an identical system.

Local Clone Sellers

A *clone PC* is compatible with the IBM/PC standard, yet has a lesser-known or unknown brand name. Local clone dealers may have one or two stores in a city, or in a region. Their PCs are assembled on-site from inexpensive or commodity components. The result? Low prices and, usually, fairly decent systems. To keep inventory down and cash flow up, local clone dealers may build a system only after you order it.

In general, it's good to shop dealers as carefully as you shop PCs. Check any store's reputation with the local Better Business Bureau, local user groups, and computer societies.

A little research and homework into why systems and components differ will pay off if you decide to buy a computer this way.

Local clone dealerships should offer dealer-supported, one-year parts and labor warranties; on-site service; and after-sales support. Some might even offer "free" classes. (*Nothing* is *free*.)

Bob's Basement Bargains

Individuals who build custom-configured, "homebrewed" systems will make you a system to order. Locate these "brewers" through user groups, local computer publications, and computer fairs. In general, it's best to leave this buyer channel to those shoppers who know what they want—and how to tell whether they got it.

Because my philosophy is to teach you enough in this book so that you can shop even from a brewer, some guidelines apply if you choose this route:

☛ First, read every chapter in this book and visit computer stores to examine components. Get a price quote in writing. Make sure this price beats local clone dealerships and mail-order vendors. Ask about on-site service. Look inside the PC's case. Get each component brand, speed, capacity, and so on, in writing.

☛ Make sure the brewer services the warranty, and negotiate for a two-year parts and labor warranty. When the system's ready, ask the brewer to sit down with you and run a diagnostic software program like Norton's System Information program. Diagnostic programs examine a PC and list its specific parts, speed, and so on, right on the screen.

Computer Superstores

High-volume sales ensure low prices. Still, it's worth a try to negotiate a price reduction on the brand-name PCs these huge national chains typically stock. Selection is great here—especially on extras like books and cables.

Membership Warehouse Stores

Stores such as Price Club or Office Club may not offer as wide a selection as stores dedicated only to selling computers, but there are some advantages. Prices are among the lowest anywhere, and these stores carry nationally recognized brands. Some Price Club stores offer Tech Centers where trained staff help you select a system. Salespeople staffing warehouse stores' electronics departments might not be knowledgeable on the very latest products, although stores differ widely. Ask for details on the type of support a membership warehouse offers.

The Appliance Store

Selection can be sparse in an appliance store. Besides, will you be buying a computer from someone who sells vacuum cleaners for a living? Just who will repair the computer if it breaks down?

The University Bookstore's Computer Corner

Courteous and knowledgeable salespeople who take time to listen to your needs count here. If you're a student, find out what discounts you can negotiate (these can be sizable). Name-brand systems are the rule. Check for details on repair, warranty, and support.

The Least You Need to Know

The misadventures of Bob Bungle showed you how *not* to buy a computer. Buying one the right way is easy if you follow these steps:

1. Decide what you need a computer for.

2. Find the software to accomplish those tasks.

3. Track down a software package you like, and see what type of hardware it needs to run best.

4. Price and compare similar hardware components and PC systems, as well as warranties, support, free classes, and so on.

5. Buy the best PC system you can afford.

Chapter 2
Mail-Order Shopping for a Computer

In This Chapter

- ☛ The right and wrong ways to buy mail-order
- ☛ Selecting a reputable mail-order house
- ☛ Using a credit card to protect your purchase
- ☛ Comparing warranty and repair services

Chapter 1 showed you how to (and how not to) shop in computer stores. In this chapter, you'll learn about another way to shop that's far from foolproof.

Mail-Order Maladroit

Bernice Bungle put down the letter from her brother, Bob. Sheesh! What a mess he'd gotten himself into when he bought a personal computer! She almost laughed out loud when she thought of all the times Bob's hasty, slapdash nature had gotten him into hot water as a kid.

Bernice wanted a PC, too—something to help her run her small retail outlet, Bernice's Beauty Barn. She knew that her rival across town, Eunice Euler, used a computer at her place, Eunice's Elegance Emporium. Hah, the nerve! Bernice bristled. (The very name *Eunice* sent Bernice into fits.)

To be sure, Bernice wasn't quite clear about what her competitor *did* with the machine. No matter. Bernice wasn't about to watch Eunice and her high-tech contraption corner the beauty-supplies market in their town.

Why Not Buy Mail-Order?

Bernice decided that buying a computer through mail-order was the way to go. Rather, Cousin Louie decided for her. Years ago, Louie bought his computer through the mail, and he never let anyone forget what a great deal he got. If mail-order computers were good enough for Louie, they were good enough for Bernice, she reasoned.

Just Look at That One!

Dragging a stack of computer magazines home one afternoon, Bernice could hardly contain her excitement. Everything looked so good. Once in a while, she'd come across articles offering advice on how to buy a particular component, but they looked too dull.

Bernice decided to skip the articles, opting instead to look at the pictures in the ads. Besides, who has time to read these days? There she'd be, holed up reading computer articles, and meanwhile, Eunice would be grabbing up all her hard-won business.

Just then, Bernice Bungle landed on a page that really caught her eye. That's the computer for me!, Bernice told herself—and it's a real bargain to boot. She dialed the ad's phone number, credit card in hand.

A pleasant salesman answered the phone. After a short talk (with him doing all the talking), Bernice headed over to her bank to get a cashier's check. The nice young man on the phone said that was the best way to pay for her new computer system—the one that would really put Eunice in a snit.

"For Technical Support, Please Hold . . . "

It's probably just a minor glitch, Bernice thought, as she navigated the computer company's voice mail. She'd had her computer only three weeks—a week and a half just getting the neighbor kid to set it up—and already it didn't work right.

Funny how I didn't have to hold this long when I called to order the darn thing, Bernice fumed under her breath. The recorded voice droned on about which extensions to press.

After two days of fruitless phoning, Bernice fired off a complaint letter. A week later, the mailbox held a familiar looking envelope, marked "No Forwarding Address."

And Now, the Right Way to Buy Mail-Order

Bernice Bungle ended up with a fancy doorstop and (hopefully) a lesson learned. It didn't have to be that way.

If only Bernice had thought a little about what she needed the computer to do, she could have researched software, compared hardware, and phoned a few vendors to assess their reliability, purchase policy, and support.

Poor Bernice. At least she and brother Bob will have something to talk about at family reunions.

Reputation Comes First

Hunt down local computer groups, often called *user groups,* and attend one of their meetings. Ask members to relate all mail-order experiences, good and bad. Take notes.

Call the mail-order vendors that interest you, and ask how long they've been in business. Have them send you a brochure or price list with their sales and support policies in writing.

> ## By the Way . . .
> You might try calling the vendors and asking outright for (recent) customer references. This may seem outlandishly bold. On the other hand, computer vendors are a competitive breed, and they want your business.

Courtesy Pays

Call a few vendors and discuss the system you have in mind. Use these preliminary conversations to assess the sales staff for important qualities such as knowledgeability, friendliness, willingness to take time for you, and skill in communicating. These qualities will blow up to gargantuan proportions once you buy a system.

Sales and Service, Warranties and Repairs

Accept nothing less than a 30-day, unquestioned, money-back guarantee. That means that if you don't like the computer for any reason, you can return it.

Many mail-order dealers charge a *restocking fee* for returned merchandise. Don't agree to such a fee, especially if you return the PC in new condition. And find out who pays shipping costs. You shouldn't—even for returns.

Will the service department be easy to reach? You can test this. Ask the salesperson for the toll-free technical support number, and then call it and see how long you have to wait before you are connected to a real human.

What's their repair policy? If an electrical component is going to fail, it's usually within the first 30 days. Insist on a one-year parts-and-labor warranty, at least. Some vendors offer two-year warranties, although the extended version might include either parts or labor—usually not both. Try to negotiate a two-year parts-and-labor warranty when you're dealing.

Ask who will honor the warranty. Make sure it's the dealer—not the manufacturer. Typical PC systems contain components made by many different manufacturers—a monitor from one, a hard disk drive from another. Imagine having to keep track of phone numbers, addresses, shipping records, and technical support for each one!

If you find a problem with your new system, whose dime do you spend to call technical support? Make sure tech support keeps accessible hours, preferably some periods on weekends or during evenings. Obtain a toll-free number.

Make sure the mail-order company has on-site repair facilities—that's where the repair person comes right to your house. You don't want your PC enduring any more shipping than is absolutely necessary. And insist on reasonable turnaround time on repairs.

Ask About Bulletin-Board Support

Perhaps the mail-order company offers customer support on a computer *bulletin board system*, often called a *BBS*. If so, the company runs special *bulletin board* software on a dedicated computer that's connected at all times to a phone line. Computer bulletin boards give a company an easy way to distribute information, helpful programs, and news to customers.

Here's how it works, in brief. (For detailed information about bulletin boards and other computer communications, check out Chapter 17.) You dial the phone number of the bulletin board computer using a special device known as a *modem*, which connects to your computer and to an ordinary phone line. Give two computers a modem each and they can talk to each other. The modems break down the computers' digital instructions into signals that can travel over phone lines, and then they put the signals back into computer-readable shape at the other end.

Your computer can connect to the bulletin board computer anytime it's receiving calls, no matter how distant the mail-order company's location. Once you're connected, you can navigate the company's bulletin board computer as if it were your own. You can dig up special software and read customer comments and informational bulletins. You can even *download* (bring into your own computer) utility software that the manufacturer wrote to make your computer run better.

Merchandise Ready to Ship

When ordering a computer through the mail, nail down a firm ship date. Make sure the merchandise is ready to ship soon after you place your order. If a company is seriously backlogged with its orders, chances are good that they're going to get careless when assembling your system.

Pay with a Credit Card

At some point in the shopping process, you may be offered a discount if you pay cash. Don't do it. Buying with a credit card means your bank card company will back you up in case of a dispute or, worse, a no-show. Credit card purchases guarantee many other consumer rights. Check with your credit card bank to see just what you're getting for that annual fee you pay for your credit card.

Make sure the vendor charges your account only after the system is actually shipped. Determine how billing takes place in advance so there won't be any surprises.

Refuse to Pay Extra for Credit Card Purchases

Some mail-order houses try to tack on an extra fee for credit card purchases, typically 3 to 7 percent. If this happens to you, report it immediately to your credit card company. Depending on what card you use, you may not have to pay the surcharge. American Express is one company that allows surcharges. Most don't. Check with your bank card for their policy.

The Least You Need to Know

Mail-order shopping can be a convenient cost cutter, but only if you check out the seller in advance and get the facts straight while you're buying. When shopping mail-order, follow these guidelines:

- ☞ Make notes of all telephone conversations, and be sure to get the names and extensions of all employees you talk to.

- ☞ Pay by credit card, if at all possible. You'll be protected with the consumer coverage many cards provide (check with your company before you assume any coverage).

- ☞ Get a money-back return policy of at least 30-days, no-questions-asked.

- ☞ No restocking fee should be charged if you choose to return the PC.

- ☞ Do not allow them to charge you a fee for paying by credit card.

- ☞ Your credit card should be debited when the order ships, not before.

- ☞ Get at least a one-year warranty on parts and labor, two years if possible.

- ☞ The mail-order house should have accessible telephone tech-support.

This page unintentionally left blank.

Chapter 3

What Do You Want to Do with Your Computer?

In This Chapter

- ☛ Why you should choose your software before buying a computer
- ☛ How to assess your software needs
- ☛ Possible software scenarios you may encounter

Bob and Bernice "bungled" their computer purchases by not taking the right steps. That won't happen to you. You're about to take the first step in buying a computer right now—thinking about the types of software you'll want to use on your new PC.

First, you'll list all the tasks you want your PC to help you accomplish. Then you'll read about six typical PC situations. You'll see the tasks these PC owners do each day. You'll learn the types of software they use, and you'll see why each user has chosen a particular PC to run that software.

By the time you leave this chapter, you'll have an idea of how you might use a PC. You may want to hang around for Chapter 4, where you'll find details on the different kinds of software, as well as what PCs run each software type best.

Sit Down, Take Your Shoes Off . . .

Find an easy chair and relax with a cool beverage. Grab a pen and some paper. This step doesn't involve driving anywhere or looking at complex equipment. Instead, sit back, breathe deeply a few times, and focus on you—and the tasks *you* need to accomplish.

Many computer shoppers get the wrong computers because they neglected one basic rule: **The only reason to buy computer hardware is to run software.** That's because it's software that actually performs the tasks. Without the instructions contained in software, computers would qualify for the paperweight-of-the-month club, and little more.

Right now, don't worry about software, or anything else. Just list whatever tasks come to mind when you think of being productive with your new computer.

Now it's time to don your wizard's cap and grab your crystal ball. What do you see yourself accomplishing with your computer two years from now? Find your pencil (first put down the crystal ball) and jot down as many ideas as you can.

Okay. Enough predictions for now. We'll use your task list throughout this book, so make sure the dog doesn't eat it. (The list, not the book. Well, actually both.)

What's Software and Why Is It So Important?

Software is the cushion between you and the nuts-and-bolts machinery. It's the "personal" in personal computer. The only way to get a computer to do something is to load it with purchased, prepackaged software. Software contains all the instructions to make a computer accomplish a particular task, such as printing a memo or playing a game.

Software Is Like Music

People use lots of comparisons when they try to explain software. Perhaps the most useful one likens software to the audio cassette or CD you load into your stereo system to play music. A music publisher records an artist's music onto the cassette's magnetic tape and sells it in a music store. Well, a software publisher records a computer application onto a form of magnetic media known as a *diskette* and sells it in a software store.

A music lover buys a stereo system knowing it will play many different kinds of music: country, jazz, classical, and even Weird Al. Likewise, someone who buys a PC from the IBM-compatible family can look forward to "playing" hundreds of types of software: games, word processors, and even garden-design programs.

> ## By the Way . . .
> Of course, a hard-core Weird Al fan might choose to listen to nothing else on his stereo; just as a dedicated doodler might use only a drawing program on her PC. These people are generally avoided at company picnics. . . .

The similarities extend all the way to legal issues. When someone buys a tape, dubs it, and gives a copy to a friend, that person is breaking the music publisher's copyright and depriving the artist of royalties. When a person buys a software program and copies it onto diskettes for a friend, that person is breaking the same basic laws.

Why Can't I Just Buy My Software After I Get My Computer, Like Everyone Else?

Not all software packages are created equal. PCs differ, too. Hoggish, complex programs strain even the biggest machine's capabilities, while other more elegant programs hardly consume any computer resources.

Big or small, each software program has certain minimum hardware requirements that it needs to run properly. Since these requirements are listed on the software's box, if you know what software you want to use, you'll know the minimum-strength PC to buy.

The kinds of software you'll load onto your new computer determine whether you need a color monitor, how much hard disk space you need, how fast the computer runs, how much expansion room you'll need, and even the type of printer you should buy.

Six System Scenarios

The following situations describe different, typical PC user scenarios. You may find your needs overlapping into two or more of these examples. Even better. Just don't forget to jot down all the other tasks you find to do on your new computer. (For more details on the software mentioned in the examples, scurry over to Chapter 4.)

I Want to Bring Work Home from the Office

Ed's an accountant. At work, he runs a spreadsheet program that calculates his company's financial status. Since large spreadsheets tax the average computer with heavy numeric calculations, Ed uses a fast 486 computer. Ed bought a similar PC for home, where he's running a purchased copy of his spreadsheet software.

The software runs under a program called Microsoft Windows, so Ed bought a copy of that, too. The Windows program works by letting users point at pictures (*icons*) on the screen, instead of typing commands with a keyboard. The pointing device, known as a *mouse* (Chapter 15), eases spreadsheet work on Ed's home computer setup.

Ed may want to buy a *modem* that works with communications software to send computer data over the phone line to another computer. This way he could *telecommute*, sending completed work to his office computer without leaving his den.

We Need a Family Computer for Writing, Using Educational Programs, and Organizing Stuff

Specialized database software helps the Trujillos keep track of their huge record collection, as well as their prized recipes. They use a low-priced word processor to write letters to Grandma. The kids enjoy playing math arcade games that boost their test scores while improving hand/eye coordination.

One of the most useful additions to the family's software arsenal was an inexpensive home printing program called The Print Shop. It's designed to be easy for kids to use, but they all find themselves creating simple greeting cards, stationery, banners, and invitations with this program and their inexpensive, 9-pin dot-matrix printer.

The family is interested in an *on-line service* they've seen advertised, called Prodigy. Prodigy, and services like it, enable families to meet and to share interests with other families, via modem, across the nation. The Trujillos will need a modem to use Prodigy; they'll also pay a monthly fee of about $15. If they do buy a modem, they're planning to investigate a software program called CheckFree, which will let them pay their bills electronically.

The family manages with a 386 computer equipped with an 80 megabyte hard disk to store programs on, a VGA color monitor, and an inexpensive dot-matrix printer that can print nice-looking letters.

I'm a College Student and Need a Computer for Schoolwork

Whatever major Mary chooses, she figures she'll always have a term paper due. Unfortunately, Mary is short on cash, and can't spend a lot on a fancy computer. She bought a word processing program, and she uses a personal finance program to keep track of tuition hikes. She's thinking of hooking up her black-and-white monitor and low-cost 386 PC with a modem to run communications software. That way she can grab term-paper fodder from research databases, and even access the library's card catalog.

Because a modem works with the ordinary phone line in her off-campus apartment, Mary must choose her modeming sessions carefully so she won't tie up the phone when her roommates need to use it.

A Computer Could Help Us with Our Small Business

Writing business letters and invoices, spitting out mailing labels and memos: the high-end word processing software works almost as hard as Carl and Susan to keep their small business afloat.

The partners use an *integrated* software package to cover their other computing needs. Integrated software offers several different modules rolled into one low-cost package. It runs great on their low-priced 486 computer. Carl and Susan use its spreadsheet for finances, its database for client records, and the communications module with their modem to converse with other users on small-business-oriented computer bulletin boards.

By the Way . . .

Small businesses should buy a larger system than they need, or an upgradable system, in case the business expands. Never fear success!

I'm a Graphics Designer and I Want to Do Desktop Publishing

Leah and Kay run a custom publishing business that provides graphic design and layout services for their clients. Their complex desktop publishing software demands a fast 486 computer with the capacity to store lots of software and data, plus a mouse to highlight text and manipulate page design. They might also consider a PC based on Intel's new Pentium processor—they'll pay more but they'll get the speed they need.

A large, two-page display monitor with excellent resolution helps, too. A sharp laser printer helps them design effective layouts. A device called a *scanner* lets them transform ordinary photographic slides into computer graphics, ready to be inserted into documents.

They use a modem, too, to send files to service bureaus for processing. All of their programs run under the graphic user software Microsoft Windows. They also use a contact-management software program that helps them prospect for new clients.

Our Whole Family's Addicted to Computer Games— We Need One with the Works!

The entire Chou family enjoys sessions with their state-of-the-art computer golf game. Arcade games attract the more agile family members, and adventure games with movie-quality color and sound are popular, too. That's why they invested in a powerful 486DX PC with a large hard disk.

They bought an oversized color monitor and a video card capable of showing hundreds of colors at once. A sound card and stereo speakers add realism by letting them hear the many digitized voices, musical scores, and sound effects incorporated into today's games. Their computer is equipped with a joystick, similar to the controller in an arcade game, that lets them dodge spacecraft and blast the bad guys without using the clunky keyboard.

The Chous recently bought an electronic music keyboard that attaches to their PC. They use it with their sound card and music-composing software to write their own songs. What fun! Next on the family's list is animation software that will let them create and play back their own movies.

By the Way . . .

Believe it or not, a music program has bragging rights to being the first *monitor* on the very first personal computer.

The computer, the Altair 8800, also discussed in Chapter 5, came in one of those kits that electronics enthusiasts were always building (back in the days before they all became computer nerds). The trouble was, it had no keyboard, and certainly no mouse. The only way you could get information into the thing was by force-feeding arcane commands by way of tiny switches along the machine's front.

Worse yet, the Altair had no monitor, or even a speaker. The only way you could get information out of the thing was to read bizarre code in the base 8 number system off a tiny, flashing LED light. Then you had to translate that into decimal, or base 10, numbers!

continues

continued

All this changed the day a guy left his radio on while working with his Altair one night. He was surprised to hear the radio wail after he'd pushed the computer's run button. One more try yielded the same, baffling results. It seems that the radio frequency interference resulted from the bits switching around inside the Altair.

A light came on in the guy's head. If he sat down with his electric guitar and mapped out all the sounds, he could figure out the computer memory locations of all the notes and write a music program. At the next meeting of the Homebrew Computer Club, the proud Altair owner set his computer down and set it up to sputter the notes to "Fool on the Hill." The crowd cheered: the tinny little tune confirmed their dreams of a home computer that could do something.

`The Least You Need to Know

This chapter shows that your computer choice is based on an assessment of your computing situation, and that the only reason to buy a computer is to run software. Keep the following in mind when deciding your software needs and wants:

- ☛ Software gives instructions that tell the computer to perform a particular task.

- ☛ It's important for you to define your needs and to think of what types of software will accomplish your goals.

- ☛ Decide what you'll be doing with your computer in two years to accomplish your goals.

Chapter 4
To Run This Software

In This Chapter

- ☛ What an operating system is and what it does
- ☛ How DOS controls your computer
- ☛ What PC you need to run Microsoft Windows
- ☛ Other operating systems
- ☛ Ideal computer systems for various software packages
- ☛ Shareware programs ease the strain on your software budget

The first part of this book showed how crucial it is to take the right steps when buying a PC. In the last chapter, you saw why choosing software is the first step. Then you thought about possible software program types for your own computing situation.

Let's learn more about the various software packages: what they can do for you and what PC systems run them best.

First, the Operating System

Software differs greatly from one package to the next. Some programs are deadeye straight and serious. Others are whimsical and madcap. Because they vary, programs can't be installed directly onto a computer. The computer hardware could never anticipate the many diverse, often quirky, ways each program chooses to talk to the rest of the PC.

Instead, software communicates with a special type of middleman software called an *operating system*, which then communicates to the PC. The operating system (often shortened to *OS* and pronounced *oh-ess*) provides a way to organize files, to copy data to and from diskettes, and to perform other housekeeping tasks.

MS-DOS (pronounced *em-ess-dawss* and often seen as just *DOS*) is the name of the operating system that runs on most PCs. It stands for Microsoft DOS, one brand that's available.

What If I Don't Want DOS?

No fair! You don't even get to choose it, like you do the other types of software. When you buy an IBM-compatible computer, the dealer generally sets up DOS on your computer. Unless, of course, it's a Macintosh computer, in which case this book won't help you.

By the Way...

If you buy one of IBM's PS/2 line of computers, you'll get an operating system called OS/2. OS/2 is in many ways the same as DOS and in many ways similar to Windows (which you'll learn about next.) Whether you're computer has DOS or OS/2, the guidance in this book should help you choose the right computer for your needs.

So, there MS-DOS sits on your PC's hardware, like the first layer of a chocolate cake sitting on a platter. When you install and run a "real" software package, it runs right on top of DOS. This software is the cake's second layer. (Yum.) When you finish using your software program and tell it you're ready to quit—Boom, Thud—you're back to the bottom layer, DOS.

Make sure you've purchased a licensed copy of DOS and you get the full set of user's manuals. Otherwise you won't be able to look up what's wrong when you encounter an error or problem.

Once you're face-to-face with DOS (alone in a cheap hotel room, with only the blinking Eat at Joe's sign outside to relieve the oppressive darkness), you'll see why DOS is legendary for being difficult. In DOS, you type cryptic, short commands that hardly ever spell real words. Worse yet, you have to memorize these blurtings. That's why another layer for the cake was invented: *Microsoft Windows*.

What Does Windows Need (and How Come It Needs So Much)?

Microsoft Windows isn't an operating system, technically, because it still needs MS-DOS to run underneath it. It's called an operating *environment*. It runs in a layer between DOS and the application program, making the Windows cake a three-layer extravaganza (Mmmm).

If you choose to run it, Windows does away with the complex, heartless DOS prompt by stepping in between DOS and you, the user. Windows lets you get things done by pointing to pictures (icons) with a mouse, instead of typing cryptic commands. Because it has pictures and it's an interface between you and DOS, Windows is known as a *GUI* (pronounced *gooey*), or *graphical user interface*. The figure on the next page shows several aspects of the Windows interface.

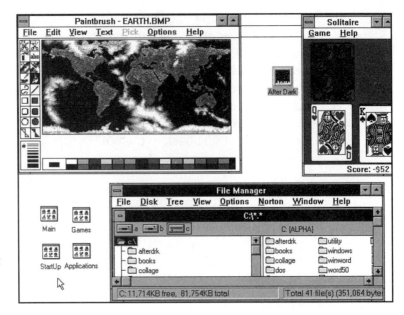

Microsoft Windows lets you run programs in friendly, easy-to-use window panes.

Graphical User Interface, or GUI (pronounced gooey), is a type of program that uses a mouse (a computer mouse, that is) and graphic images to make it easier for you to tell the computer what to do. Your files, documents, and other works are represented by small pictures, called icons. You open, move, and copy your files by moving and manipulating the icons. There are tons of other advantages to using a GUI, but we won't get into that right now.

If Windows Makes Computing So Easy, Why Doesn't Everybody Use It?

Partly because it works with pictures instead of text commands, Windows and Windows-compatible software programs are generally large and quite demanding on a PC's hardware. Expect to pay more for your computer, monitor, and hard disk (even your printer, if you do it right) if you choose to run Windows the way it should be run. You'll be satisfied with the performance of a fast 486 PC running Windows. If you decide to go with the less expensive 386 processor, you might find yourself wishing for more speed. Check out Chapter 6 for the details on all these numbers and speed issues.

Why Aren't There Other Operating Systems?

Plenty of other operating systems vie with each other for designation as the bottom layer of choice. UNIX, OS/2, and DR-DOS are some other IBM PC-compatible operating systems.

Whatever operating system you run, your software programs must be compatible with that operating system. While you're looking at software, you might see a package that looks interesting, but it turns out to be *Macintosh-compatible*. That means it runs under the Macintosh operating system (which runs on a different type of personal computer), and you can't run it on your MS-DOS PC.

Here's another example. In the unlikely case that you wanted to run UNIX on your PC, and you liked the WordPerfect word processor, you'd need to buy WordPerfect for UNIX. (The DOS version of WordPerfect wouldn't find the bottom layer it was expecting, and it would sulk and refuse to operate.)

MS-DOS was the original operating system for IBM PCs and PC-compatibles. (*DOS* stands for Disk Operating System, by the way.) It's deeply entrenched in the PC marketplace, because most of the software for PCs is MS-DOS-compatible. And it's the one you'll probably start with (even stay with).

Ideal Computer Systems for . . .

Here comes the software! Search the following subheads for tasks on your list, and you'll find a description of additional tasks the software can do. You won't find recommendations on which software to buy, or lengthy descriptions on each software's features, because this book focuses on hardware shopping.

You can skim over the hardware suggestions in each section for now because many of the terms, letters, and numbers are still unfamiliar. Remember where to find them for later, though.

Newsletters, Articles, Books

If your tasks include writing business or personal letters; writing articles, books, or poetry; or doing minor page layout for simple newsletters or even business cards, you need a word processor. Word processors let you easily change a document, reformat it, even change the style of the lettering—without ever having to retype a draft or drag out the correction fluid. Some include grammar checkers to sharpen your pencil a bit; simple spelling checkers and a thesaurus are also features to look for.

Word processing software runs from simple to feature-laden and huge. The PC for a simple, no-frills word processing package might dip as low on the cost and performance scale as a 386SX PC with a monochrome monitor and an 80MB hard drive.

If you plan to run the massive GUI programs such as Ami Pro, Word for Windows, or WordPerfect for Windows, buy at least a 386/33 (a 486/33 if you can) with an 100MB hard disk and a VGA color monitor. A mouse is crucial for any Windows program. These high-flying word processors also take full advantage of a laser printer.

Checkbooks and Business Data

If you plan to work with numbers, you'll want a spreadsheet software program. Spreadsheets work like a multiplication grid, only you can perform any operation (even complex scientific formulas) on a number.

Spreadsheet software programs are great fun for playing "what if": what type of mansion can you afford if you land that 25 percent raise and then interest rates fall 3 percent? Even if you don't need one for your primary tasks, spreadsheet programs are essential for budgeting. High-priced packages, such as Excel, Lotus 1-2-3, and Quattro Pro for Windows let you transform numbers from your spreadsheet to pie charts, bar charts, and so on—perfect for slide presentations.

Simple spreadsheets that you'll use only occasionally require at least a 386SX. Frequent spreadsheeters will want a more powerful computer, as will those who plan to use Excel or another spreadsheet that runs under Windows. A mouse helps to navigate a spreadsheet program. A 386DX with a math coprocessor or a 486 will give you enough computing horse power to really crunch the numbers.

Address Listings, Inventories, Client Data

Database software lets you organize collections and client lists; produce mailing labels and membership records; even track your garden seeds. A database arranges data of any kind. Think of a database as an electronic filing cabinet that sorts itself and retrieves information at the press of a button.

Very simple databases look like index-card files and perform like electronic address books. (You'll never have to use correction fluid again for that friend who moves every year.)

More complex database software breaks down each *record* (index card) into *fields*—one field for last name, one for first name, one for street name, another for ZIP code. After typing in data, you can sort fields in endless ways. You might produce a list of all your clients named Smith with Iowa ZIP codes who bought something from you in June, for example.

Like spreadsheets, occasional database users don't need beefed-up PCs. If using large databases, or database programming, is in your plans, however, be sure to get a faster PC with lots of hard disk storage and plenty of memory: a fast 386 or even a 486 PC with at least 8MB of main memory and a 100MB hard disk would be about right.

Page Layout and Graphic Design

The many types of software in this category let you publish newsletters, design flyers, create computer art, or remodel a kitchen. Desktop publishing software provides the user with the ability to lay out documents without having to physically cut and paste pieces of paper. Graphics software arms the user with an electronic paintbrush and canvas. Computer-assisted design programs come with rooms already planned for you to modify. Some programs allow photo retouching and image reduction or reversal. This ever-changing field presents some of the most exciting uses for a PC.

Although low-end programs put less strain on a PC, the results from the cheaper programs might not be satisfactory for a professional. The high-end desktop publishing and graphics software programs are large and memory-hungry because just displaying a picture is hard work for a PC. A professional desktop publisher needs a fast PC with a large, two-page color monitor; a mouse; a hand-held or flatbed scanner; and a hefty hard drive. The truly serious professional would consider a tape-backup device for safekeeping large files, as well as a CD-ROM drive for accessing large collections of digitized pictures (also called *clip art*).

As you can see, desktop publishing and graphics are among the most hardware-intensive tasks a PC can accomplish.

Taxes, Education, Home Design, Writing

Designing a new deck? Tracking tax deductions? Writing the great American novel in your spare time? Household software can be any "business" software that's applied to home use.

A low-priced 386 computer with plenty of hard drive space, a color monitor, a mouse, and a joystick will see the family through many hours of rewarding PC time. Consider a sound card and some stereo speakers to enhance a home PC. If communicating with others over the computer seems like fun, you'll want to try out some communications software and buy a modem.

Writing Programs, Tinkering with Your Setup

If making a computer do your bidding sounds appealing, you'll enjoy computer programming. For that you'll need to buy one or more *programming language* software packages, and teach yourself by writing small programs at first—and then larger and more complex programs.

Utilities (another type of software) help your computer run better. If there's a lack or deficiency with PCs, someone out there has programmed a utility to fix it. These programs will optimize your hard drive, make your printer print sideways, check a diskette for viruses, or make your keyboard easier to use.

As with the other types of software, buying the best PC for programming and utilities software depends on the amount of time you'll devote to these pursuits. A midrange 386 might be a good place to start. You can migrate to a bigger system in a few years if you find yourself writing huge programs or running large utility software packages. (Or writing large utility packages—utilities are among the first programs programmers write.)

Playing Games and Making Music

Computer games abound; if you get even the slightest pleasure from cards, board games, video arcades, or mystery novels, there's a computer game somewhere for you. As with the other types of software, games range from simple and undemanding to huge, colorful, expensive, and PC-intensive. Read the individual packages to be sure of the requirements.

> ## By the Way . . .
> Although it may seem foolish to invest money in a home computer dedicated solely to gaming and music, your home PC can be the source of ongoing, rewarding family fun. Computers are much more stimulating and interactive than television.

Many of the high-end games take full advantage of sound cards. Some games offer sophisticated synthesizer scores throughout their duration, as if you were "playing" a computerized movie. Once you have a sound card, you can write and play music if you invest in an electronic keyboard and a music program.

Where to Learn More About Software

Read computer magazines to learn about other types of software you might want to use. These magazines run articles about new products and offer detailed software comparisons that are written by experienced users. Look for ads that offer demo programs. Send away for these, even if you have to try them out on a friend's computer.

Visit software stores and get in the habit of reading a software box for its system requirements. Ask if you can try out a package (most stores will be happy to oblige).

Plan on at least one session at a computer *user group*, where people with similar PC interests gather monthly and exchange ideas, tips, and even horror stories. Try out more software here. Ask questions and ask those who share your software interests what type of PC they own.

Don't forget your friends. Grill them about their software experiences. Sit down at their PCs and check out the software they like. Ask what makes their favorite software better than the others. (People love showing off their PCs.)

Shareware: A Different Way to Buy Software

Some software publishers make their software available on a try-before-you-buy basis. This software is called *shareware* because it can be passed around (or *shared*) for free, unlike commercial software.

You pay for a shareware program when you find yourself using it regularly and enjoying it. Then you're on your honor to send a fee (usually lower than what you'd pay for commercial software) to the program's author. User groups and electronic bulletin boards are great sources for shareware. The one drawback to shareware is that, because it travels around to so many PCs, you must screen it for *viruses*—destructive programs written by bad people—using a special anti-virus utility program.

The Least You Need to Know

The only way to accomplish your goals with a PC is to find software designed for those goals. Within each software category, you'll find a range of programs that perform both simple and complex tasks. The more complex a program is, the more strain it puts on the PC hardware.

- ☞ Before you buy a PC, determine the tasks a software package can accomplish.

- ☞ Look at the software's box to get a rough idea of the PC system you'll need for it. The PC required to run the software should be listed under the heading System Requirements.

- ☞ Narrow down your software choices by reading reviews, trying out software at stores, and visiting user groups. Try out your friends' software, too.

- ☞ Shareware's a great resource if you're cautious.

- ☞ Desktop publishing and graphics programs are among the most hardware-intensive applications.

This page unintentionally left blank.

Part II
Come On Inside!

Take a look at the rows of different computer models at any computer store or warehouse club. Have you ever wondered why two computers that look identical from the outside are priced $2000 apart? It's because of the parts you can't see— the components buried within the computer casing.

Time to pull the lid off these mysteries! In this part, we'll dive head-first into the innards of a PC, and find out what makes one component better than another. When you surface at the end of Chapter 11, you'll be able to use techie terms like Megahertz, serial ports, and read/write heads with confidence.

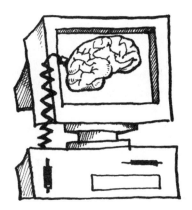

Chapter 5
The Processor Process

In This Chapter

- ☞ What is a microprocessor?
- ☞ The microprocessor determines the capability of your computer
- ☞ Why do chip numbers almost always end in 86?
- ☞ What chip brand should I look for?

In Chapter 4, you found out that software, like a puppy, will make you aware of its needs (although it won't soil your carpet). You skimmed the main types of software, with stuffy names like word processors and spreadsheets, and you learned what is the ideal computer system to run each software happily. Wisely, you didn't focus too much on the systems' specifics right then, instead saving the whole discussion in the secret now-I-know-for-later area of your brain.

Even so, you probably discovered a pattern in the system descriptions. They all had numbers that ended in 86—such as 386, 486, and so on. (Could it be? Order and consistency in the computer world?) Miracles have happened.

What Is a Microprocessor, and What Does It Do?

It's been described more ways than I can count: the "brain" of the computer; the "heart" of the computer; the "camp counselor" of the computer. . . . Why confuse things?

The *microprocessor* is a small black wafer, about the size of a Triscuit. The microprocessor is tightly packed with circuitry that controls a computer's ability to know what to do, and to do it. It's nestled deep inside the computer's system box on a flat green thing called a *motherboard* (turn to Chapter 7 to see a picture of this thing). Other circuits on the motherboard are connected to the microprocessor with pins, by which the microprocessor reaches out to more remote parts of the computer (say, the keyboard) and tells them what it has done and what to do now. Over and over again, the microprocessor processes these instructions, all in the inconceivably fast time frame of millions of instructions per second (MIPS).

Even the 8086 chip claimed an ancestor: the Intel 8080. The 8080 drove the Altair, a personal computer circa 1974 whose name came from a "Star Trek" episode. The Altair had neither monitor nor keyboard—not because they came as extras, but because these extras didn't yet exist. To make it do something, Altair owners spent hours flicking zillions of tiny switches (only to lose all their work when they turned the machine off). Oh, and they had to build it themselves from a kit. Even so, early electronics enthusiasts were enthusiastic about the Altair. Up until then, nobody had thought there was any need for a computer you could use in your house.

286, 386, 486, and the Pentium: What the Numbers and Weird Names Mean

Why start here? Well, more than any other single element, these numbers point to how fast and powerful a computer will be and how much it will cost. They're short for bigger numbers (somehow, that doesn't surprise you) that tell you which microprocessor is driving the computer.

Why Do Chip Numbers Always End in 86?

The microprocessors you'll see when shopping for a PC hail from the Intel Corporation's 80*x*86 (eight-oh-ex-eight-six) chip family, a hoary clan whose most prominent ancestor was the 8086 chip used inside the first IBM PC-compatible computers. And, in case this is sounding too consistent to possibly be about computers, the first real IBM-brand personal computer housed not an 8086, but a chip called 8088.

Why Are There So Many Chip Numbers?

Each new *xxx*86 number represents a new generation—the higher the number, the more advanced the chip. That's progress for you. And since the PC industry has been going strong for about 10 years now, and since they seem to come out with a new chip every 2 years or so, simple addition would tell us that there are about 5 different chip families out there now: the 8086, 80286, 80386, 80486, and Pentium.

By the Way . . .

The microprocessor itself is a landmark. Before Ted Hoff thought of putting it on a single chip back in 1969, a computer's central processing unit (CPU) was a boxed unit about the size of a large desk, connected to all the other computer stuff. The old CPUs had to be big, because wired inside were integrated circuits (one to each function) driving the computer. Combining these circuits onto one chip was a stroke of genius. But even then, it took the experts at Intel about four years to realize just what they had.

So What's the Point?

This is all leading up to one thing: You can't stop progress, so don't worry about it. No matter what chip you buy, trust that a bigger, better chip is just around the corner. There's no use waiting for that one chip that every-body will agree is the standard for our time.

Computer chips become faster, smaller, and more feature-packed with each new generation. And the time between generations grows smaller, too. Chips took a huge leap forward when Intel used a technology called Very-Large-Scale Integration (VLSI) to squeeze a math coprocessor and something called a memory cache onto the 486 chip. The Pentium, Intel's newest microprocessor, packs even more features into one chip. And beyond that, Son of VLSI will someday pack up to 1 billion components—a computer's entire central electronic complex—on a single chip.

The PC "river" keeps on rolling, so jump right in. No one ever gained anything from the power of personal computers by waiting to buy one.

Are There Other Types of Microprocessors?

Microprocessor families abound, and each type of chip has a different PC, mainframe, or even supercomputer to boss around. But the 80x86 microprocessor clan is the one that concerns you most right now.

By the Way . . .

Until recently, which brand of chip you should buy just wasn't an issue. Intel made the chips for IBM-compatible PCs. Motorola made the chips for Macintoshes and some other personal computers. That was that. It was easy—even for computers.

In the early days, Intel decided to open up its 8086 and 80286 chip technologies by licensing them to other companies. Intel hoped to standardize the industry and create a bigger market, and it did. But Intel stopped its "open" approach in 1985 after it introduced the 80386 chip. Too much money was at stake.

Even after it closed down access to licensing rights, the giant chip maker was challenged by a tiny startup called Advanced Micro Devices (AMD) for the right to use the 386 name on their clone chip. Intel took its case to court, claiming copyright infringement, but the judge ruled in favor of AMD, saying that "386" had become a generic term.

That broke Intel's monopoly on the 386 and caused the company to push its 486 technology even harder. (The ruling also resulted in huge price wars—and big breaks on 386 prices for the rest of us!)

Today, numerous companies manufacture unauthorized 386 and 486 chip clones. Intel has learned its lesson: The 586 isn't the name of its newest chip. What did they name it? The Pentium, of course. The Pentium is the biggest, fastest, baddest chip in Intel's line up, and it's name is easier to defend in court against those unruly clone companies. You'll learn more about this chip in the next chapter.

The world can only mourn the passing of the "86" chip lineage: An island of consistency in the normally chaotic computer seas.

It really doesn't matter what brand chip you buy if you're careful to find out how long the manufacturer's been in the chip-cloning business. A rule of thumb in the computer industry is that the first few products are bound to have some bugs. Wait, don't rush; do your homework and *finish reading this book* before you buy anything.

The Least You Need to Know

When you're shopping for a PC-compatible microcomputer, you'll be evaluating systems whose chips belong to the 80x86 family. Keep the following thoughts in mind when evaluating microprocessors.

- ☞ If you're buying a PC (not a Macintosh or Commo dore, etc.) you'll be evaluating the computer's cap- abilites based on Intel's 80x86 line of microprocessors.

- ☞ Older chips can't handle some of the new software, which may require more *megahertz* (the chip's clock speed), or some of the other design improve- ments featured in the new chips.

continues

continued

☞   The class of microprocessor required by your
     software is typically indicated on the software's box.

☞   If your software requires a stronger class of chip
     than you can afford, a less demanding software
     package could do the trick.

☞   If the chip's a clone (made by a company other than
     Intel) be sure the chip has a good reputation for
     reliability.

Chapter 6
Shopping for a Microprocessor

In This Chapter

☛ How various microprocessors differ

☛ What DX and SX mean

☛ Megahertz: How fast is your computer?

☛ When you'll need a math coprocessor

As you walk through a computer store or thumb through mail-order ads, it's easy to compare features and to decide what monitor or keyboard you want. Microprocessors aren't as easy to peg. They're not very outgoing, because they're too busy doing "important stuff."

Here's the Lineup

The computer's chip is housed deep inside the system box, where it snaps into a socket on the motherboard. (The motherboard is home to some other computer vitals, too. We'll look at those in Chapter 7.)

Even though you can't see it, don't worry; you'll never have to guess which microprocessor's inside a given computer because computer vendors love to crow about the speed and the power of their systems (if the chip's a powerhouse). Or they tout the system's affordability, if the chip's a more unassuming type. Either way, you'll see chips like the ones in Table 6.1 proclaimed loudly in ads, signs, and sales pitches.

Here's what it all breaks down to:

Table 6.1   PC Chips on Parade: Bigger numbers mean newer, faster, costlier.

"Street" Name	Chip	Bits	MHz	Comments
586	Pentium	32	60/66(+)	32-bit chip; 64 bit data-path capabilities.
486DX2	80486DX2	32	50	The Doubler: doubles 25MHz clock to 50MHz.
486DX	80486DX	32	25,33,50	Another name for 80486 below; powerful.
486	80486	32	25,33,50	Math coprocessor and memory cache on chip.
486SX	80486SX	32	20	No math co-processor; fine for most users.
386DX	80386DX	32	25,33,40	Another name for 80386 below; adequate.
386	80386	32	25,33,40	A good value; fast enough for most needs.
386SX	80386SX	32/16	20,25	Less expensive, scaled-down 386.
286	80286	16	6–12	Aging technology; rarely seen for sale.
088 and 086	8088/8086	8/16	4.77/8	Ancient; first IBM PC.

In a Nutshell, What's the Big Difference Between These Chips?

Each chip in Table 6.1 has a *bits* number. Because the function of a computer chip is to process data, it's useful to be able to measure the amount of data a chip can handle at any one time. The more bits a chip can handle at one time, the better. A 32-bit chip can move twice as many numbers as a 16-bit chip, and moving numbers is what computing is all about as far as the chip is concerned.

Exactly How Do the 386DX and the 386SX Differ?

The Bits column in Table 6.1 shows two numbers for the 386SX. Here's why. The 386SX came about because, at the time, the 386 cost way too much for the average person. When the Intel Corporation designed the 386 chip, one of the improvements they made was to beef it up to 32-bit capability.

Soon, everyone wanted a 386 so they, too, could shoot data around in big, 32-bit-wide streams. But only the big-business tycoons could afford one. Put simply, Intel released a more affordable chip by disabling some of the 386's 32-bit capability. They called the more affordable chip a 386SX.

Those of you who'd like to understand just how the two chips differ need to know a little more about how chips work. Bits travel down two data "hoses" on a chip. One's called the *internal data path*, where bits of information are processed. The other's called the *external data path*, where bits of processed information shoot over to the system memory and around the motherboard to other parts of the computer.

SPEAK LIKE A GEEK

The word *bit*, which stands for *BInary digiT*, is the basic unit of measurement for describing a chip's data-handling power. The bit number tells how big a stream of instructions the processor can process. It also tells how many bits of data the chip can move to other key components, like memory and the keyboard.

Think of the early 8-bit computer as a drinking fountain spout, a 16-bit as a bathtub faucet, and a 32-bit as a fire hose. And soon, the 64-bit capabilities of the Pentium will clamor for a comparison (a culvert?). Each time a different number shows up in the Bits column, that means that particular type of PC broke the previous bit limit and advanced personal computing just a bit!

Well, to boost sagging 386 sales, Intel decided some people might not need or want a full-size, 32-bit external data path. So, they scaled it back to 16 bits and called it macaroni. (No, they really called it a 386SX.)

It worked. Computer makers bought the hybrid chip in droves and stuck them in cheaper systems that could process 32-bit streams of instructions, just like the 386, yet which transferred data around the motherboard in 16-bit streams, just like the 286.

And the Difference Between the 486DX and 486SX?

The quest for a better, faster chip continued. The hard-working chip developers figured out a way to cram not only a more efficient CPU but also a math coprocessor (a chip dedicated solely to math calculations) into a single package, and they called it a 486. And it was good. It was not only faster than a 386, but it had this wonderfully efficient coprocessor built in. With the 386, you could buy a coprocessor separately and install it in another slot on the motherboard. But having it all in one chip made the 486 extra special.

Well, the same people who called the shots on the 386SX decided some 486 users might not need the coprocessor but might still want the better CPU. Why should they have to pay for the coprocessor? Impressed by their own marketing finesse, they took the 486 chip, disabled the math coprocessor, and sold it as a 486SX. ("But wait," you're probably saying. "It's not any cheaper to manufacture a 486SX than to manufacture a regular 486. So why does a 486 cost more?" Marketing, my friend, marketing.)

Math coprocessors have been around for years. They cheerfully calculate the national deficit or the fluid dynamics of a boogie board—as long as your software supports the extra boost in power. Until the advent of the 486, if you found your computer balking at big jobs, you went out and bought a math coprocessor. Then you pressed it into your motherboard, if your motherboard even sported the proper socket.

What Else Does the 486 Family Have Over the 386?

Even though it doesn't have a math coprocessor, the 486SX shares with the 486DX some other advantages over the 386. The 486-family chips have a memory-management unit, 8 kilobytes of *cache memory* (an area where the CPU can go to find frequently used data), and a built-in *cache controller*, which speeds the CPU's access to the cache area. This means they remember instructions they've already seen much faster than any other chips.

What's a Pentium and What Can It Do for Me?

If you were paying attention back in Chapter 5, you learned that the Pentium is the latest and greatest microprocessor from Intel. And if you thought the 486 could stomp on the poor little 386, you'll really be charged up by the Pentium. As you can see in Table 6.1, the Pentium has a 32-bit internal data path and a 64-bit external data path. More bits is better right? Right.

TECHNO NERD TEACHES

Budding technical wizards out there will be interested to know that the Pentium's circuitry has 3.1 million transistors. Big deal you say. Well, the 486's circuitry only has a measly 1.3 million transistors, but it can't fry an egg.

But this chip is not just twice as good as it predecessors. Intel has poured some more magic into this one. The Pentium can process two instructions at one time, has a bigger and better math coprocessor, and can cook you breakfast in bed. Well not quite breakfast in bed, but it does get hot. Which is one of the biggest problems with this baby. If you choose to fork out the big bucks to get a PC with a Pentium, make sure there is a cooling fan on the chip. It really does get hot.

PCs built around this chip will be blazing fast and you'll pay for the performance. Also keep in mind that much of the software out there will not take full advantage of the chip's capabilities. The same software will run faster on a Pentium than on a 486, but not as fast as it could if the software was *recompiled* (rewritten) for the Pentium.

Clock Speeds, Megahertz, 33MHz: What Does It All Mean?

One more number begs to be compared when you're chip shopping. That's the chip's clock speed, or *megahertz* (MHz) rate.

Hertz is a measure of cycles, or clock ticks, per second. Megahertz means one million clock ticks per second.

You'll see the chips' megahertz numbers advertised in all sorts of ways at the computer store or in ads: 486SX/25, 486SX 25MHz, and so on. They all mean the same thing. The first number is the processor, and the second number is the clock speed. The clock regulates operations—the chip performs a certain number of operations per clock tick. So if the clock ticks faster, more operations are performed per second.

By the Way . . .

Don't get this "clock speed" rating confused with the clock that keeps the date and time in your computer's memory when you shut it off at night. The date and time clock in your computer always runs at normal, real-time speed.

Generally speaking, the faster the clock speed, the faster your computer will operate. The 386 family ranges from 16 to 40MHz, and the 486s range from 20 to 66MHz. Here's a loop, though: MHz (megahertz) only tracks how fast the clock ticks, and is not an absolute measurement of performance. A PC's actual performance depends on both the clock speed and the number of instructions per tick of the clock that the chip can process. A 25MHz 386 and a 25MHz 486 may both have the same clock speed, but the 486 will process more data per tick and thus will appear to run your programs a lot faster.

The DX2: Doing Double Duty

When is a 486/25 not a 486/25? When there's a 486DX2 chip inside. Intel's *486DX2/50* chip, also known as *The Doubler*, doubles the 486/25's system clock's 25MHz rate within the CPU, so that it "ticks" twice as fast. Since the processor relies on the ticks to tell it how fast to process the data, speeding up the ticks makes the processor work harder.

How does The Doubler work? Recall the two types of data paths in every microprocessor: *internal* and *external*. A special integrated circuit called the *phase-locked loop* on the Doubler chip allows internal data path speedup of 50 percent. External cache, peripherals, RAM, and other stuff on the motherboard accessed by the external data path are still tied to the PC's standard bus rate (in this case, 25 MHz), so you won't see a full 50% improvement in overall speed.

Although the 25/50MHz Doubler was first, there's a version that accelerates 33MHz systems to 66MHz as well. Intel is planning a 16/32, 20/40, and even a 50/100MHz Doubler.

Do I Even Need a Math Coprocessor?

If you have a 386 based PC running certain software packages, such as CAD and animation programs, you'll benefit from a math coprocessor. Remember, you don't need one if you buy a 486, because it already has one built into the chip. Furthermore, stay away from a 486SX if you need a math coprocessor. Recall the SX means the chip has some limited features (as compared to the fully operating DX line.) The limited feature of the 486SX is the math coprocessor—it doesn't have one.

If you have any doubts, read over some of the user scenarios in Chapter 3. Do any of them sound like you? If you're still not sure whether you need a math coprocessor, turn to Chapter 4 to learn the needs of some of the software you think you'll be running. And if that doesn't tell you, hunt down a computer store or a user group where you can test drive the software you have in mind—with and without the coprocessor.

What If I Want to Add a Math Coprocessor Later?

If you think you'll need a math coprocessor down the road but you don't want to shell out bucks for a 486 just this minute, be sure to mention your concerns in any information-gathering calls you make to dealers and mail-order houses. Make sure there's a place on your motherboard for the coprocessor once you need it.

Will I Ever Want to Upgrade to a Better Chip?

The best way to avoid an unhappy match is to use a little foresight in planning your purchase. That means thinking a bit, now, about how soon you'll want to boost, or *upgrade*, your system's power. (Trust me; you'll want to upgrade someday. No matter how fast a computer is that you buy today, someday it's going to seem woefully slug-like—fit only for the kids' baseball card database.)

Questions to Ask When Buying an Upgradable Model

Ask if its memory architecture will be compatible with the new chip. You'll never have a true 486 if you try to access data from a 386SX memory layout, because the chips differ so in their bit-width capability. You'd hold back the 486 to the 386SX's 16-bit limits. (Check Chapter 7 for more details on bus architectures.) If an upgradable has a 16-bit data path to memory, keep shopping.

Ask if the upgradable comes with flash BIOS. (*BIOS*, covered in detail in Chapter 7, runs the computer's basic operations.) *Flash BIOS* enables you to electronically update these instructions. That makes it easier to tell the rest of the computer there's been an upgrade.

A growing trend in system design makes upgrading even easier by leaving the vendor out of the loop later on down the road. The latest upgradables feature motherboards that let you simply pop out the old CPU and snap in the new one. That way, you don't pay for the special CPU upgrade card—only for the new chip. And you don't have to depend on any particular vendor for the chip.

Compare the Cost of an Upgradable Computer

Be sure to compare the cost of upgradable versus non-upgradable models. Buying the basic system and upgrading can cost more than buying the higher-powered system in the first place. Ask pointed questions, such as how long the vendor will sell and support the upgrade card—and your machine, for that matter.

Design Factors Count

Another good question: Just who will perform the upgrade? Will you be performing a brain transplant on your dear old computer? If so, ask how the upgrade is installed. If it's through an expansion card, sometimes you have to remove all the other cards in your system before you can begin. Be sure the design makes sense.

I know what you're thinking: Why don't they make all computers upgradable with a simple pop/snap of a chip? You can always hope. If you think about it, though, the cost of personal computers would shoot way up if computer makers had to maximize every box's potential for memory, bus, hard drive space and expansion slots, and even extra cooling power— at birth. There's no guarantee everybody would take advantage of these extras, and yet we'd all be charged for them.

The Least You Need to Know

- The 286 and 386SX microprocessors are old and slow compared to today's standards. Only buy a computer with these chips if your budget is severely limited. A 386DX is probably the minimum you should get these days.

- It takes the 386 three times longer than the 486 and 486SX to do a particular task

- The 386DX has a 32-bit external data path; the 386SX has a 16-bit external data path. More bits is faster, fewer bits is cheaper.

- A chip's megahertz (MHz) number determines how fast it can process instructions. The higher the MHz, the faster your computer runs. Processor type counts too, though: a 486/25 runs faster than a 386/25.

- The 486 chip has a math coprocessor built in. A 486SX doesn't. That's the only difference between the two of them.

- The Pentium chip is Intel's fastest processor, but it costs a great deal and requires special cooling systems to keep it running properly.

This page unintentionally left blank.

Chapter 7
Meet the Motherboard

In This Chapter

- ☛ Understanding the role of the motherboard
- ☛ The basics of ROM and ROM BIOS
- ☛ Determining your expansion slot needs
- ☛ Understanding the different kinds of expansion busses
- ☛ Shopping for a Local Bus computer

You've come a long way from Chapter 1! You've learned that wise shoppers first decide what they want to *do* with their computers, and then they find the software that will accomplish their goals. You discovered many different types of software, and you saw which software runs best on the various ranks of PC systems. In Chapters 5 and 6, you learned that the microprocessor is the first big hardware decision to face. And you're just about to find out what else goes on in the system box. You're almost an expert, or at least you will be once you meet the motherboard.

Let's continue by heading back to the store's PC display. We can pry open one of the system boxes and view a motherboard, as well as some other neat stuff, close-up.

What's a Motherboard Again?

It's big; it's green; it's the *motherboard*—a nickname for the large printed circuit board underlying everything else in the system box. System boxes come in a vertical orientation, too, called a *tower*. Towers have the motherboard along one side. To see what that looks like, turn the book on its side and look at the figure below. There.

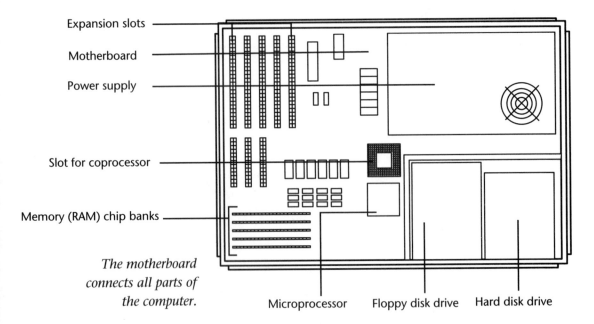

Expansion slots

Motherboard

Power supply

Slot for coprocessor

Memory (RAM) chip banks

The motherboard connects all parts of the computer.

Microprocessor   Floppy disk drive   Hard disk drive

The most important thing to know about the motherboard is that everything else in your computer plugs into it—including the microprocessor. You've heard the comparison: The microprocessor is the computer's brain. If so, the motherboard's the skull. Choose carefully. Skull transplants are possible, but are best saved for experts. If you already have a computer and you think it might benefit from a new skull, check out Chapter 25. The motherboard houses other essential components, like ROM and the BIOS, expansion slots, and DIP switches.

What's ROM?

Even the self-important microprocessor has a boss: the ROM chip. *ROM* stands for *read-only memory,* a permanent set of instructions etched onto the ROM chip. These instructions set the computer's basic personality.

Computer manufacturers can store many
types of instructions in ROM. But once in
place, a ROM chip can't be altered. That's
why it's called read-only: The instructions
can be read but not written over with other
instructions.

Where Does BIOS Fit in?

BIOS stands for *basic input-output system.* It
is one of the groups of instructions
preprogrammed onto a ROM chip. The BIOS' job is to see the computer
through the identity crisis it suffers each day. When you flick your
computer's power switch first thing each day, the machine panics. It can't
do a thing without instructions. Right away, the BIOS kicks in and reas-
sures the computer. The whole process of turning on a computer is known
as *booting up.* That's when the machine performs something called
bootstrapping, a term that comes from the old expression "to pull yourself
up by your own bootstraps."

Shopping guidelines for a BIOS? Not too many, since you don't get to
choose the ROM chips that come in a particular PC. Even so, ask what
BIOS version the PC is running. Get the latest version possible, since
different BIOS' can affect the performance of otherwise similar PCs. For
example, certain new hard drives won't work with a BIOS that was made
before 1989.

How Much RAM Will It Hold?

As you'll learn in the next chapter, random access memory (RAM) is where
the PC holds information it's working on—programs, word processing
documents and so on.

Few computers come fully loaded with RAM. But the computer you buy
should have sufficient RAM chip slots, so you can add more later. Once the
motherboard's RAM slots are filled, even more RAM can be added via RAM
expansion cards. A 386 motherboard should accept a minimum of 16MB
of additional RAM. A 486 should allow for at least 32MB of main memory,
plus a 256KB RAM cache.

Ask about a computer's memory configuration. RAM chips come in different sizes; the motherboard should accept both 1MB and 4MB memory chips. You might hear the chips called SIMMs—it's just a techie term for a certain type of RAM.

Expansion Slots

Your computer provides several ports (interfaces) to connect devices to the motherboard, as you'll learn in Chapter 9. But there are some devices that cannot be plugged into any of the normal ports that come with the computer. In many cases, the problem is solved because the device comes with its own interface card. The interface card plugs into an expansion slot on the motherboard, creating the port that the device needs to plug into the computer. A cable then connects the device to the new port.

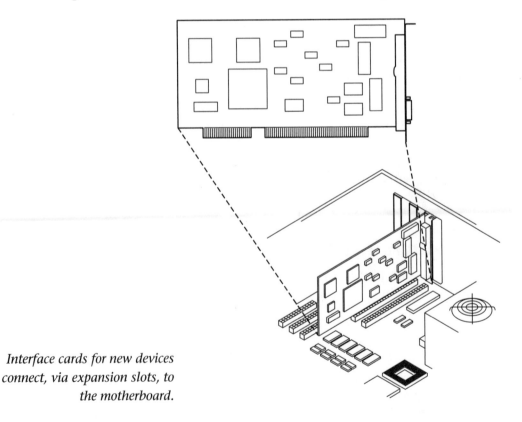

Interface cards for new devices connect, via expansion slots, to the motherboard.

> ## By the Way . . .
>
> Devices such as scanners and CD-ROM drives usually come with their own interface cards, but monitors usually do not. That's because many scanners and CD-ROM drives require special, non-standard interfaces. Most monitors, on the other hand, are standardized and will function with any of a wide variety of video interface cards (usually called just "video cards").
>
> Whenever you are buying a new device, make sure you interrogate the salesperson about the interface cards and cables you might need.

How Many Expansion Slots Do I Need?

Obviously, you can't plug in a new interface card if your computer doesn't have any open expansion slots. When you buy a computer with three open expansion slots, it may seem like more than you will ever need. But when you start buying computer gadgets, these slots fill up fast. You'll need to plan ahead to make sure the computer you buy contains enough open slots for your future needs.

You may see the terms *interface card, expansion card, card, daughterboard, add-on board,* or even just *board.* It's all the same thing—a neat new toy for your computer.

Since a computer's expansion capacity is rarely mentioned in ads or placards, it's something you'll have to ask about. Generally, the more expansion slots you get, the more you'll pay (and the bigger your system box will be).

8-Bit, 16-Bit, 32-Bit?

You know that microprocessors differ in how big a stream of data they can handle in a given time. Well, expansion slots differ, too. As with microprocessors, higher bit widths mean a bigger data stream flowing to and from the card. Faster access. More time for the fun stuff.

Interface cards come in a range of bit sizes. Make sure your motherboard has at least one 32-bit and several 16-bit slots open. That way, you'll have a large enough slot for any device you might set your eye on in the computer store later.

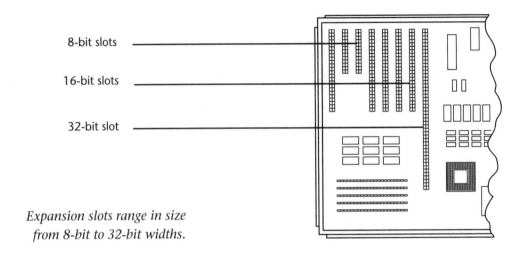

8-bit slots

16-bit slots

32-bit slot

*Expansion slots range in size
from 8-bit to 32-bit widths.*

By the Way . . .

Bigger slots can hold smaller cards, but the opposite's not
true. For example, if you have an 8-bit interface card, it can
plug into any slot: 8-bit, 16-bit, or 32-bit. Don't be wasteful,
however: if you have an open slot that matches the card, use
it rather than a higher-bit slot.

What's an Expansion Bus?

An expansion slot's capability is often measured in bus size instead of bits.
It's basically the same thing. *Bus* is short for *data bus*, the circuitry on the
motherboard where data travels to and from the microprocessor. The
entire grouping of expansion slots and circuits on the motherboard is
called the computer's *expansion bus*.

By the Way . . .

When 32-bit microprocessors came on the scene (the 386s and above), computer manufacturers found that the rest of the system lagged behind the blazing chips. The original AT bus, called *Industry Standard Architecture (ISA)*, was just too slow. Manufacturers set out to resolve this dilemma, but quarrels arose about how best to revise the bus architecture.

IBM's plan, *Micro Channel Architecture (MCA)*, involved costly licensing fees, so nine other computer makers joined forces and agreed to develop and support their own new world order: the *Enhanced ISA (EISA)* bus. Unlike MCA, EISA is compatible with older expansion cards, and is fast becoming a high-performance standard. EISA costs more than ISA, but prices are beginning to level out, and if blazing performance is important, you may find EISA a good investment.

Some Ads Say Local Bus—What's That?

Local bus is a new technology that links the microprocessor directly to one or two expansion slots so the devices connected to them can run at full speed without getting bogged down in the data bus. These slots also move information in 32 bit chunks, rather than the typical 16 bit chunks. Video cards are the most popular devices to come with the local bus option.

The direct link between the microprocessor and the video card significantly increases the speed at which your monitor can display images. If you plan to work with a graphical interface, such as Microsoft Windows, strongly consider the local bus option. It may cost you a little bit more, but the speed improvement will be worth the strain on your pocketbook.

What Are DIP Switches?

DIP switches are tiny switches sometimes found on the motherboard and also on interface cards. Hardware devices, like printers or

OOPS!

It's wise to leave DIP switches alone unless you know what you're doing. Even then, make sure you write down the original setting before you begin, so you can put things back the way you found them if necessary.

modems, can sport these, too. When you add new interface cards to your system, the newcomer's DIP switches must sometimes be set to a particular setting so the newcomer's BIOS does not try to occupy a space in memory that is already taken by an existing device.

There may be DIP switches on your motherboard too; these can perform many different functions depending on where they are located. For example, some motherboard DIP switches tell the motherboard how much memory is installed.

The Least You Need to Know

As you've learned, the motherboard is a busy and sometimes confusing place (or thing.) It brings together all the components that make up the PC, from the processor to the ROM chips and all those slots. Review the key points below to help sort out all this motherboard info.

- ☛ The motherboard, housed in the system box, connects all the computer's components.

- ☛ ROM chips contain the BIOS, which directs your computer's start-up routine.

- ☛ Get the latest possible BIOS version you can get.

- ☛ Expansion slots are part of the motherboard's expansion bus.

- ☛ Slots provide a place for you to add new devices to your computer via expansion cards.

- ☛ If you'll need fast video display, consider a PC with LocalBus slots.

- ☛ DIP switches are found on expansion cards, devices, and the motherboard.

Chapter 8

Pump Up the RAM!

In This Chapter

- ☞ How your computer remembers what it's doing
- ☞ What RAM is and what it does
- ☞ Deciphering three kinds of RAM
- ☞ What is a RAM cache?

The motherboard holds another key to a computer's speed and power: *random-access memory*, or *RAM*. The amount of RAM on a computer—along with the power of its microprocessor, the width of its bus, and the size or speed of its hard disk—determines how well your software will run.

What Is RAM?

RAM gives the microprocessor a place to dump all the data, the instructions, the input mumbo-jumbo, and the stray socks it's not using at the moment. The information waits patiently in RAM until the busy microprocessor comes to retrieve it. This holding tank eases the microprocessor's load, so processing takes place more quickly.

Recall from Chapter 7 that after ROM's BIOS prodded it into action, the microprocessor loaded its operating system. Loaded it where, you ask? Well, the microprocessor itself doesn't have that much memory space. And ROM chips are off-limits—no new stuff can be written there. So the operating system was "written to" RAM for the short term. RAM, unlike ROM, can be read from and written to.

Random Access means the microprocessor takes an equal amount of time to access any one of RAM's memory cells. These cells are organized in a special, two-dimensional grid. It's like a wall of post office boxes, or a bingo card. The microprocessor gets the scoop on a piece of information's address (B-12), and goes to the B column and down to the 12 to grab the data from that cell. Bingo!

RAM is notable for one other thing. It's fast, because all the data access or storage takes place electronically. Electronic streams of bits and bytes (pronounced *bites*) move much more rapidly than bulky, slow, mechanical devices such as disk drives.

RAM Is Volatile; ROM Is Not

When is information not safe in RAM? When the computer is turned off. Because it's electronic and not mechanical, RAM needs constant refreshing by a stream of electrical pulses. When the computer's turned off or accidentally unplugged, the electricy stops and RAM empties its contents. Swoosh! That's why they call RAM *volatile memory*.

How Is RAM Measured?

Like software, hard disks, and the mileage left on your teeth, RAM is measured in bytes. One *byte* equals eight bits, and a *bit*, as you'll recall from Chapter 6, is the smallest unit used to measure data.

The fact that RAM needs a steady supply of electricity to hold information explains the existence of two customs: turning off a computer during an electrical storm, and saving your work to floppy disks and hard drives (see Chapters 10 and 11). If you don't follow these practices, you could lose your data. Oops!

A byte holds a character's worth of data, such as a letter of the alphabet. Each of RAM's cells holds a single byte and gives this byte a particular memory address, ready for the microprocessor's retrieval.

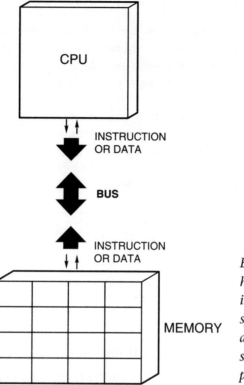

Each of RAM's cells holds a single byte of information at a specific memory address, in a system similar to a grid of post office boxes.

The byte is a pretty small unit of measurement. Bytes are so small that even in the early dawn of computers people tended to clump bytes into thousands, or kilobytes (K, KB or Kbyte, for short). A *kilobyte* equals 1,024 bytes.

Early PCs held 64KB of RAM. Computers sold today have at least 640KB of RAM (usually even more). Most PCs now count their RAM capacity in *megabytes* (meg or MB). One MB of RAM equals about a million bytes, or 1,024KB. The PCs on the market that are equipped with the 386, 486, and Pentium processors can access as much as 4GB (*gigabytes*, or billion bytes) of memory.

What's Your Memory Address?

When considering a computer's RAM, you may see the terms interleaved memory, static-column memory, page-mode memory, and row/column memory. These design differences are attempts to increase the speed at which the CPU accesses, or addresses, the memory cells.

Interleaved memory divides it into equal portions and processes them alternately. *Static-column memory* finds one column to store data, and then stores subsequent data in that same column. With *page-mode memory*, memory access occurs back-to-back in blocks called pages. And *row/column memory* is a Bingo card-like, grid-accessing method.

The memory chips you'll encounter most are the *dynamic RAM chips*, which are often referred to as DRAM (pronounced *d-ram*.)

What Are Static and Dynamic RAM?

RAM chips come in two styles. *Static RAM chips* are slower and more expensive than *dynamic RAM chips*.

Three RAMs: Conventional, Expanded, and Extended Memory

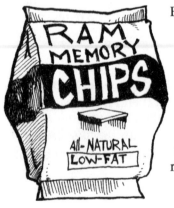

Early computer designers lacked foresight: They never thought a PC would be able to use more than 640K of RAM. Even today, that early barrier is known as *conventional memory*.

Later on, computer designers came up with special memory expansion boards that could fool the computer into thinking it was grabbing the new memory from the old conventional memory range. This is known as *expanded memory*.

Extended memory chips plug directly into chip slots on the motherboards of newer computers, as shown below. Like expanded memory, it gives the PC additional memory power, but it can be accessed much faster than expanded memory.

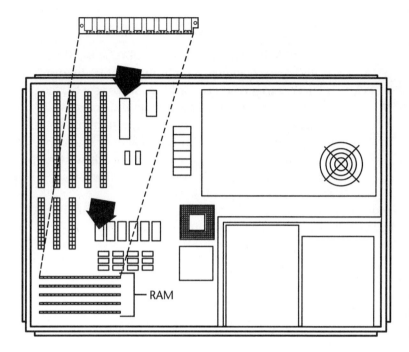

A bank of RAM chips on a 386 motherboard.

You have to be running an application program that is written to take advantage of extended or expanded memory in order to get any benefit out of them. Because most programs today are written to use extended memory (and, more rarely, expanded memory), the additional memory power is definitely worth the expense.

By the Way . . .

When buying a PC, make sure you get enough RAM to satisfy your program's requirements. Microsoft Windows, in particular, needs lots of RAM. For Windows, you can squeak by with 4 megabytes but you're better off with 8MB or more. Don't buy an expanded memory board for a new PC—if you ever need expanded memory, you can set up your extended memory to imitate it.

Shadow RAM may cause memory conflicts with other software. Make sure you know whether your computer has it, and if so, how to disable it.

What's a RAM Cache?

A good feature to look for is a *RAM cache*, also called *cache memory*. It's a bundle of fast memory chips on the motherboard that serve as a bridge between the fast microprocessor and the slower main RAM. By predicting what instructions are likely to be needed next, RAM caches reduce the computer's *wait state*, the time it spends waiting for something to do in between instructions.

If you see a computer advertised as "*zero wait-state*," chances are it has a RAM cache. A 256KB cache is sufficient for mid-sized systems.

Are They Serious? Shadow RAM?

It sounds sinister, but *shadow RAM* is just a feature to speed a microprocessor's access to the BIOS by loading BIOS directly into *fast RAM* when the computer is turned on.

The Least You Need to Know

☞ RAM chips provide memory for the computer to store stuff in while working.

☞ The more RAM you get, the better off your computer will be. It's fairly cheap, so don't scrimp in this area.

☞ The minute you turn off your computer, RAM empties itself, which explains why people store their work on floppy or hard disks.

☞ The number of RAM chip slots on your motherboard determines the amount of RAM you can add to your computer. There should be at least eight slots, and each slot should be able to take both 1MB and 4MB chips.

☞ A RAM cache helps improve your computer's performance.

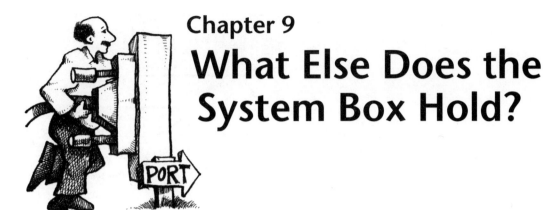

Chapter 9

What Else Does the System Box Hold?

In This Chapter

- ☞ How ports help you add devices
- ☞ Assessing your drive bay needs
- ☞ Powering and cooling your computer
- ☞ Case styles
- ☞ Is it comfortable to use?

You can deduce from Chapter 7 that the thick computer case shelters some pretty impressive parts. But before you can buy the best system, let's see how the rest of the case's contents work together.

Not-Just-Any Port in a Storm

Even the sketchiest computer ad lists ports as part of the system package. *Ports* are connectors on the back of the system box where you plug in a printer, a modem, or other devices. They're called ports because they're gateways into your computer's innards.

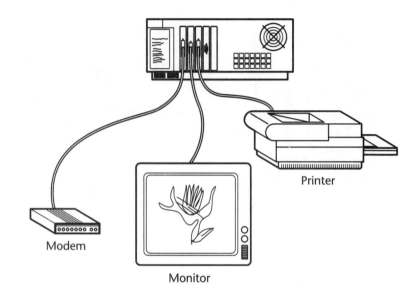

Printer

Modem

Ports are gateways into your computer's innards.

Monitor

How do ports differ from expansion cards inserted into expansion slots, as discussed in Chapter 7? They're actually not that different: some ports come preinstalled with your computer, and others come later when you purchase interface cards.

TECHNO NERD TEACHES

Some PCs sport a separate game card, or you can buy one yourself and plug it into a spare expansion slot. Then you have a game port, and you can plug in a joystick and blast invaders until it's time for "Star Trek" reruns.

Almost all computers come with at least two ports: a parallel and a serial. Rather than including two separate interface cards with your computer, the manufacturer commonly uses a single multi-function card to give you the ports you need. A *multifunction card* holds a combination of ports, usually two serial ports and a parallel port.

The important thing to remember about ports is that each type of port handles devices made only for it. You can't plug a joystick into a serial port, for example, nor a modem into a parallel port. When buying printers, modems, or tape-backup units, be extra careful to match the device with the port type.

Serial Ports

Serial ports provide a place to connect serial printers, a mouse, a modem, or another serial device. A serial device gets its name because of the way it transmits instructions—one bit at a time (serially). Figure 9.2 shows typical serial connectors. They usually come in 25-pin and 9-pin models.

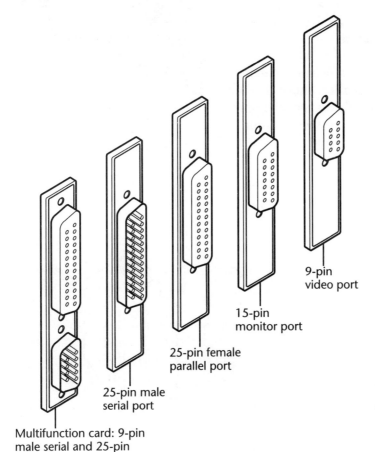

9-pin
video port

15-pin
monitor port

25-pin female
parallel port

25-pin male
serial port

Multifunction card: 9-pin
male serial and 25-pin
female parallel

*Serial and parallel
ports sport 9-pin
and 25-pin connec-
tors.*

Parallel Ports

Parallel ports transmit information over eight wires (in 8-bit, or 1-byte, chunks). They're faster than serial ports in the same way you saw that 32-bit data buses transmitted information faster than 8-bit buses: more bits can be sent at once.

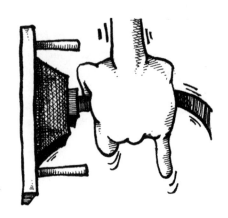

A parallel port usually attaches to a parallel printer, although other parallel devices exist. Parallel ports and devices connect with 25-pin plugs to your computer.

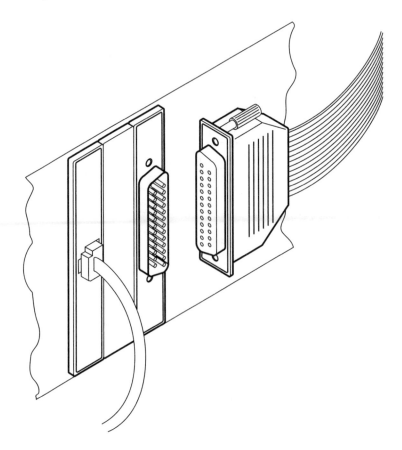

Cables plug into the ports on the back of the computer.

SCSI (Scuzzy) Ports

SCSI stands for *small computer system interface*, and yes, they're really pronounced *scuzzy*. Since they're even faster than parallel ports, they're used to attach high-capacity hard drives, CD-ROMs, and tape-backup units.

Most PCs don't come with a SCSI port installed (although Macintosh-brand personal computers do). The neat thing about SCSI ports is that you can chain up to eight SCSI devices off one port. The downside to SCSI ports is that all SCSI devices aren't compatible with the port or with each other, so you have to be careful when selecting SCSI add-ons.

> **SPEAK LIKE A GEEK**
>
> *Serial ports* should be clearly labeled at the back of the computer. The label usually says serial or COM (for communications port), because many people connect serial (external) modems to this port. Another name for serial port is RS-232 port (computer people enjoy talking in numbers and do so at the slightest provocation). Parallel ports are often labeled LPT, short for line printer port.

Driving into the Bay

Drive bays are large slots with racks inside the system box. Drive bays hover over the motherboard and harbor hard drives and floppy drives. They come in either vertical (stacked drives) or horizontal (side-by-side) orientation.

Plan for future needs by asking how many spare drive bays the system offers. Later you may want to add hard or floppy drives or even an internally mounted CD-ROM unit. Some tower cases sport up to seven extra drive bays!

What Case Style Is Me?

Check out the variety of PC systems crowding the computer store's floor. There's the desktop model, the sexy portables and notebooks, slimlines, and the hulking tower case. There's even an all-black Darth Vader Special—very sleek. But what's the best case to buy?

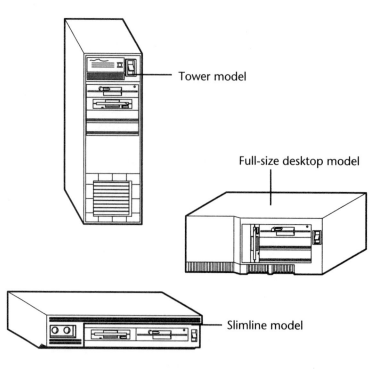

Tower model

Full-size desktop model

Computers come in a variety of styles and colors.

Slimline model

Computer cases have come a long way from their bland, desktop-hogging, boxy forebears. Small-footprint computers save space and look tidy, but they forfeit expansion slots, drive bays, and other room to grow. The same is true of slimline models, which offer side-by-side disk drives. Tower models offer lots of room for expansion but take up floor space.

By the Way . . .

Look critically at the various models available. Assess the amount of room you now have and how likely you are to expand your system later. Then try to strike a compromise.

Looks are important, it's true. And that all-black model would look great in your high-tech computer nook. But the question to ask yourself is: "What components will combine to build the best solution to my current and near-future computing needs?" As you continue reading this book, keep that question on your lips. The system-box dilemma is sure to solve itself.

Pump Up the Power

No sense in owning a super hot-rod computer if its *power supply* can't keep up. Power supplies are measured in watts and range in strength from 80 to 300 watts. Even though every computer system comes fitted with a power supply, make sure it's powerful enough—especially if you plan to add things later on, such as tape back-up units.

When shopping, ask if the power supply will be sufficient should you choose to expand the machine to its maximum capacity. Table 9.1 provides some power supply guidelines. As in every area of life, use common sense: If a desktop model you're looking at offers gobs of drive bays and expansion slots, go with the power recommendation for a tower model.

Table 9.1   Typical power supply requirements

Case Size	Minimum Power Supply Needed
Slimline	80–100 Watts
Full-size desktop	100–150 Watts
Minitower	100–150 Watts
Tower	200–300 Watts

An Ounce of Protection

A computer's not just something you plug into the nearest extension cord. Before deciding where to put it, ask yourself if there's a free outlet nearby. Then plug a power strip or surge supressor into the outlet, and plug your computer components into that rather than plugging them directly into the outlet.

A *power strip* is like a heavy-duty extension cord. One end plugs into the wall, and the strip sits on the floor, ready to supply your components with juice. Power strips provide seven or eight sockets—one for the system box, printer, monitor, modem, lava lamp, boom box. . . . You won't have any trouble filling up the spare sockets.

Power strips may offer some surge protection. If so, they will shield the computer's sensitive parts against fluctuations in electrical current, which are known as *power surges* or *power spikes*. Not all power strips guarantee protection, so it's wise to make sure you know if you have it or not. (Some people don't opt for surge protection, opting instead to save their work to disk frequently and turn their computers off in electrical storms. It's probably safer and wiser to invest the extra bucks.)

Because even the slightest power cuts can mean hours of lost work, many experts recommend *only* plugging a computer into a special surge suppressor unit. Some offer separate power switches for each component. You pay for surge protection: Units average $25 to $130.

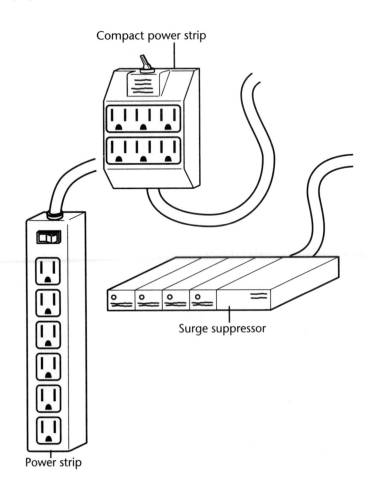

Compact power strip

Surge suppressor

Plug your new computer into a power strip or surge suppressor unit.

Power strip

Finally, make sure the computer comes with a heavy-duty, three-pronged power cord.

Keeping Cool

Large, powerful computers such as the 486-50MHz model generate lots of heat. Ask about cooling methods. Some models sport a second cooling fan in the power supply; others use a heat sink method. Some high-powered computers offer both.

FCC Approval: Does Your PC Pass?

As computers become more powerful, they emit strong electronic signals that interfere with other transmissions over the airwaves. To minimize electronic interference, the Federal Communications Commission (FCC) regulates electronic emissions that escape from PC cases. Systems rated Class B emit the least interference, so they're approved for home use. Class A systems pass muster only for office or industrial use.

Portable computers come rated Class B only. And yes, the Federal Aviation Administration is on record as saying they do believe laptops pose "a potential for interference to aircraft avionics."

One exception to this rule: Super high-powered PCs (486-5 MHz models and above) aren't required to meet class B approval. (Go figure!)

The Touch Test

When you think you really like a system, it's time to give it the touch test. Sit down. Make yourself as comfortable as can be expected, considering the salesperson is glaring over your shoulder, and the system next to you is occupied by a 5-year-old who's busy programming the Space Shuttle's next orbital.

Floppy Drive Location

Floppy drives are almost always found within easy reach along the front of a computer system. You'll be reaching for the floppy drives often; double-check to be sure they're in the best spot for you.

The Power Switch

Check the position of the power switch. A front switch is easiest to reach and allows more range in where you put the system (against a wall, for example). Side switches mean you won't turn the computer off accidentally—but they're not as easy to reach. A power switch along the back of the computer can be a real pain.

The Reset Button

The reset button gives you a way of emptying RAM and resetting the system without shutting off the power. You might want to reset the computer after installing a new program, or when your computer locks up or acts strangely. You can always turn the power off and on again (called a *cold boot*, but this throws a giant strain on the computer's electronic components). The reset button is the better alternative. Obviously, you'll want this button to be within easy reach. Front placement is best, but recessed, to avoid accidental resetting.

The Turbo Button

A turbo feature lowers or raises the megahertz rate with the touch of a button. Often, an indicator light on the system box tells you when you're in turbo mode. Why wouldn't you want to run at maximum speed at all times? Well, a few programs, notably older computer games, won't work at the highest speeds, or they work so fast that they're not any fun. The turbo switch toggles from fast to slow(er). Chances are you won't be using this feature often, so it's okay along the side.

LED Read-Outs

Some models sport *Light-Emitting Diode (LED)* read-outs that monitor megahertz rate. Other lights advise hard drive and turbo status. Think of where you'll place your new computer once you get it home, and make sure these lights are easy to see.

The Least You Need to Know

Before you buy, consider the computer's system box. It may seem superfluous now, but when you get the PC home, the system box will be the main part that you see every day. Think about these things:

☛ The number of ports that come with a computer are clearly listed in ads or at the store. Your computer should come with at least one parallel port and two serial ports.

☛ You might have to add more specialized ports, such as SCSI or game ports, if you purchase specialized devices.

☛ Ports are exclusive creatures; you have to be careful when shopping to match port with device type.

☛ It's essential that the case style you select fits your available space, as well as your expansion needs.

☛ Your computer should have a large enough power supply to accommodate the number of expansion slots your computer comes with. (The number of expansion slots is dictated primarily by the case type; slimline has the fewest; tower has the most.)

☛ All systems need FCC approval; you're better off with a Class B-approved computer to minimize radio interference.

Recycling tip: Tear out this page and photocopy it.

Chapter 10
Floppy Diskettes and Drives

In This Chapter

- ☛ Understanding floppy disks and floppy disk drives
- ☛ Determining floppy disk densities
- ☛ Shopping for floppy disks

The last few chapters provided a look at almost all the parts inside a computer's case. Yet, no matter how many cool gizmos it has, without any software the computer sits there blankly. In this chapter, you'll learn about the *floppy-disk drive*, the mechanism that reads the software from disk into memory (or copies it to your hard disk to be read into memory later).

Floppies for Reading and Writing

Think of your floppy disk drive as a special-purpose tape deck like the one in your stereo cabinet. Floppy disk drives are mechanical gizmos that are able to "read" floppy disks, just as a stereo's tape player can "read" the music recorded onto audio tapes. Just as you can buy audio tapes prerecorded with an artist's music, you can also buy disks that contain various software programs you want to run. And just as you can buy blank tapes for your stereo on which to record music, you can buy blank disks on which to store your work for "playing back" later.

Blank audio tapes enable you to make illegal copies of copyrighted music; blank diskettes enable you to make illegal copies of the software you purchased. In both instances, it's against the law, except to make backup copies for yourself.

Why Write?

You learned in Chapter 8 that RAM provides a place for the microprocessor to store data and instructions while you're running a particular program. Well, recall what happens to RAM when your computer's power goes off (or when you exit the program that is using the data and instructions): all the contents of RAM go swoosh into data heaven.

Floppy disks (and hard disks) are where you save your work while you're using your PC, to avoid losing the contents of RAM permanently. When you issue a "save" command in a program, the data file you are working on is copied to a disk for safekeeping. Later, when you need the data file, you can use the program's "open" or "retrieve" command to copy it from the disk back into RAM.

By the Way . . .

Why do they call them floppy disks? Well, the circular wafer inside the semi-rigid casing is actually quite flexible; the casing is what makes them seem un-floppy.

Hard disks, on the other hands, are metal plates. Even if they weren't in their casing, they would still be pretty darned hard.

Two Sizes, Four Capacities

Floppy disks and disk drives come in two sizes: 5 1/4-inch and 3 1/2-inch. That measurement is the diameter of the disk casing that goes into the drive. Some people call the 3 1/2-inch versions *micro floppy disks*. (You don't have to say this silly word if you don't want to.) On your new PC, you choose what size floppy drive you want and what capacity disks it handles.

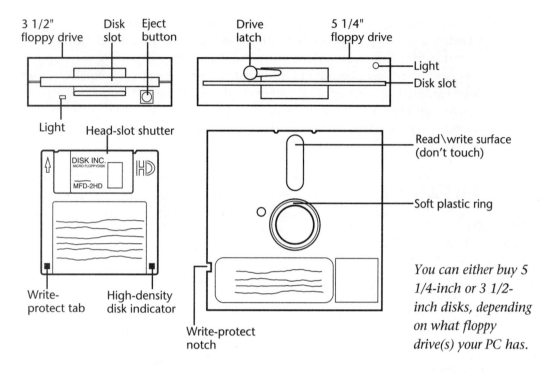

You can either buy 5 1/4-inch or 3 1/2-inch disks, depending on what floppy drive(s) your PC has.

Like RAM, a disk's capacity is measured in bytes. Disks come in four different byte capacities, measured either in kilobytes (KB) or in megabytes (M or MB).

Density	*5 1/4-inch*	*3 1/2-inch*
Double Density	360KB	720KB
High Density	1.2MB	1.4MB

There is a less-common type of 3 1/2-inch diskette called an extended density diskette. It can hold 2.88MB of data, twice as much as a high-density diskette of that size. However, you must have a special, expensive disk drive in order to use these diskettes; for most people, it isn't worth the expense.

What Kind of Disk Drives Should I Get?

A PC should come with at least one floppy disk drive, either 3 1/2 inch or 5 1/4 inch. The 3 1/2-inch drives are more popular these days because the disks are sturdier and hold slightly more data.

For maximum flexibility, consider a PC with two floppy drives: one high density 5 1/4-inch drive and one high density 3 1/2-inch drive. Double-density drives are nearly obsolete; they are seldom sold with new computers anymore. That's because high-density drives are not very expensive and can read high-density or double-density disks just fine. (Double-density drives can read only double-density diskettes.) Make sure that the computer you purchase comes with high-density drives of whatever size you choose.

Most software comes on one size of disk; rarely does a package contain both. Although most software publishers offer to exchange disks for the right size, this is a slow process and may cost you a few extra bucks. This is one good reason to have a PC with drives of both sizes.

If you buy a PC with only one floppy drive and later decide you need another, don't despair. You can always have a second drive added, or add one yourself, with the help of a book on upgrading your computer. Just make sure you buy a PC with enough available *drive bays* (spare drive compartments in the system box) for later additions.

Determining a Disk's Density

Unfortunately, there's no reliable way to tell the high- and low-density 5 1/4-inch disks apart, except perhaps by looking at the label on the box or the diskette. Some low-density disks sport a reinforcing hub ring around the center hole, but that's not a reliable indicator.

The 3 1/2-inch disks look different. Often the high-density ones have an HD symbol to the right of the *head-slot shutter* (the part you stick into the computer's drive first). The head-slot shutter may say MFD-2HD under the brand name. (HD stands for high density.) Here's another way to tell: a high-density disk has a hole in two corners, one of which is closed by a sliding tab. A double-density disk has the hole with the tab, but not the second hole.

Stocking Up on Disks

Mail-order companies are the least expensive sources for disks. Some mail-order houses sell nothing else. If you take this route, know that the mass-quantity, El Cheapo brand in the big plastic bag really does differ in quality from the more expensive brand-name disks. Your data is usually

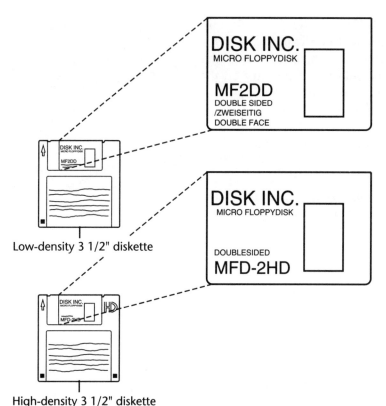

Low-density 3 1/2" diskette

High-density 3 1/2" diskette

Here's how to tell if a 3-1/2-inch disk is high-density.

safe enough, but each disk may not hold the full capacity marked on the label.

Also, as computers have been with us for a longer period of time, people are starting to discover that the stuff they stored on their very oldest disks is slowly fading away. It's no one's fault—it just happens. Always keep plenty of blank disks on hand so you can make backup copies of your most cherished backup disks every year or so.

Don't forget to buy at least one box of name-brand disks when you buy your computer, so you'll have them there the same day the PC shows up. In the excitement of buying a new computer, many people forget all about dull things like blank disks.

Where to Store Disks

When you buy your computer, buy a disk storage unit. Keep your disks in the unit, away from magnets, extreme heat and cold, and (of course) any food or drink that might spill onto them.

On the 5 1/4" disks, there's a slot in the casing where the disk is exposed. Never touch the exposed area, or the inside hub. Fingerprints can leave oil and dust on the diskette that can partially erase or garble the information stored on it.

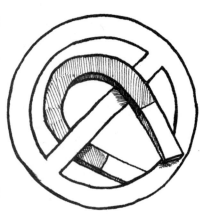

The 5 1/4" disks come with paper dust jackets—use them. The 3 1/2" disks often come in plastic sleeves; you can use these sleeves for storage as extra protection, but they're rather awkward to handle so most people just throw the plastic sleeves away.

The Least You Need to Know

Whether you're buying a new computer or just considering an upgrade of an existing one, you should carefully consider the computer's floppy drive setup. Scan through these reminders to review floppy disk issues.

- ☞ Floppy disks and disk drives come in two stylish models: 5 1/4-inch and 3 1/2-inch versions.

- ☞ Each disk size can be further divided into two different capacities: higher capacity (room for more data and program stuff) and low capacity.

- ☞ Consider buying a PC with two floppy drives, or at least an open drive bay to install a second drive later.

- ☞ When handling disks, keep your fingers off the exposed parts of the disk, and keep the disk away from heat, cold, food, drinks, water, and magnets.

Chapter 11
Hard Disks Aren't So Hard

In This Chapter

- ☞ What a hard drive can do for you
- ☞ How fast is fast with hard drives?
- ☞ Different types of hard drives

In case you haven't noticed, a certain theme has popped up in every chapter so far (it's okay to sing along): To buy the best computer, you first need to decide what tasks you want to perform, and then you need to find the software that can help you accomplish these tasks. Then buy the hardware that runs that software best. Tra-la. Nowhere is this more true than when you choose a hard disk drive for your PC.

A Faster, Easier Way to Store More Stuff

You read in Chapter 10 that floppy disks provide a more permanent way than RAM to store data and programs. But a larger, faster, more convenient storage place exists for your programs and all the work you do with your computer: a hard disk drive.

Because your PC's hard disk will hold the software and data you use regularly, choose the hard disk only after you have a good idea what software you'll run. Your choice of software will affect two important shopping decisions:

- ☞ How much the hard disk holds
- ☞ How fast the hard disk operates

Also, since "bigger" and "faster" almost always translate into "more expensive," know that the hard disk you choose will make a big difference in the price you pay for your PC.

Do I Need a Hard Drive?

You'll find yourself hamstrung pretty quickly without a hard drive. The time waiting for floppies to spin goes by torturously slow. And picture yourself swapping floppies every time you want to spell-check a report or save updates to your database. What's more, programs are quickly outgrowing even the largest hard drives. A ten-second voice sequence in one of today's advanced computer games takes an entire 360KB disk. Finally, the price of a good hard drive starts at around $1–2 per megabyte. A hard drive is no longer a luxury.

There are some hard disk drives on the market that have removable disk cartridges. When you fill up one hard disk cartridge, you can remove it from the drive and insert another one. These drives are a bit slower than their non-removable counterparts, but the speed sacrifice is small if you need lots of disk storage space. Typical cartridge sizes are 44MB, 88MB, and 105MB.

So, no—the computer store's alarm won't blare if you try to leave without a hard drive in your new PC. But my conscience won't rest unless I do my best to persuade you how much you need one.

How Does a Hard Disk Work?

Like floppies, a hard disk's capacity is measured in megabytes (MB or M). A hard disk drive works like a floppy drive, except the disk and drive are one unit; the disk doesn't pop out of the drive to be switched with

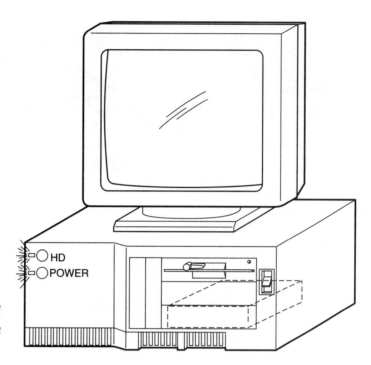

A look at the system box's front will not tell you if the system has a hard drive or not.

another. There's another difference: You can't tell if there's a hard drive in a PC just by looking at the front of the system box, as you can with floppy drives. You'll see only a hard disk indicator light, which comes on whenever the hard disk is being accessed.

The hard drive unit fits inside the system box, in the same kind of drive bay as the floppy drive(s). The disk is made of the same magnetic recording material as a floppy, but is *fixed*, or permanently sealed, in its casing. A disk stores your data on one or more platters, stacked up like pancakes. The bigger the hard disk's capacity, the more pancakes, in general, although some of the newest models squeeze all their capacity onto a single platter.

Each platter is accessed by a *read/write head* that is connected to a *head arm*—sort of like a bizarre jukebox. The platters spin while the head hovers over them. The head floats on a cushion of air that's 20 times thinner than a human hair.

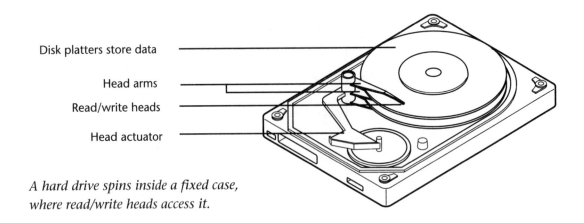

Disk platters store data

Head arms

Read/write heads

Head actuator

A hard drive spins inside a fixed case, where read/write heads access it.

When a hard disk (or a floppy, for that matter) comes off the assembly line, it's smooth and clear, a blank slate. In order to help the read/write heads find your data, a disk needs to be divided into sections, or *formatted*. Formatting a disk lays down on its smooth surface the physical addresses for data, known as tracks and sectors. In the case of hard disks, each platter surface is subdivided.

Tracks can be likened to the concentric grooves on a 33-rpm record album. (Does anybody remember these?) Well, imagine taking the album and etching thin pie slice lines into it. These pie shapes further divide the tracks into sectors, which organize the disk in preparation for data storage. Even though sectors around the outside of the pie cover more physical area than the ones around the inner pie, each sector stores the exact same amount of data, usually about 512 bytes.

Each track, and each sector on that track, is numbered. When you tell your PC to store a data file on the disk, the PC gives your file its own address on the disk.

When you tell your computer to retrieve a file, the DOS software gives special signals to the hard disk controller, telling it exactly where to access the data. You can actually hear your hard drive spinning away, grabbing the data you need and transferring it into RAM. Impressive, eh?

How Much Does the Hard Disk Hold?

Even the smallest hard disk holds about 20 times more megabytes of programs and data than the highest-capacity floppy disk. If you're shopping for a preconfigured PC, it's important to verify not only how big its hard drive is, but details about the drive's controller, access time, transfer rate, physical size, and brand name.

A typical PC system usually comes with its hard drive preformatted. Check with the dealer to ensure yours will be ready to roll (or spin).

How Fast Is It?

Even the older hard drives spin at 3600 rpm, ten times faster than a floppy drive. Two measurements must be considered when you're comparing hard drives: a drive's *average access time* and its *data transfer rate*.

How much disk space do you need? The minimum hard drive for a moderate user is a 100MB model. If you plan to use graphics, sound files, or Windows and Windows compatible software, spring for a 150 to 200MB drive. A power user would jump right into the 350MB–600MB range.

Average Access Time

The *average access time* is the time it takes the drive head to reach and read a random cluster on the disk. Access time is measured in milliseconds (ms), or one-thousandths of a second. The lower the number, the faster the access time.

A fast hard drive is anything less than 20 ms. Here are some general guidelines: a 286 PC should be able to access hard drive data at between 20 and 30 ms; a 386 PC should access between 16 and 20 ms; and a 486 PC should access between 15 and 18 ms.

Data Transfer Rates

The *data transfer rate* refers to how quickly data moves from the hard drive to your PC's RAM memory. A slow data transfer rate can bog down even the fastest access time. Hard drive transfer rates vary with PCs, but the higher the number the faster the rate. A 386/33, or higher, will sport a high transfer rate—700KB per second is fast. For 286 systems, anything over 500KB per second is fine.

What Do Half-Height and Full-Height Mean?

The casing around the hard drive comes in two basic sizes. Half-height, about 1 1/2 inches high, is the standard. Full-height, an older standard, is still used for the largest capacity drives. Some computers sport third-height bays. Tiny 1.3-inch drives are just appearing in the marketplace.

If you're planning to add a bigger hard drive to your PC later, and perhaps add devices like internal CD-ROM drives or tape backup drives (discussed in later chapters), make sure you have the right size bays available for the models that have caught your eye. To be safe, look for models with at least one full-height bay open.

Different Types of Hard Drives

Hard drives use a *controller* to direct data access. The controller technology determines the drive's type.

The most popular type of hard drive is the IDE drive, which stands for *Intelligent Drive Electronics*. The IDE's controller has been integrated onto the drive itself. Older, ST-506 drives (named for their original way of accessing data) had separate controllers. Another type of drive with a built-in controller, *ESDI*, or *Enhanced Small Device Interface*, is the current high-end favorite; it offers high data transfer rates and large capacities.

The SCSI drive is becoming increasingly popular. You might recall the SCSI interface from Chapter 9's discussion of ports. As with other SCSI devices, up to seven SCSI drives can be "chained" together. (There'd be a whole lotta storage goin' on!) To use a SCSI device, like a SCSI disk drive, you must have a SCSI interface card for the drive to plug into (see Chapters 9 and 27).

Confused? Table 11.1 is a quick hard-drive type reference chart that should clear some of this up.

Table 11.1   Type of hard drives

Type	Features
ST-506	Older, slow
	Cheaper
ESDI	Large capacity
	Fast
	Expensive
IDE	Controller on drive
	Good value
SCSI	Allows device chaining
	Controller and processor on adapter card
	Expensive
	Good in multiple-drive systems

Hard Disk Cache Memory

As you learned earlier in the chapter, the speed of a hard disk depends partially on its data transfer rate. But what if you could avoid some of the data transfer entirely?

A *cache controller*, pronounced "cash" controller, cuts down on the amount of data transfer that needs to be done by stashing data in its high-speed memory chips. Then, if you need that same data again, it's available without going back to the hard disk.

Cache controller cards come in two bus styles: ISA and EISA. ISA cards typically can be upgraded to 16MB of RAM, and the EISA cards hold roughly 24MB of RAM. As you know from Chapter 7, the ISA bus design is more common on PCs, while computers that sport the enhanced ISA, or

TECHNO NERD TEACHES

Look for hard drives that use a voice-coil actuator to position the read/write heads. These mechanisms are found on the better drives. Steer clear of earlier stepper motor head positioners; they lose alignment over time, which can grate more against the drive's head and affect a drive's overall performance.

EISA, are more expensive—as are EISA-compatible cache cards. Unless you have abnormally heavy hard disk use in mind, you'll find an ISA-compatible cache sufficient for your needs.

Some SCSI adapters offer cache capabilities. It's becoming more common to see some type of buffers onboard IDE drives, as well. Read-ahead buffers help, but better still are read/write or segmented buffers.

Built-in Caches

Some newer hard drives come with built-in cache capabilities, which speed up data access considerably. Be sure to ask about a hard disk's caching abilities before you buy. These come in two flavors: read-ahead buffers or read/write buffers, also called segmented buffers. This last type is the best type to have.

A less expensive way to benefit from a disk cache is to install special software that uses some of your PC's RAM as a disk cache. Ask a techie friend about this neat use for RAM.

What Is a Stacked Hard Drive?

You might hear the term *stacked hard drive* at user group meetings or when talking with friends who have PCs. Microsoft's DoubleSpace utility and Stack Software's Stacker are a few of a number of commercial products that squeeze down the size of data on a hard drive so the drive can hold more—sometimes up to twice its former capacity. Hard drives that have been compressed in this manner are referred to as "stacked" or "compressed."

Although Stacker and products like it work well for people who have underestimated their storage needs, it's more a "fix" or a last resort before springing the big bucks for a new, larger hard drive. Be sure to carefully estimate your storage needs, and then double this number to allow for expansion.

Removable Hard Drives

Removable hard drives are cartridges that plug into a slot, much like floppy disks fit into a disk drive. They combine the storage capacities of a hard drive with the portability of a floppy disk. If you have compatible drive units in two different computers, for example, you can transport your entire hard disk from one computer to the other.

However, removable hard drives are expensive: $500 to $2,000, depending on capacity, speed, extra disks, and so on. They're also bulky and heavy: even the lightest drives tip the scale at 3 pounds. External models (which most are) can take up a parallel port. And finally, these hard drives are slower and less efficient than regular hard drives.

The Least You Need to Know

In this chapter, you learned about the essential details of hard drives. Consider the items below when evaluating your hard drive purchase or selection.

- ☛ Hard drives are significantly faster than floppy drives and they hold many times more information than floppies.

- ☛ Hard drive storage is measured in megabytes. A typical drive size is 200 megabytes.

- ☛ Your hard drive's average access time should be between 15 and 20 milliseconds.

- ☛ Data transfer rate refers to how quickly data moves from a hard drive to your PC's memory. A rate of 700KB per second is a typical (and acceptably fast) data transfer rate.

- ☛ A cache controller uses fast memory chips to speed up the data transfer rate between your hard drive and your PC's memory.

**Recycling tip: tear this page out
and photocopy it.**

Part III
The Right Accessories

No matter how good the goodies in your system box are, they're worthless without the devices that attach to it. You have doubts about this? Just try to figure how you're going to get any work done on a PC that doesn't have a monitor, keyboard, mouse, or printer. If there's no way to get info in, there's not going to be any info coming out.

This part of the book focuses on ways to get info into and out of your PC. Most PCs, of course, have a keyboard and a monitor, but you may be surprised at the plethora of toys and gadgets available to add that extra oomph of control to your system!

Chapter 12
The Monitor Aisle

In This Chapter

- ☞ How a monitor works
- ☞ Evaluating your need for color
- ☞ Resolution, pixels, and dot pitch
- ☞ Monitor sizes and related considerations
- ☞ Other important monitor considerations

Pay no attention to those swirling, colorful screens! Seductive and enticing, a state-of-the-art video display sells PCs like nothing else. It's the trump card used by PC stores and mail-order ads to tempt people like Bob and Bernice Bungle into impulse buys.

Ahem! All eyes this way. . . Shall we continue?

Most books on shopping for a computer tell you more about choosing between video standards than about selecting a good monitor. This book gives step-by-step instructions on buying both a video card *and* a monitor.

So far, we've covered the components inside the PC. This chapter focuses on the most noticeable part outside a PC: its video display, or *monitor*. The monitor provides a way for you and the computer to communicate. You see your work and the computer's responses to your commands on the monitor.

To learn more about letters like VGA, EGA, SVGA and the like, flip over to Chapter 13, "Video Modes to Max Out Your Monitor." To learn how to buy the best monitor for your money, stick around.

By the Way . . .

The earliest *monochrome*, or single-color, monitors (*MDA*) displayed text in one color, but no graphics. A color monitor released at the same time, *CGA*, could display four colors at a time from a possible 16, or one color with a crisper image. A *Hercules graphics card* enabled fairly crisp monochrome graphics. *EGA*, the next standard, allowed 16 colors with an even crisper image. *VGA*, *Enhanced VGA*, and *Super VGA* (today's standards) offer at least 256 colors and photo-graphic-quality images. Details on each of these standards, plus tips on which to buy, appear in Chapter 13.

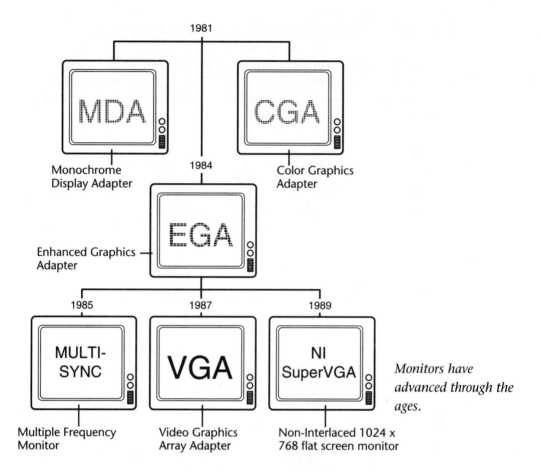

Monitors have advanced through the ages.

How Does a Monitor Work?

Just as on a TV set, everything takes place inside a vacuum—the *cathode ray tube*, or *CRT*. Electron guns shoot beams through the tube to scan the inside of the monitor, which is lined with tiny phosphors that glow as they're struck by these electron beams. When you look at your screen, you're actually watching the peaceful glow of thousands of phosphors.

A color monitor features hundreds of thousands of groups, or *triads*, of three phosphor dots: one red, one green, and one blue. Color monitors also come with three electron guns inside the CRT: one for each color in the triad. When a beam increases its electron rate, the triad takes on the hue hit by the strongest beam. Each beam hits the screen many times per second, continuously scanning the inside of the monitor. If you look at the side of the monitor, you can see the subtle scan flicker.

A Monitor and Its Video Card

A monitor is only as "good" as the video card inside the PC. Monitors are usually *downward compatible*. That means it's usually possible to run a new color monitor with an older, less-advanced video card. But the results will be crude.

Think of the monitors we meet in this chapter as if their corresponding video cards were "driving" them. In Chapter 13, you'll see why most people buy a video card that corresponds to the monitor they buy.

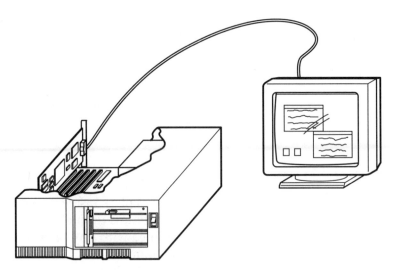

A video card inside the PC controls the monitor's display.

There are lots of factors to consider before picking out a monitor—and there's no universal answer. The rest of this chapter will introduce you to the important concepts—and help you decide what you need.

Color or Monochrome?

Computer monitors come in two basic styles: *color* and *monochrome*. You can choose a monochrome monitor with either amber/black or green/black hues. These inexpensive models are still on the market. They display sharp text and are adequate for very simple applications.

Color monitors come bundled with most preconfigured PC systems today. They display a spectrum of colors, commonly 16 or 256 at once, depending on the monitor/video card combination. The shopping tips discussed in this chapter pertain mostly to color monitors.

Do I Need Color?

You don't need a color monitor to get your work done, unless your application involves color desktop publishing, computer art, or graphic design. On the other hand, a color monitor enlivens the many hours you'll spend deep in computing sessions. Color is fun. Most business software uses color to highlight functions or otherwise ease computing tasks. In fact, Microsoft Windows and Microsoft Windows software are much harder to use without color, and these programs demand a monitor that's capable of graphics.

Paper-White monitors provide extra-crisp, black-on-white displays used in specialty fields like desktop publishing and computer-assisted design (CAD). The display technology behind these often-oversized beauties represents an advance over color monitors, so expect them to be much more costly than a more mundane, monochrome model.

Text or Graphics?

Most monitors (including all color ones) can operate in either of two modes: *text-only* or *graphics*. Very few monochrome monitors today are text-only. Of course, text-only monitors, if you can find them, are dirt cheap because they're not very versatile. If at all possible, however, spend the extra money and get a graphics monitor. Later, you'll be glad you did.

Even monochrome monitors can display single-color graphics with a Hercules graphics card installed in the PC. (Hercules is a brand name.)

What Resolution?

Resolution determines how crisp an image looks on a given monitor. Four factors decide a monitor's resolution: *pixels, dot pitch, convergence,* and *refresh rate.*

> ## By the Way . . .
> Perhaps a fifth element is the most important of all: your subjective judgment. If you don't think a monitor looks that good, all the numbers and benchmarks in the world aren't going to change your mind.

What Are Pixels?

One of the biggest factors affecting resolution is the number of *pixels* that run across and down the screen. Pixel is short for PICture ELement. The more pixels, the sharper the picture.

Although a monitor is advertised as having a given "resolution," that's a maximum, theoretical number based on the best possible video card connected to that monitor. The actual number of pixels in a given display is determined by the software and the video card—not by the monitor alone.

For example, video cards of the VGA standard enable VGA or Super VGA monitors to display 640 x 480 pixels. A Super VGA video card enables a Super VGA monitor to display images with a crisp 800 by 600 resolution or even higher, but a regular VGA monitor would still be limited to 640 x 480, even with this souped-up Super VGA card attached. Check Chapter 13 for more on video cards and the resolutions they provide.

What Is Dot Pitch?

The color monitor's red, blue, or green electron beams hit their corresponding dot color with the help of a Swiss-cheese-like shield called a *shadow mask*. Tiny holes in the mask guide the beams, so the "blue" beam hits the blue dot, for example.

The distance between the mask's holes is known as *dot pitch*, measured in millimeters (mm). Dot pitch determines how grainy or tight the picture will be. Look for a dot pitch of .28 mm or less. Smaller screens in particular look much more focused with a tighter dot pitch.

What Is Convergence?

When all three electron beams hit a triad evenly, a monitor is said to have perfect *convergence*. Differences in the alignment of the electron guns or a distortion in the shadow mask can throw this off, causing color imperfections and a blurry looking screen.

Ask the dealer to show you the monitor displaying a pure white background. If the monitor looks pinkish or bluish, ask to see another model by the same manufacturer. If it's still off, look at another brand.

What Is Refresh Rate?

A *refresh rate* is the rate that electrons scan the screen from top to bottom to restore the tiny phosphors. Refresh rate, also known as *vertical scanning frequency*, is measured in hertz (Hz). The higher the hertz, the less flicker you'll see on-screen.

Look for refresh rates above 70Hz. The big-screen monitors require even higher refresh rates; anything below 90Hz will cause noticeable flickers and eye fatigue.

Multi-Scan or Multi-Frequency Refresh Rate

All graphics monitors have two frequencies: a *vertical scan rate* (see previous page) and a *horizontal scan rate* (the rate at which a line draws across the screen). Each graphics mode requires different frequencies. *Multi-scan* monitors, also known as *multisync* or *multi-frequency*, can adapt to suit any scanning frequency and are compatible with a wider variety of graphics standards.

If a monitor's billed as multi-scan, make sure it's able to switch back and forth between a variety of modes—not just one or two. Look for automatic resizing when the resolution switches from one video mode to another. Some monitors only offer manual switching. Look for a monitor that has a broad range of horizontal and vertical scanning frequencies: from 30 kilohertz (kHz) to 64kHz horizontal and 50 hertz (Hz) to 90Hz vertical.

How Software Affects Resolution

Before you sink $1,200 into the finest monitor in the store, remember this: it's the software that creates those dazzling images. If the software you plan to use does not support your monitor's fancy Super VGA modes, you're no better off than the guy down the street with a regular VGA monitor.

However, support for high-resolution video modes, like Super VGA, is becoming more and more common in software packages. Even if most current software can't take advantage of it, shoppers with an eye to the future should investigate Super VGA (discussed in Chapter 13).

Look for a non-interlaced monitor, which won't flicker and cause as much eyestrain as an interlaced model will.

Interlaced or Non-Interlaced?

Interlaced means the monitor's electron beams scan alternating lines on the monitor, a method of displaying images which speeds up the refresh rate of cheaper monitors. Non-interlaced monitors scan the entire screen at once, and they're becoming the standard.

Big Screen or Standard Size?

If your application requires you to see two pages of a document at once, as in desktop publishing, or to see many programs simultaneously in Windows, consider buying a large-screen monitor. These monitors measure 20 inches or more, but you'll pay for the added convenience: They run between $2,000 and $4,000. Make sure you have enough desk space for one of these honkers, too.

To be prepared for the future, buy at least an 800 x 600 resolution, .28-dot pitch, non-interlaced Super VGA color monitor with a refresh rate of 70Hz. This monitor, along with an SVGA adapter card, can keep up with anything your software can dish out—right now and for the next few years.

Other Monitor Issues

Besides the major factors you've learned about so far, there are a number of "extras" to look for in a monitor. While not as performance-critical as resolution or color, they do make a difference, especially after you get the monitor home and start using it.

Flat Versus Curved Screens

Flat-screened monitors are quickly becoming standard. These screens reduce glare, a major source of eye fatigue. Expect to pay more for the flat screen than the rounded one.

Anti-Glare Coating

Increasingly, models offer anti-glare coating to combat sore, red eyes. Inspect these models closely to make sure the coating doesn't degrade the color quality or image sharpness.

By the Way . . .

If your monitor gives you glare problems, you can buy a special anti-glare screen that fits over the glass of your monitor. These $25 glass plates reduce glare and eyestrain significantly, but are not as attractive, durable, or effective as built-in coating.

Low Radiation

If you're concerned about monitors emitting radiation, look for compliance with the Swedish MPR-2 standard. Radiation studies are inconclusive at this point, so protection's not guaranteed, but you might feel better knowing that you're doing all you can to lessen your exposure to electromagnetic rays.

Easy-to-Use Controls

Ideally, the monitor's controls should be along the front, where you can reach them easily. Some newer models offer digital controls, with buttons instead of knobs for more precise tuning of contrast, brightness, and sizing. The most advanced monitors offer adjustable tint and LCD status readouts. These fancy features may not be worth the extra price you'll pay.

Make sure you can turn the monitor and tilt it to your optimum viewing angle. Add-on products that accomplish the same thing are available; they're recommended by computer-health experts as one way to prevent a sore neck while computing.

The Least You Need to Know

Chances are good that you'll choose a color monitor, but it will be an informed decision—not the result of a wide-eyed stroll down the monitor aisle!

- ☞ Monitors come in either monochrome or color models. Color models correspond to several video card standards, discussed in Chapter 13.

- ☞ Check a monitor's resolution, size, and control layout before you buy.

- ☞ In deciding between color and monochrome, keep your present and future software requirements in mind.

- ☞ If you buy a multisync model, be sure it automatically resizes at different resolutions.

- ☞ Make sure the monitor comes with all cables and connectors.

Special bonus virtual text page.
(Virtually no text on it.)

Chapter 13
Video Cards to Max Out Your Monitor

In This Chapter

- Video cards and display quality
- EGA, VGA, SVGA: What do all those letters mean?
- Video card memory
- Windows accelerator video cards
- Getting the best video card for your money

In Chapter 12, you learned that a monitor was the most visual way for a user to communicate with a PC, and for the PC to communicate back. Since no monitor can function without a corresponding video adapter card inside the PC's expansion slot, consider this a "companion" chapter to Chapter 12.

This chapter details the various PC graphics cards. As you read, you will learn to decipher the mumbo-jumbo you'll encounter when making the important decision of what video card and monitor to buy for your PC.

Resolution Revolution

Like the monitors they control, video cards have improved through the years. Early color graphics modes look primitive compared to today's. Although speed and colors count, the *resolution*, or image sharpness, that's possible with current video cards really points to the advances in PC displays.

Chapter 12 explained how a monitor's advertised resolution is a theoretical number, something like 640 x 480 (the numbers vary depending on the type of card). This number stands for the maximum number of *pixels*, or picture elements, the monitor could display across and down if it had the perfect video card for its needs. The higher the numbers, the sharper the picture.

Resolution's a Group Effort

Although maximum resolution is important, a monitor's true resolution depends on two other factors. First, the monitor's video card must be able to reach that same maximum resolution. Second, a software program must be able to recognize and make use of this resolution.

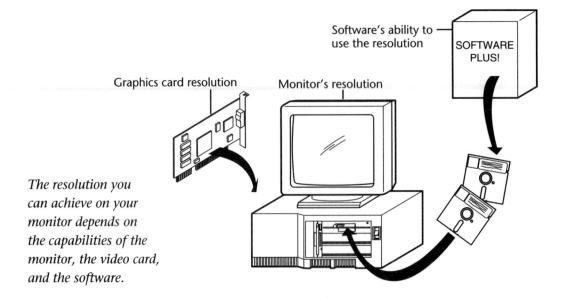

Software's ability to use the resolution

SOFTWARE PLUS!

Graphics card resolution

Monitor's resolution

The resolution you can achieve on your monitor depends on the capabilities of the monitor, the video card, and the software.

Resolution Evolution

Higher resolutions display clearer, more realistic images on your monitor. As monitors and cards have progressed in quality, they've driven advances in software, input devices, and even printers. This section will tell you about the major kinds of video cards, from the oldest technology to the newest.

MDA—Plain Vanilla

The earliest standard, *MDA*, offered a clear monochrome text display (no graphics) at a resolution of 720 x 350 pixels. This was a great improvement over the TV sets and terminal displays available to the earliest PC users.

Hercules Graphics

In 1982, an enterprising grad student developed a monochrome graphics card so he could use his PC to write papers in his native Thai alphabet. When a major software package started to support it, the card gave rise to a new standard, *HGC* or *Hercules Graphics Card*. Hercules cards enabled graphics at 720 x 320 resolution. This monochrome graphics standard is still supported by many programs.

CGA—C Is for Crude

As color grew more affordable, it's amazing how many users flocked to a crude, blurred, blocky-looking standard called *CGA*, or *Color Graphics Adapter*. CGA offered a few different graphics modes, depending on how many colors were displayed. The most common resolution was 320 x 200 pixels (quite a step down from monochrome) in four dreary colors: cyan blue, weird magenta, glaring yellow, and basic black. Reading the chunky, ill-formed text this mode provided made deciphering the Rosetta stone seem easy.

Enter EGA

The *EGA*, or *Enhanced Graphics Adapter*, appeared in 1984 and boosted color graphics up to 16 simultaneous colors at CGA's resolution. Later models sported memory chips and were capable of 16 colors out of a *palette* (color range) of 64, at 640 x 350 resolution. You can still find EGA monitors and cards on the market. For those on a budget who don't need to run graphics-demanding Windows or other GUI software, EGA is a decent "make do" alternative.

VGA

Chances are, at this stage in the game, you'll buy a card from the *Video Graphics Array*, or *VGA* standard. Out of a palette of 262,144 colors, you get either 256 simultaneously, at 640 x 480 resolution, or 16 at full 800 x 600 resolution. Most preconfigured PCs come bundled with VGA monitors that have VGA cards already planted inside the system box. Most of today's software packages take advantage of the VGA standard.

Super VGA

Super VGA offers all the colors of VGA but at an even higher resolution: 1024 x 768 pixels or more. This standard isn't very standardized. For all the other standards we've talked about so far, the software you buy usually comes with video driver files that make the program work on that type of monitor. (Some software comes with a hundred or more video driver files.) This works because no matter what brand the video card is, it conforms to one of the standard formats.

With SVGA, though, there is no established standard. Each manufacturer does his own thing, resulting in a video card that requires its own special video drivers for each program you want to run in SVGA mode. That's why each SVGA card comes with a disk full of special driver files for the most popular software (such as Windows).

Keep in mind that these intense levels of resolution can cram too much detail onto a smaller monitor. Consider going all the way to a 20-inch screen if your graphics requirements demand a video accelerator. Talk to users and jot down their experiences with different brands. Read reviews in magazines, too.

The 8514/A Standard

Also known as *Hi-Res SVGA*, this standard offers a tightly focused 1,024 x 768 display, at least 1MB of video memory, and a graphics coprocessor chip that hastens drawing. Monitors supporting this standard are up there in the price range, but they'll start becoming more affordable soon. Software, too, is only starting to come around to this level of graphics quality.

Resolution vs. Color

No matter how far PC graphics have come, users still face the same dilemma as in the old HGC/CGA days: resolution vs. color. Table 13.1 shows the evolution of resolutions and colors offered by different monitor/video card combinations.

Table 13.1   Resolution and Color Evolution

Graphics Standard	Colors	Resolution
MDA	single (text only)	720 x 350
CGA	4	320 x 200
	2	640 x 200
HGC	monochrome	720 x 348
EGA	16	640 x 350
VGA	16	800 x 600
	256	640 x 480
SVGA*	256	1,024 x 768
	16	1,280 x 1024
8514/A	256	1,024 x 768

Note: SVGA, not being a true standard, varies in its capabilities from brand to brand.

Video Cards Need Memory, Too

Graphics cards fly when equipped with memory chips, which take the graphics processing load off the main processor and speed up the rate at which graphics display and screens refresh.

Typically, you'll see a card advertised with 512KB or 1MB of RAM, although some cards hold several megabytes of video RAM. You'll pay extra for more RAM, but it may be worth it for your graphics-intensive applications, or if you plan to run a lot of Windows programs.

Before you buy, find out how much memory a card comes with, and what the card's maximum memory capacity is. You may want to upgrade later.

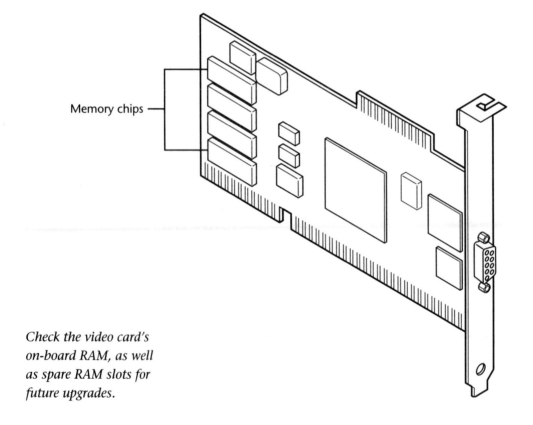

Memory chips

Check the video card's on-board RAM, as well as spare RAM slots for future upgrades.

The type of memory chips makes a difference in a card's speed. *DRAM* chips, also known as *Dynamic RAM*, are slower than special *VRAM*, or *Video RAM* chips. But cards with VRAM cost more.

What's a Bit Number Doing on the Card?

Chapter 7 discusses how a PC motherboard's expansion slots differ in size, or bit width. Recall that a bit is the name for the smallest unit that data can be broken down into. Video cards also differ in bit widths. As with other types of expansion cards, higher bit widths ensure that information can travel at a higher rate through the card. Because graphics can really bog down a PC, if you'll be doing lots of graphics, invest in a video card with a higher bit width.

An altogether different "bit number" exists with video cards (just to confuse shoppers). If you see "4-bit color" in a video card ad, this refers to the number of bits it takes for the screen to show pixels. This is extremely technical, so for now, know that the higher the "bit color" number, the more colors it can show and the more expensive the card! Currently, the high-end cards run up to 24 bits, enabling more than 16 million possible colors. That's neat . . .except that most software can't take advantage of it!

Video Accelerator Boards

Video accelerator boards, also known as Windows accelerators, take the place of the PC's normal video card to enable souped-up graphics capabilities, thanks to on-board graphics coprocessors (and often VRAM

TECHNO NERD TEACHES

What does the ad mean by VESA? VESA stands for Video Electronics Standards Association, a group of companies that sets standards for video cards and monitors. A card touted as VESA-standard means its manufacturer complies with VESA's specifications. The VESA folks are working on a standard meant to speed up image loading. Creating a standard should ensure that different manufacturers' local bus video cards can fit into any brand of PC.

video memory chips). Video accelerator boards should offer 1,280 x 1,024 resolution, in non-interlaced mode, with refresh rates of 70Hz or higher to reduce flicker.

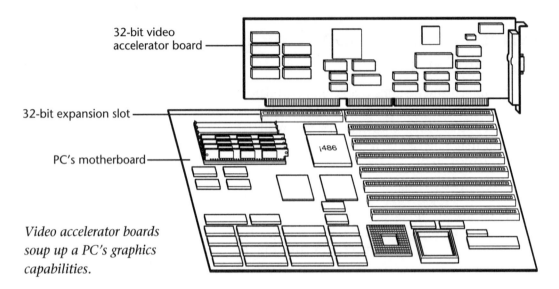

32-bit video accelerator board

32-bit expansion slot

PC's motherboard

Video accelerator boards soup up a PC's graphics capabilities.

The best card for your money is a 16-bit Super VGA card with at least 1MB memory and a money-back guarantee. If you get a Super VGA, make sure the video card comes with a disk of software drivers to run your planned software—or else you'll see them in plain old VGA mode. And make sure you buy from a reliable company, so you'll be able to get updated driver files in the future.

Video accelerator boards differ from local bus video boards, which give you another way to improve a PC's graphics capability. A PC system with a local bus has moved the video circuitry from a card in the expansion slot directly onto the motherboard, so it's connected right to the CPU, or the local bus, rather than the expansion bus.

Although local bus video can load images quickly into video memory, they still place the video grunt work on the CPU's shoulders. For now, the video accelerator meets the advanced user's needs best.

Which Video Card Should I Buy?

Look at different card/monitor combinations in stores. See what your planned software requires, and try out a couple of the applications with the video card.

Get a monitor that matches the capability of your video card. Make sure the two are compatible in areas like non-interlacing, multi-frequency modes, and vertical scan rates, covered in Chapter 12.

If you buy a multi-frequency monitor, make sure the card enables mode-switching through software, so you don't have to fiddle with dip switches on the card whenever you want to change modes.

The Least You Need to Know

Choosing a video card can be daunting, but if you take your time and review your video needs you will make a good choice. Run through these reminders as you evaluate your video card needs:

- ☞ The video card inside your PC drives the monitor.

- ☞ A display's quality represents the combined capabilities of the monitor, video card, and software you're running.

- ☞ The best card for your money is a 16-bit Super VGA card with at least 1MB memory and a money-back guarantee.

- ☞ For truly intensive graphics, you may want to investigate graphics accelerator boards, often called Windows accelerators.

This is not a printing error. The page is <u>supposed</u> to be blank.

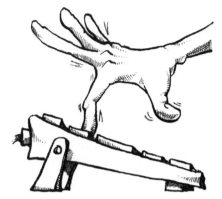

Chapter 14
Not Too Bored with Keyboards

In This Chapter

- ☞ Standard and enhanced keyboards
- ☞ Alternative keyboards
- ☞ Keyboards with built-in trackballs
- ☞ Accessories for your keyboard

A keyboard helps you put information into the PC where it can do some good. A keyboard's not as glamorous as a monitor, to be sure, but it's just as important to get one you like. You'll be looking at the monitor you choose for hours on end—and you'll be tapping your keyboard for just as many hours.

Aren't All Keyboards the Same?

A computer's keyboard is based on a typewriter keyboard, with some extra keys for certain computer chores. The keyboard connects to a special port in the back of your computer.

Keyboards come in different styles of two basic models, but beyond that, they all seem to *feel* different. Some people like a keyboard with a little resistance to it. Others prefer a "loose" keyboard that performs at the slightest tap.

By the Way . . .

Keyboards made by the Compaq company are notoriously firm. And people still rave about the touch on the original IBM keyboard. (In fact, IBM has recently started selling a replacement keyboard that they're billing as "The Original IBM Keyboard" to cash in on people's fond memories.)

The original IBM PC keyboard sported such a small *Enter* key that users often accidentally hit the Print-Screen key instead. If they slipped and tapped the adjacent Shift key, too, the PC immediately sent their screen's contents to the printer.

You can't enjoy your computer as long as you hate the feel of your keyboard, so try out a few different brands. Mail-order shoppers will have to try some out at a store—and then ask some very detailed questions over the phone! You might buy one that feels exactly like the one you use at work—or one that's just the opposite!

Standard or Enhanced Keyboard?

One of the keys used most often on a PC is the Enter key. It works like a typewriter's carriage return (in word processing) and sends instructions of every type to the PC.

The Standard Keyboard

Like the keyboard on the original IBM PC, the standard keyboard lines up the *function keys* used in working with a software program along the left side. This keyboard improved upon the original keyboard by labeling the Tab and Shift keys and by beefing up the Enter key size. Standard keyboards come in two versions: an *XT-compatible model* and an *AT-compatible model*.

The 101-Key Enhanced Keyboard

One big difference between the standard and enhanced models is the function key placement. On the enhanced keyboard, they've been moved from the left side to a row along the top, above the number keys and far out of reach of most touch-typists. (Not an enhancement in my book!)

> ### By the Way . . .
> Northgate brand keyboards were the first to offer enhanced keyboards with function keys in both spots, so people didn't have to relearn typing inside their favorite software just because they got a new keyboard. (Many bought Northgate computers just for the keyboard.) These days, Gateway and many other computer manufacturers offer the same thing.

Another difference is that the enhanced keyboards offer a bank of *cursor movement keys* separate from the *numeric keypad*. (*Cursor keys* let you move the typing point, or *cursor*, around the screen. A numeric keypad works as a calculator to perform operations on numbers.) Standard keyboard users must press a *NumLock* key to toggle between cursor or numeric keypad modes, so they can't simultaneously work with numbers and move their cursor around—a big hassle for regular spreadsheet users. In this respect, the enhanced keyboard is a big improvement over the standard keyboard's combined numeric keypad/cursor keys.

If you have an older computer (below a 286), it's important that you get an XT-compatible keyboard; an AT-compatible keyboard will not work. Conversely, if you have a 286 or above (an AT computer), make sure you get an AT-compatible keyboard. A few keyboards have a switch you can flip that lets them work with the opposite type of PC.

Original

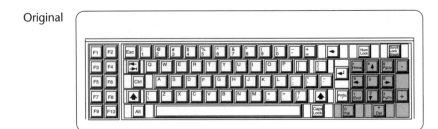

Standard

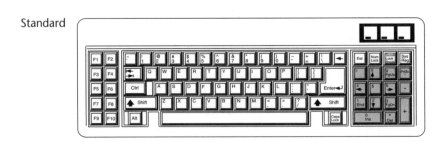

Enhanced

Original IBM PC, standard, and enhanced keyboards.

Another Alternative: The Dvorak Keyboard

The original typewriter layout was designed to befuddle speedy typists enough to keep the old mechanical keys from jamming. Today's electronic keyboard poses no such pitfalls for users with agile fingers. You can overcome this interesting remnant of the machine age by buying a Dvorak keyboard, like the one in Figure 14.2. It's specially designed to take advantage of the stronger fingers on the right hand. To avoid confusion, make sure keyboards you use elsewhere are of the same layout.

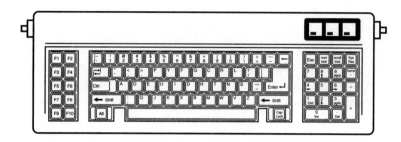

If you'd like to type faster, the Dvorak keyboard optimizes every stroke.

Built-In Trackballs and Other Keyboard Extras

Keyboards, once simple and predictable, are gaining in features and in cost. You can buy a model with a built-in trackball device that lets you position the cursor by rolling your fingertips instead of pecking at the cursor keys. Trackballs, like the mice discussed in Chapter 15, speed your movements in graphics applications.

Other keyboard models sport built-in calculators and even rubbery touch-pads to replace the numeric keypad. Many new models offer a row of programmable function keys along the top. These let you record keystrokes you find yourself repeating often. You assign the sequence to one of these keys and then press the one key instead of several. Imagine typing your name and address with a single keystroke. These high-end keyboard features sport high-end price tags, however, so be careful to assess what features you'll truly need.

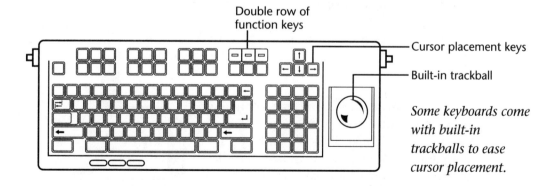

Double row of function keys

Cursor placement keys

Built-in trackball

Some keyboards come with built-in trackballs to ease cursor placement.

Wrist Protectors

On a long-term basis, the repeated motion of typing can cause a range of painful conditions to hands and wrists. Fortunately, most computer stores and mail-order companies carry products that ease the blows. A keyboard wrist protector, a thick strip of rubbery wet suit material, may be all you need to cushion the impact from hours of typing.

Keyboard Covers

Clear plastic devices on the market sit over your keyboard and protect it from dust, crumbs, and even beverage spills, while still allowing you to type. Some find typing atop one of these devices just as easy as typing without one—but it's one of those things you have to try out before you buy.

Keycaps

Most software programs enable you to reassign keys and their functions in that program. Special plastic key caps fit over normal keys on the keyboard, giving you a way to label the reassigned keys. Colored keycaps let you color-code frequently used functions.

Pre-Purchase Keyboard Tests to Perform

When shopping for a keyboard, check for the position of the most frequently used keys, such as Enter, Backspace, the Shift keys, and the Function keys. Make sure they're in the right place for you—you'll be pressing them a lot.

Test the keyboard's ergonomic-awareness by seeing if you can raise or lower its back end to a better angle. Sit down and type a few paragraphs on a variety of keyboards to see how the "touch" appeals to you.

Check the keyboard's fitness with the trusty *N-key rollover test.* A quality keyboard should let you strike another key while holding down the first one and making it repeat. To test the keyboard, press down the "j" key and make a whole row of j's. While still holding down "j," press "f," "g," and "h," too. A good keyboard will throw something besides j's on the screen.

The Least You Need to Know

Finding the right keyboard is a subjective process. Just because a keyboard comes bundled with a PC doesn't mean you have to take it home. Try out a range of models and buy the one that feels right. Review this list of reminders before you jump into buying a new keyboard:

- Almost all computers come "bundled" with a keyboard.

- Enhanced keyboards have cursor keys and a numeric keypad to assist you with cursor navigation and number entry.

- Function-key placement and the general keyboard layout should suit you.

- Most keyboards allow you to adjust the keyboard's angle for comfort.

- Before buying a keyboard, try it out!

This page unintentionally left blank.

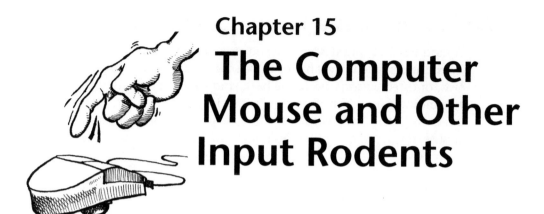

Chapter 15
The Computer Mouse and Other Input Rodents

In This Chapter

- What is a mouse?
- How the computer mouse works
- Choosing a mouse interface
- How many mouse buttons should you have?
- Looking at other input devices

Despite the cute name, a computer mouse can boost your efficiency in a decidedly no-nonsense way. Like the keyboards described in the last chapter, a mouse is an *input device*. Positioning the cursor with a mouse gives you another way of telling the PC to do something. Paired with a keyboard, a computer mouse gives you quick, smooth control over your applications.

Although a mouse is the most common of its genre, a range of input devices exist. If you want to spice-up your interaction with your computer you might try a mouse pen or a trackball—popular alternatives for cursor control.

But a Mouse Is a Furry Rodent, Right?

A mouse is an input device that moves a pointer on your PC's monitor. White and shaped like a bar of Dove soap, the computer mouse has one, two, or three buttons along the back, and a ball in its underbelly. The tail-like mouse cord connects to the PC's serial or mouse port. The whole effect, with the "tail" cord, the white shape, and the buttons, looks like a mouse. (Okay, so computer designers *have* been sitting too long in front of their PCs!)

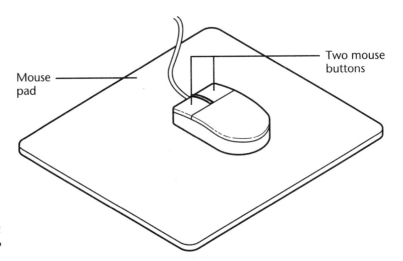

Mouse pad

Two mouse buttons

It's a bar of soap, it's a plane, it's a . . .mouse?

By the Way . . .

Neanderthal Mouse: Back in 1967, a researcher came up with the mouse prototype while working on ways to make computers more understandable and easier to use. Softball-sized, the device had three control buttons where eyes and mouth belonged, plus large wheels underneath for "feet." Embellished with a tail-like cord, the device was quickly dubbed "mouse." The name stuck.

How Does It Work?

You place your hand atop the mouse and roll it around over a mouse pad, pressing buttons along the back, as your software requires. As the mouse rolls up and down, across and back, the cursor on screen scuttles around correspondingly—pushed by a signal that reads the mouse motion.

In some software applications, the mouse pointer looks like an arrow; in others, a bar. When you maneuver the mouse pointer to a desired object on-screen (whether it's a block of text, a cell in a spreadsheet, or a command box in Windows), you hold down a mouse button to *select*, or highlight, text. You can press-and-release, or *click* (even *double-click*) the button to activate a software command.

Not all software supports a mouse. If it does, you can use the mouse's pointer instead of tedious cursor keys to highlight text, invoke commands, view menus, drag objects, and navigate around the program.

Who Needs a Mouse or Other Input Devices?

Some computer users go their whole careers without ever touching an input device except the keyboard. But more and more these days, mice and other "alternative" input devices are cropping up. Who might use one? Here's a few ideas:

- ☞ **Windows Users**   Although Windows and other GUI programs come with keyboard commands, forget it! You need a mouse if you plan to run Windows and Windows-like programs. Period.

- ☞ **Desktop Publishers**   Designers wouldn't think of trying to navigate their software without a mouse. Dragging and sizing images, making subtle text adjustments, creating type styles: a mouse improves all these functions. Many desktop publishers opt for a trackball instead, and scanners help these professionals add graphics to their work.

☛ **Computer Artists and Multimedia Producers**   Mouse pens, scanners, and mice ease the production of computer art and multimedia efforts.

☛ **Accountants and Business Professionals**   Mice make even the most ho-hum business applications zing. Once you select a spreadsheet's rows and columns with a mouse you will never go without again.

Mouse Comparisons

The mouse family is sizable, with many subspecies. Whether country mouse or city mouse, an easy way to compare them is by *ppi*, or *points per inch* resolution. A ppi of 200 lets you select objects more precisely; 400 ppi requires even less wrist motion to move the pointer across the screen.

Two Interfaces: Bus Mouse or Serial Mouse

A serial mouse connects to a PC's serial port. A bus mouse comes with an expansion card, or plugs into the PC's "mouse" port if it has one. (If you forgot ports, head back to Chapter 9.) The type of mouse you buy depends on which slot is free on your PC. If your computer is long on expansion slots, buy a bus mouse. If you have few free slots, but you do have a free serial port, your best buy is a serial mouse.

Bus mice cost a bit more, but some users report more responsiveness and better circuitry within. Plus they don't take up one of your serial ports, which could be better filled by a modem (discussed in Chapter 17).

Cheap mechanical mice can be had for as little as $30 by mail order. Expect to pay more for an optical mouse, which is better constructed and will need less care and maintenance.

Optical Mouse vs. Mechanical Mouse

All mice glide around on a rubbery, cushiony mouse pad. But an optical mouse sports optical sensors that "read" a special pad printed with an optically detectable grid. The higher-priced optical mouse offers increased precision over the mechanical mouse, which works by means of a roller ball that can clog up with dirt or lint.

The Cordless Mouse

Cordless mice come in two species: *radio-controlled* and *infrared*. Both types liberate you from a mouse cord, since they work via a receiving unit, which connects to the PC via a serial port or expansion slot. The cordless mouse shoots waves back to the unit recording its position; the unit then communicates to the PC.

The radio mouse costs more than the infrared—and both cost more than a normal mouse. For both types, the required mechanics lead to a larger-than-normal mouse, which some users say is too big to grasp comfortably. The infrared model works fine until an object like a coffee cup is inadvertently placed between the mouse and its receiving unit. Then the beam is blocked and mousing ceases.

Wait until the novelty of your new PC has worn off before you buy one of these toys, even if it will unleash you from the mouse-strings.

Mini Mouse

Where's Mickey? Wrong fictional character. A tiny, 2 1/4-inch mouse called the Gulliver hopes to take mousing to new levels of portability. Held with two fingers, like a piece of chalk, the Gulliver works with a friction-activated, floating-ball movement that lets a user mouse around anywhere, even on the sleeve of a jacket.

What's Mouse Compatibility?

Most software supports a variety of mouse types, but there are certain standards in the industry that many manufacturers follow. Microsoft-compatible is the most common standard; Logitech-compatible is another.

Why Do Some Models Have Three Buttons?

Mice that are *Microsoft-compatible* have two buttons, while mice that are *Logitech-compatible* have three. Very few software packages allow you to use the third (middle) button. Windows itself recognizes only one mouse button, but some Windows applications allow you to use two or even three buttons.

What Mouse Should I Buy?

Look for a mouse with a 200 points per inch resolution or above. As with keyboards, mice are a matter of comfort and usability, so make sure you buy one with a money-back guarantee.

Whatever you buy, make sure it's Microsoft-compatible.

The mouse you buy should come with special software, called a device driver. This software tells your PC that you have a mouse by putting a line in one of two crucial files in your PC, either the CONFIG.SYS file or the AUTOEXEC.BAT file. Have a techie friend help you install your mouse, or ask nicely at the local user group. If all else fails, a good DOS book should help, like *The Complete Idiot's Guide to DOS,* by Jennifer Flynn.

Often, a mouse's software includes special menu or graphics programs. It's fun to play with your mouse's graphics program, especially if you have a color monitor.

Other Input Devices

Portable and laptop computers have spawned a nest of mouse substitutes. When shopping for one of these pointing devices, make sure it comes with a Microsoft-compatible mouse driver. It's essential to look at connectors: If the device requires a serial port, do you have a spare? If it requires an expansion slot, do you have an extra one? Make sure the cord's not too long . . .or too short! No matter how small the ball is in one of these devices, make sure it moves freely and feels right.

Trackball

Take a mouse and (very gently!) flip it on its back. Now roll the mouse ball around with your fingertips. Voilà! That's the basic idea behind a trackball—all that's left is to pry the mouse buttons off the bottom and glue them on either side of the ball. (Do not try this at home.)

The advantage to trackballs is that, being stationary, they take up less desk space. You can buy trackballs attached to high-end keyboards, as you read in Chapter 14. They're also available in stand-alone models that sit next to your keyboard, where a mouse and mouse pad would be. Trackballs are mouse balls on steroids; most average about the size of an eight ball. Miniature trackball units clip onto the side of a desktop or laptop keyboard.

Mouse Pen

Imagine a pen with a mouse's rolling ball where the ball-point tip should be. Now feed the pen a steady diet of coconut ice cream and cheesecake so it bulges into behemoth stage. Stick some miniaturized mouse buttons down the front and you've just imagined a mouse pen. Mouse pens are a perfect choice for people who want the agility, but not the bulk, of a true mouse.

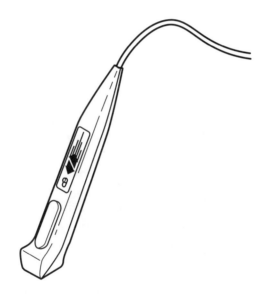

Mouse pens present a compact alternative to mice.

Scanners, Joysticks, and Other Input Toys

Besides the mouse family, there are many other input devices on the market. Some are more practical than others. As with any computer add-on, check to see what your software requires before you buy anything.

Hand-Held Scanners

A hand-held scanner lets you put pictures into your PC, ready to be added to a newsletter or transformed into Windows wallpaper. You hold down the scanner and guide it over the image to be scanned, kind of like the bar-code scanner at the grocery checkout counter.

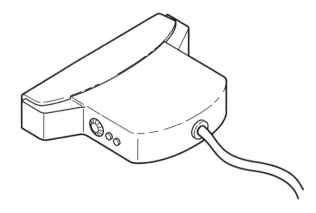

Scanners transform pictures into information your PC can process.

If you need super-high resolution from your scanned images, investigate the next level of scanner, called a *flatbed scanner,* which works like a copy machine. Instead of moving the scanner over the image you want to scan (as you do with a hand-held scanner), the flatbed scanner handles the scanning process. The precision mechanical mechanism in the flatbed scanner is far more accurate than even the steadiest people-powered hand-held scanner.

The wider the scanner, the wider the picture it scans. Most can scan either a half-page width (4 inches) or a full-page width (8 inches). Special software lets you "stitch" the strips together to form a complete picture. More expensive scanners can also handle text, when teamed with optical character recognition (OCR) software. Imagine being able to scan a document into your word processor instead of typing it!

Hand-held scanners vary in their image quality, measured in a type of resolution termed *dots per inch (dpi).* As with monitors and printers, discussed in the next chapter, sharper output costs more money.

Joysticks

Joysticks sport a padded, upright arm similar to the controls on video arcade games. They connect to a game port on a PC system. Joysticks can move up, down, right, left, and diagonally, and sport two or three buttons that let you blast Klingons with aplomb. Did I say "blast Klingons?" Sadly, joysticks are used for little more than computer games. But what a difference a good joystick makes. This is another one to test out for the right feel.

Flight Yoke

Flight simulators rank among the best-selling software programs. An inventive company markets a special device tailored to the many flight-simulator fans, called the Maxx Yoke. The Yoke looks just like an airplane's steering mechanism, or yoke, complete with optional foot pedals. The steering wheel even slides toward and away from the "pilot" to add an extra air of realism to the in-flight experience.

Most PCs don't come with game ports, so you have to install an interface card— see Chapters 9 and 27.

The Least You Need to Know

Mice, trackballs, and the more offbeat input devices team up with a PC's keyboard to enhance your control over software applications.

- ☛ There are two types of mouse interfaces, serial and bus.

- ☛ Make sure your mouse is Microsoft-compatible.

- ☛ Computer gamers wield joysticks to demolish asteroids, or simply to navigate the screens of an adventure game.

- ☛ Scanners help you embellish your work with pictures, and can even input text.

- ☛ Hand-held scanners will do for the amateur, but if you're serious about your scanning, get a flatbed model.

No, this is not a printing error. This page is truly blank.

Chapter 16
Printing with Pizzazz

In This Chapter

- ☛ General printer wisdom
- ☛ Dot-matrix printers: an inexpensive alternative
- ☛ Laser printer basics
- ☛ Inkjet printers and beyond

By now, you've gained an appreciation for how hard the PC's components work together to accomplish your tasks. You've worked hard, too, learning about PC hardware and how to choose the best components for your needs. You have more work in front of you, as you learn your operating system, your software, and—as time passes—discover even more about your hardware.

Wouldn't it be neat if there were a way to show off all this hard work? There is, once you buy a printer for your PC. A printer provides a way for you and your PC to produce printouts, or *hard copy*, so you can proudly share your hard-won efforts with the rest of the world.

This chapter describes several printer families. Within each family lies a range of choices to ensure that you find an efficient, cost-effective printing solution.

Let's Begin with General Advice . . .

As you're looking at various printers, keep in mind these things:

- ☞ Some printers have both *parallel* and *serial interfaces* (that is, they're capable of hooking into either a parallel port or a serial port on your PC). Some printers are capable of only one or the other. Parallel is faster, but the printer must be within about 10 feet of the PC. Serial is slower but the cable can be much longer.

- ☞ Some printers are designed to be used with a non-IBM-compatible computer, such as an Apple Macintosh. If you're interested in one of these printers, find out up front if it will work with your PC.

- ☞ Printer cables (the cables that connect your parallel or serial port to the printer) are sold separately from the printers themselves; make sure you buy the appropriate cable. Ask the salesperson for help in selecting one.

- ☞ If you're buying a less-popular brand of printer (that is, a printer other than an Epson or Hewlett Packard), make sure your software will support the printer. Many off-brand printers can emulate (imitate) a popular model to work with your software.

Dot-matrix printers come in 9-pin and 24-pin versions. They get their name from the number of pins (either 9 or 24) arranged in a matrix inside their print heads. When the print head is in position to create a letter, the pins scramble to form the number, letter, or symbol needed. Each pin of the matrix adds a dot to the character image.

Dot-Matrix Printers: The No-Frills Standard

Dot-matrix printers offer decent text and graphics output—and even color, with the right ribbons— at a reasonable price.

Making Your Resolutions

There's that word *resolution* again! Printers, like many other computer accessories, measure their graphics quality in resolutions of dots per inch, or dpi, where higher dpi rates ensure sharper print quality.

Although 9-pin dot-matrix printers sport a switch that jumps to "near-letter quality" mode, the result leaves something to be desired. The print heads on the 9-pin models try to top their personal best by making several passes over each dot. Though darker, the result does not exactly epitomize high resolution, as the figure shows.

Because more dots make up each character, 24 pins produce a finer character than nine. Accordingly, a 24-pin dot-matrix printer usually costs two to three times as much as the 9-pin variety.

```
Before you can run any program, you have to boot your computer.
Boot is a fancy term that means you have to turn on your computer
with the disk operating system files in place: the files have to
be on your computer's hard disk (if it has one) or on a floppy
disk that is in one of the floppy disk drives.
```

24-pin output

```
          Before you can run any program, you have to boot your
computer. Boot is a fancy term that means you have to turn on
your computer with the disk operating system files in place:  the
files have to be on your computer's hard disk (if it has one) or
on a floppy disk that is in one of the floppy disk drives.
```

9-pin output

A 24-pin dot-matrix printer produces a sharper image than a 9-pin model.

The 24-pin models can print great-looking letters. But laser and inkjet printers—and older daisywheel models, the original letter-quality printers—leave dot-matrix in the dust.

It's Not Exactly Speed Racer

Dot-matrix printers' speeds are measured in cps, or characters per second. The higher the cps, the faster the print job. Because ads broadcast only the biggest numbers, many brag about the printer's speed while printing in draft mode, a faster, but lower quality printing mode good for printing first drafts. Ask the salesperson what the model clocks in LQ (Letter Quality) or NLQ (Near Letter Quality) mode, especially if you'll be using these high-quality modes consistently.

Dot-matrix printers race along anywhere from 30 cps for a 9-pin model in NLQ or LQ mode to 430 cps for the newest 24-pin models in draft mode. Some of the high-end models also offer a *quiet mode*, at the expense of speed.

A business letter needs to look as spiffy as possible. That's why the highest ranking printers tout their ability to spit out letter-quality documents. The term *near-letter quality*, or NLQ, evolved when printer marketing types needed a way to say their dot-matrix printers were almost capable of letter quality output.

What? Did You Say Something?

Dot-matrix printers belong to the *impact printer* family. This means the print head bangs (loudly) against the print carriage. After half a page or so of printing takes place, you'll begin to see why *non-impact printers*, like the laser printers discussed later, are so popular. Dot-matrix printers often sport pause buttons that let you interrupt the print job long enough to talk on the phone, and then resume.

Impact printers do have one advantage though: They print well on multipart forms, where you must bear down on the top page hard enough to leave an impression on the pages underneath.

Dot-Matrix Bells and Whistles

Most dot-matrix printers provide attachments that accommodate *continuous-feed*, or *tractor-feed*, paper. That way, you don't have to feed in each individual sheet—the paper automatically advances and feeds through.

The more expensive 24-pin models offer extra plastic noise shields. They also may sport wider carriages that accept paper up to 14 inches in width. Also dubbed 132-column printers, these wide-carriage models offer more versatility in printing odd-sized forms than their 80-column wide, standard siblings.

A printer with easy-to-use controls on the front will make adjustments easier for you; avoid printers that force you to open a panel and flip switches to make simple changes.

Many models offer various built in type styles, or *fonts*. These fonts come in handy when you're working with a software package, such as WordPerfect, that relies on your printer's fonts. If you're using software with its own fonts, such as Windows 3.1, you'll probably never use a printer's built-in fonts.

Most printers also come with a small *print buffer*. A print buffer is a small amount of RAM in the printer (8KB is common) that holds data until the print head catches up. You can pay extra for larger print buffers, but there's little reason to with a dot-matrix printer. (Printer RAM is very important with laser printers, however.)

And finally, some dot-matrix printers offer color output. The quality of dot-matrix color printing often leaves something to be desired, especially on complex images, but it's fun, especially for families with children.

Is Dot-Matrix for You?

Dot-matrix printers are noisy. But they offer decent print quality and versatility—including multipart and extra-wide form printing—unmatched by the other printer families.

In general, look for the highest resolution at the lowest price, with the features that are important to you. If you need an inexpensive, simple printer next to your PC for drafts and quick, almost-near-letter quality printouts, buy a 9-pin dot-matrix printer. High-volume users and small businesses may opt for a 24-pin model, still a versatile, affordable printer solution.

Count on paying about $150 for an average 9-pin model. A good 24-pin model runs about $300, and you can pay up to $800 for a high-end model that prints multipart forms.

A Dazzling Laser Show

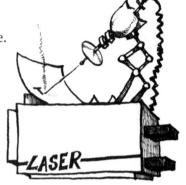

A *laser printer* works similar to a copy machine. It quickly and quietly produces high-quality text and graphic printouts. A million amateur desktop publishers were born the day laser printers appeared on the scene.

Laser is the most expensive printer type on the market, sometimes costing as much as a computer. But if your needs include large print jobs, high-quality graphics, a mixture of type styles, or just great print quality, look at a laser printer.

Making Your Laser Resolutions

Laser printer output quality rates in dots per inch, or dpi. Most models on the market offer up to 300 dpi. As with other devices, higher dpi means a sharper looking printout. Graphics are affected by dpi more than text is; with text, you probably can't tell much difference among the various resolutions.

```
        Before you can run any program, you have to boot your
computer. Boot is a fancy term that means you have to turn on
your computer with the disk operating system files in place:  the
files have to be on your computer's hard disk (if it has one) or
on a floppy disk that is in one of the floppy disk drives.
```
Draft mode output

Laser printer graphics quality improves as dpi increases.

```
        Before you can run any program, you have to boot your
computer. Boot is a fancy term that means you have to turn on
your computer with the disk operating system files in place:  the
files have to be on your computer's hard disk (if it has one) or
on a floppy disk that is in one of the floppy disk drives.
```
Near-letter quality output

By the Way . . .

There are some fancy high-resolution laser printers on the market that offer up to 1,000 dpi. Of course, their prices aren't in the range of most users' budgets.

Thinking "Fontly" of Lasers

Laser printers typically come with several fonts, from as few as 15 to as many as 50. Fifty fonts seem like a lot, but each type size is considered a separate font, as well as each combination of attributes. For example, 12-point Courier is a font, 12-point bold Courier is another, and 14-point bold italic Courier is another. In reality, a printer with 50 fonts may only offer 3 or 4 type styles.

You can spice up documents and fliers with different fonts in two ways: through font cartridges and downloadable fonts. Although faster, *font cartridges* cost more than the many software fonts, also called *downloadable* fonts, that are available free (or very cheap) from various sources.

Fast As a Speeding Laser

Laser printers clock output in *ppm*, or *pages per minute*, averaging about 6 ppm. That number refers to the printer's maximum speed; if you're printing graphics or special fonts, it'll take longer.

How Much Memory?

Laser printers sport their own memory chips to speed the printing process. Low-end laser printers come with 512KB of RAM standard, which is not enough to print a full-page graphic image. Buy as much extra RAM for your printer as you can afford, at least 2MB or more if your applications require mixing a variety of type styles on one page.

Keeping Up with the Upkeep

Besides the expensive initial price, laser printers tally high upkeep costs to replace toner cartridges and other consumables.

When shopping, find out if the toner cartridge, developer, and drum are one unit, or come separately. Ask how much each replacement component costs, and how long each one lasts. Combination units usually cost more to replace, but they don't have to be replaced as often.

Once you start looking at laser printers, you'll find the word *PostScript* cropping up repeatedly. PostScript is a page description language built into some printers. PostScript printers include 17 or 35 scalable fonts (fonts that will print in any size) and give you the ability to print Encapsulated PostScript (EPS) graphics files.

PostScript Emulation

PostScript capabilities can boost a printer's cost significantly—by as much as $1,000. Some printers offer PostScript emulation (imitation) at a reduced cost. It's best to see what your software requires before springing for this sophisticated extra. Most home users will not benefit enough from PostScript to justify the extra cost.

By the Way . . .

For many years, PostScript was prized for its scalable fonts. A font cartridge stores each size of each typeface with each attribute (like bold or italic) as a separate entity. PostScript printers, on the other hand, sport built-in fonts that the printer can print at any size "on demand." Users of PostScript printers are not slaves to cartridges and downloadable fonts—all the fonts they need are stored neatly in the printer's memory! For a long time, this seemed like a great deal.

When Microsoft introduced Windows 3.1, however, a new technology called TrueType entered the market. TrueType fonts are stored in the computer, like downloadable fonts, but they're scalable, like the PostScript fonts—so each typeface can be printed in any size. Because TrueType fonts don't take up very much hard disk space, a Windows 3.1 user can have hundreds of scalable typefaces—instead of just 17 or 35—available all the time.

TrueType did not give Windows 3.1 users the ability to print Encapsulated PostScript graphics files, however, and Post-Script is still the language of choice among most professional desktop publishers, because it was the standard for so long.

So, Should I Buy a Laser Printer or Not?

Quiet, high-resolution printouts at a speedy pace can be yours with a laser printer, but at a price. Expect to pay at least $500 for a rock-bottom model. PostScript compatibles start at $1,500, and soar way up there, depending on output speed and resolution, among other factors. This family of printers is quickly becoming the small-business standard.

Other Printers

A variety of other printers round out this large family of computer peripherals. Here are a few that you might see when you're out shopping.

Inkjet Printers

Printers from this family form characters in dots, like those of the dot-matrix family. These non-impact printers shoot blobs of ink instead of striking the printer carriage, so they're quieter than impact models. They offer fine resolution, almost as good as a laser printer, but the ink has a tendency to smear if you're not careful with fresh printouts. Many of the color printers you see advertised use inkjet technology.

Prices for inkjet printers run from $450 to $800 dollars, depending on speed and other capabilities. Even some color inkjets can be had for as little as $600—check out the HP DeskJet 550c.

Daisywheel Printers

Daisywheel printers offer inexpensive letter-quality printing, plus they're impact printers, and therefore, are suitable for forms. The trade-off? They're noisier than a jack-hammer outside your window. They depend on striking a little wheel that spins and searches for each letter embossed upon it, so they're slow. Also, they usually turn up their nose at printing color or graphics. If you're on a budget and need solid, dependable "black and white" output, check out a daisywheel printer. But cover your ears.

The Least You Need to Know

Think carefully before you decide on a printer, because no matter how good your work looks on the screen, it's the printout you'll be sharing with other people. Keep these tips in mind:

- ☞ Dot-matrix printers are fine for average needs, while a laser printer provides high-quality output.

- ☞ Inkjet printers and daisywheel models both print smart-looking documents; inkjets are capable of graphics and are more expensive.

- ☞ If you require professional-looking documents, a laser printer is the way to go. They are more expensive than dot-matrix, but you'll get the quality you need.

- ☞ Many printers do not come with the interface cable needed to connect them to your PC. Be sure to ask the dealer or mail-order house which cable you need for your printer.

- ☞ Most printers connect to your PC via either a parallel or serial port. Check your computer's ports to be sure the port you need is available.

- ☞ Laser printers come with numerous built-in fonts, but don't let the number of fonts sway your decision too much. If you use Windows 3.1, you already have a vast variety of TrueType software fonts to choose from.

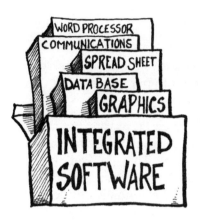

Chapter 17
Modeming and Faxing

In This Chapter

- ☞ What is a modem?
- ☞ Internal vs. external modems
- ☞ Deciphering modem speeds
- ☞ What about fax/modem combos?
- ☞ When to spring for a real fax machine

Several of the user scenarios back in Chapter 3 involved sending and receiving information through a PC linked to another computer via modems and an ordinary phone line.

- ☞ Ed the accountant uses his home PC to catch up on work he brings home from the office. He plans to use a modem to send completed work back to his office computer. That way he can *telecommute*, or work from home, on days when the traffic's particularly gnarly.

- ☞ The Trujillo family enjoys finding new ways to put their home PC to use. They plan to subscribe to an on-line service called Prodigy, through which they can meet other families and share similar interests on a variety of *forums*, or discussion areas. A service called CheckFree that offers electronic bill-paying is something else the Trujillos want to investigate.

☛ Mary, the student, has decided to hook up a modem to her low-cost PC in order to *download*, or bring into her PC, research materials for her numerous term papers.

☛ Carl and Susan depend quite a bit on their PC as they run their small business. In the evenings, they enjoy relaxing while calling electronic Bulletin Board Systems, or BBSs. They particularly enjoy calling small-business oriented BBSs and discussing issues with other entrepreneurs. Perhaps they'll eventually decide to run their own BBS, so they can automate customer support and find a better way to distribute sales information.

☛ Leah would be lost without her desktop publishing software, and the high-end, graphics-oriented hardware she has purchased to run it. She particularly enjoys the convenience and economy of using her modem to send completed layouts to a service bureau for color processing.

☛ Barry's small business is on a tight budget, and can't afford a full-featured fax machine. Barry's inexpensive fax/modem sends and receives faxes directly onto his hard disk, at a fraction of the cost of a separate fax machine.

A *modem* is a device that enables your computer to exchange information with other computers over ordinary phone lines. Two very different computers can communicate: one might be a sophisticated research-level supercomputer, and the other a humble home PC. The two computers don't even have to share the same operating system software. The only requirement is that both computers be attached to a Modulator/Demodulator, or modem for short.

A *fax/modem* is a full-featured modem with a plus—it can send and receive faxes. Just like modems, fax machines transmit data over phone lines; a fax/modem can send any document directly from your computer to either a real fax machine or to another fax/modem in another computer.

External vs. Internal?

The first question you need to answer, no matter what model you are looking for, is whether you want an *internal* or *external* unit. You probably know by now that internal means an interface card fits into one of the slots in your PC, and that external means that the device connects to one of your PC's ports. Well, you're right, but there are a few other considerations to take into account when choosing between internal and external modems and fax/modems.

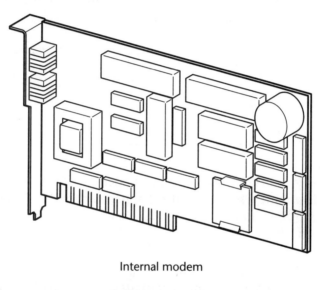

Internal modem

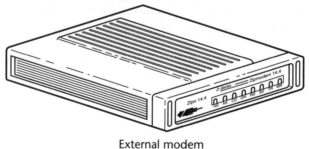

External modem

You can buy an external or an internal modem.

Why Buy External?

The advantages of an external modem or fax/modem are that it has a more audible speaker, plus a row of diagnostic lights across the front. Both of these features let you gauge the success of a transmission. The disadvantages are that the external modem takes up more desk space, and, because a modem is a serial device, an external modem takes up one of your serial ports to connect to the PC.

A row of lights embellishes the front of an external modem. The lights indicate how your transmission's going.

External modems come with diagnostic lights along the front.

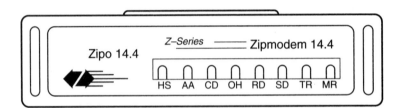

Diagnostic lights let you watch the modem send and receive data, and you can determine whether a glitch happened because of your computer or the one at the other end. Table 17.1 spells out the letters you'll find next to each light.

Table 17.1   An external modem's lights convey transmission status in a way an internal modem is unable to do.

Label	Stands For . . .	Light Is On When . . .
HS	High-Speed	The modem has achieved its highest transmission rate.
AA	Auto-Answer	The modem is ready to answer an incoming call.
CD	Carrier Detect	The modem has connected with another PC/modem.
OH	Off-Hook	The modem has taken over the phone line; the phone's "off the hook."
RD	Receive Data	The modem is receiving data you've told it to download.

SD	Send Data	The modem is receiving signals from its PC or sending data.
TR	Terminal Ready	The modem is connected to the PC and reads the communication software.
MR	Modem Ready	The modem is powered on, ready to work.

What About Internal?

An internal modem or fax/modem fits into one of your PC's expansion slots, just as any other interface card would. You plug a phone cord into a jack in the back of the card. Internal modems cost less than external models, and they take up less space because they're housed in the system box.

Internal modems and fax/modems present certain disadvantages, however. For one, you can't take it with you. An internal modem bought for one type of a Macintosh, for example, can't connect to your IBM PC-compatible computer. Second, the internal modem isn't as outgoing as the external version: It doesn't tell you how it's doing by flashing diagnostic lights, and it uses a muffled, tinny speaker to squeal its joy at reaching a modem at the other end.

Isn't an Internal Model Hard to Install?

Check Chapter 30 for instructions on installing an interface card in your PC. As long as your phone cord's nearby, installing an internal modem or fax/modem couldn't be easier. And you don't even need an extra phone line, as long as you're willing to swap phone time for modem or fax time.

By the Way . . .

If you maintain only one phone line for voice, fax, and even modem communications, fine! Many people feel the extra expense isn't worth it, especially if they fax or modem infrequently. Just remember to tell others to give you a warning phone call before they fax you something, so you can set it up.

Modems: Your Link to the World

Even if you're buying a fax/modem combo primarily for the fax part of it, you should still know a bit about how the modem part works. Who knows—maybe you'll get interested in true modeming!

When you're linked to the other computer via modem, you're at least partially in control of that system. If you type your name, it appears on the computer at the other end. That's because the modem *modulates*, or takes apart, the electronic signals from your PC and translates them into audible tones the phone system can understand. Once the tones arrive at the other end, the modem there *demodulates* those phone tones, reassembling them into electronic, digital signals understandable by computers.

SPEAK LIKE A GEEK

A *bit* is the smallest unit of data with which your computer works. Eight bits make up a byte, or one character. If you really want to geek out, tell your friends that a *nibble* is four bits or half a byte. You don't usually like to brag, but you were using nibbles just the other day when you were converting binary numbers to hexadecimal numbers. Better yet, keep your mouth shut and keep your friends.

Modem Speed

Modems transmit data to other computers in spurts called *bits per second*, or *bps*. You'll see modems rated at 1,200, 2,400, 9,600 and 14,400 bps—and each new product cycle brings higher speeds. As their speeds rise, so do their prices.
Don't even consider buying a modem in the 1,200 bps range. Even the 2,400 bps model is slow, especially if you're *downloading* (receiving) or *uploading* (sending) a large file.

Prices for 9,600 bps modems, starting at around $150, are attractive and make this model the best buy. Most modems at 9600 bps or higher these days come with fax capabilities too. Of course, there's always the glossy 14,400 bps racehorse gleaming in the corner, complete with a racehorse price tag. And even faster models beckon the unwary shopper. You can end up paying $400 and up for a super-fast, feature-laden modem.

You've heard it before, but buying the best modem for your PC set-up involves determining your needs. If a modem is a central part of your computing plan, of course it makes sense to spring for the fastest, most feature-laden model you can afford.

Modem Compatibility

As with other segments of the PC industry, compatibility counts in modems, too. Look for modems that are Hayes-compatible or that support the standards outlined in Table 17.2.

A modem company called Hayes pioneered something called the *AT command set* (also called the *Hayes command set*). The command set initiated standards in modem communications where none existed before.

If a modem is advertised as jumping to the next higher speed when connected to the same modem type, it's true, under extremely ideal conditions. Don't pay extra for this feature.

Because the AT command set caught on so widely, almost every modem on the market today supports it. Modem-related software, also called communications software, supports it too. So, in order to be able to communicate with another computer/modem, your modem must be compatible with the AT command set—whether you choose a Hayes modem or another brand of modem.

CCITT Standards

The table on the next page lists some other modem standards you'll see in ads. These features increase rates of data compression or transmission. You may pay quite a bit extra for one or more of these features, so make sure you actually need them. Here's a table of oft-seen modem standards, known as the CCITT Standards.

Table 17.2   CCITT Standards

Standard	Capability
V.32bis	Two modems equipped with this standard can communicate at 14,400 bps.
V.32	A specification for two similarly equipped modems to talk at 9,600 bps.
V.42	The standard for point-to-point error control.
V.42bis	The standard for two similarly equipped modems to compress data, enabling faster transmissions.
MNP 4	A standard for error control, contained also in V.42bis.
MNP 5	A standard for data compression.

Error Correction Is Important!

At one time or another, all of us have experienced a lousy phone connection, with so many clicks and gulps both parties agree to hang up and try again (if they make it that far). On the other hand, there are times when you're talking to someone halfway around the world, and she sounds like she is right in your kitchen.

Because modem communications take place over ordinary phone lines, they're subject to the same noises and static as any other phone conversation. In modem terms, this interference is called *line noise*. Normal modems, being the dutiful creatures they are, try to read and interpret line noise as they would any phone signal. Modems with built-in error correction attempt to verify every bit sent and received.

There's one catch: the modem on each end must have *error correction* in order for it to work. (And of course error-correcting modems cost more than models without this feature.) But if your application involves sending and receiving important files, the extra dollars you'll lay out are worth it.

Modem Extras

Many other modem extras increase the speed and the convenience of data communications. *Data-compression technology* is built into some models. When a modem capable of data compression recognizes that capability in a modem it's connected to, they agree to squeeze down data before sending it. *Programmable* modems can further automate modem sessions. But don't pay too much if programmability is touted as an extra; any good communications software can usually accomplish the same things more efficiently.

A host of tiny, portable modems flood the marketplace. These can do double duty on your home or business PC and on any portable computers you may buy in the future.

Choosing Modem Software

After picking out a modem that suits your needs, the next thing you'll need is communications software that tells your modem how to do its thing.

Most modems come with communication software that will let you talk to another computer, but these packages tend to be primitive and difficult to use. You're better off with a more full-featured package such as ProComm Plus or Crosstalk. Check with your local computer seller or ask a computer-savvy friend which software is best for your needs.

If you'll be using one of the popular on-line services, such as Prodigy, your modem software choices are made for you. The Prodigy service requires special software to use the service it's provided in a "getting started" package when you subscribe to the service.

Fax—with Your Computer?

Jack rustled through the papers in his file cabinet, looking for the fax he'd received from Acme Potato Supply last week. He also needed the Vegetable International fax from last month. Where would that be?

"Susan, have you seen that Vegetable International fax?" he called out. "Sure have," Susan said. She pushed a few buttons, and it popped up on her screen. "Want me to print you a copy?"

While Jack depended on his trusty fax machine, Susan had opted instead for a fax card inside her computer. Now Jack, his hands full of curling thermal paper, wished he'd done the same thing.

By the Way . . .

Although "fax" just recently became a buzz word, they've been around for years. In fact, news wire services and the U.S. Weather Bureau used faxes during World War II to send and receive information. Since modems and fax machines work in such a similar fashion, they've been combined to create the latest buzz-word: a *fax card*.

How Does a Fax Card Work?

A fax/modem is the same as a regular modem except it does double-duty—it also sends and receives faxes. When somebody sends you a fax, the fax/modem listens to the sounds coming in on the phone line and decides that it's a fax transaction, rather than a modem transaction. Then the fax function "grabs" the fax for you. Some will grab the incoming fax when you're not directly using the fax software, letting you continue to write letters or play computer games. Others "hijack" your computer, so you have to tap your toes for a few minutes until the fax is received.

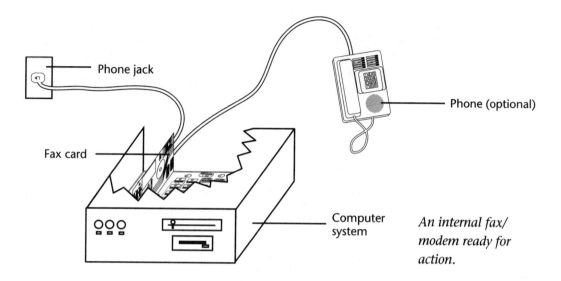

An internal fax/ modem ready for action.

Once the fax is inside your computer, you can view it on the screen. If it's important, send it to your printer. If it's a "junk fax," delete it. Faxes can be stored on your hard drive for easy reference.

Sending a fax is even easier. When you've finished composing a document, just activate the fax program. The fax card will take over, converting your text into "fax format" and sending it to the fax machine of your choice.

Fax Terminology

Fax cards come with their own bundle of terms. Here's a look at the words you'll need to know before shopping for your own fax card.

- ☛ **PCX**   A file ending in these letters (for example, SIG.PCX) contains graphics in a special format. You can import these graphics into most word processors and place them in your faxed letters.

- ☛ **bps**   Fax cards and machines measure the speed of their transmissions in bits per second. The higher the bps, the faster the machine.

☞ **fax card** In general, another name for fax/modem, but check carefully—there are a few computerized fax cards out there that don't have a built-in modem.

☞ **OCR (Optical Character Recognition)** A breed of software that looks at the faxed image and breaks down the picture of a document into legible words and letters. The fax, converted into text, can then be added to a word-processed document. The software's in its infancy, however. It can only recognize certain typefaces, and it's not yet 100 percent reliable.

☞ **scanner** A regular fax machine "scans" a document—it takes a picture and sends that snapshot to the other fax machine, which recreates it. The scanner is built-in. Fax/modems don't have this. To insert hard-copy text or images into a fax, you must use a separate scanner (sometimes called a *digitizer* since it converts pictures to computer code, or digits).

☞ **Group III** Make sure your fax card is Group III-compatible, so it will work with the majority of fax machines released in the past five years.

Don't Be Fooled! Most of today's fax/modem cards say 9,600 on the box. Check carefully! For faxes, 9,600 bps is standard, so that's nothing special. However, most fax/modem cards don't include a high-speed modem, so check the fine print. It will probably say 2,400 bps somewhere, which will usually be the speed of the modem. This is changing quickly, however, as products improve. Soon the modem bundled on fax/modem combos will be up to a faster speed, as well.

How Do Fax/Modems Compare to Regular Faxes?

Which is better, a fax/modem or a fax machine? Well, as with any other computer toy, the answer depends on how you'll be using it. Both come in handy at different times. In fact, it's best to have both a fax machine *and* a fax/modem!

Fax/Modems Don't Waste Paper

Nearly every fax machine has a wastebasket sitting right next to it. Fax machines usually waste four sheets of paper for each transmission. First, a letter is printed from the computer, fed through the fax machine, and dropped immediately into the wastebasket. A second paper copy emerges from the fax machine on the other end of the phone line. That's usually photocopied and discarded in order to convert that yucky thermal paper to "normal-paper" paper. The fourth sheet of paper, the cover letter, is thrown away when the fax is received.

Fax/modems don't use any paper at all. The document moves from one computer screen to another. Often, there's no need for a "real" paper document at all.

Fax/Modems Can Automate Your Faxes

Since a fax/modem is completely computerized, it's better at automating chores. For instance, it can be programmed to send faxes to large groups of people, and at different times, in order to avoid excessive long-distance charges. The low-person-on-the-office-totem-pole won't have to stand by the machine, feeding paper through the rollers, and trying to remember who's supposed to receive what page.

Fax/Modemed Documents Look Better

Faxed documents never look as good as a type-written page. That's because a fax machine "scans" them in: it takes a picture of the letter, and sends that picture over the phone lines. When it scans in the letter, it picks up creases and wrinkles, stray bits of dirt, thumb-print smudges and other foreign matter.

But a fax card skips that step; it transforms your letters and words directly into a picture. Since there's nothing mechanical involved, the copy is a lot cleaner. Place a fax machine's fax next to one sent by a fax card. The fax card's quality will be immediately noticeable.

Fax/Modems Don't Handle Hard Copy

Faxes are essentially pictures: pictures of letters or newspaper articles, for instance. A fax/modem's software can translate your words and letters into a picture, and send it to another fax machine. But how can it translate a newspaper clipping into a picture? It can't.

That means it can't put your signature at the bottom of your letter, either. How can you sign something that's only on your computer screen? How can you send a letter on your fancy letterhead? (Hint: recreate your letterhead in your word processor, then type your fax on that; most fax/modems can handle it.)

It's Trickier Than Pressing a Button

Sometimes using a fax/modem can be a little more complicated than using a fax machine. With a fax machine, you sign the letter, drop the paper in the bin, push the buttons, and go to lunch. With a fax/modem, you have to juggle your graphics on-screen, positioning everything in just the right place before sending the fax. You'll probably want to practice sending a few faxes to a plain old fax machine to test your work until you're sure it looks right.

Selecting Fax/Modem Software

The software accompanying the fax/modem makes a big difference. For instance, Delrina's WinFax Pro works directly with most major Windows word processors. You can create some fancy letterhead with Word for Windows by importing graphics files. When you're ready to print, select WinFax Pro from your list of printers; it will appear right there on the menu.

Faxed signatures are best reserved for your casual, day-to-day letters. The legal validity of a faxed signature is questionable, at best. (Don't use it on your will, okay?)

WinFax Pro will convert everything into a fax, and send it buzzing through the phone lines. It's great at receiving faxes, as well. For instance, sign your name on a blank piece of paper, and fax it to your fax card using a friend's fax machine. Use Windows' paint program to "grab" that signature and save it as a graphic file on your PC. When you want to sign your faxed letters, just tell Word for Windows to import that signature graphic and stick it at the bottom of your letter!

When shopping for fax modem software make sure the application can read, or import, several word processing and graphics file formats. There's nothing more frustrating than completing a long correspondence in your favorite word processor and finding that your fax software can't send the document. Also look for software that can receive a fax "in the background." That means that you can be blasting space invaders and still receive a fax. You don't want to stop what you're doing every time you receive a fax.

Faxing from the Road

Laptops can send faxes just as easily as desktop computers. Many laptops come with fax/modems built in; others offer them as upgradable (although expensive) options. But before springing for a fax/modem, make sure you'll really need one while on the road. Do you really need to send faxes? Or can you just send your data using a modem?

Also, some on-line services like CompuServe will send faxes for you. Send your letter to CompuServe using your modem, enter the fax's phone number, and CompuServe will fax it for you, even repeating the process if the fax's phone number is busy. You must have an account on CompuServe before you can go this route, however.

The Least You Need to Know

Modems expand the possibilities of PC ownership. They're primarily rated and priced according to their speed, although AT-command set compatibility affects both price and performance. Many modems are actually fax/modem combos which automate the tedious modern-day task of sending faxes. Keep these things in mind when selecting a modem or fax/modem:

- ☞ Modems and fax/modems come in internal and external forms. If you get an internal model, be sure you have a slot available in your computer. If you get an external, make sure you have a free serial port.

- ☞ Buy at least a 9,600 bps modem. The 2,400 bps modems will be cheaper, but they're too slow by today's standards.

continues

continued

☞ Error correction and data compression are important modem features and are commonplace in today's modems.

☞ If you need to send documents that are not created on your PC (existing hard copy documents, that is), you'll need a scanner to get the image of the document into your PC before you can fax the document.

☞ OCR (optical character recognition) software allows you to edit faxes you've received. It breaks down the fax picture into letters and words your word processor can understand.

Part IV
The Upgrade Experience

When you bought your computer—was it only six months ago?—it seemed like the top of the line. But now, suddenly, your neighbor is bragging about his new super-speed Multimedia Pentium Powerhouse with a 25-inch monitor. You aren't going to let a guy who left his Christmas decorations up until Easter show you up, are you?

Of course not. This part will help you decide what you need (or want) and locate the best deal on it. It'll also breeze you through some info on those cool little laptop and portable models. Just imagine your neighbor's face if you came home with one of those! Ha!

Chapter 18
Is It Time
to Upgrade?

In This Chapter

- What is this thing called upgrading?
- Knowing when to do it
- Common upgrading scenarios
- Accessing your PC's accessories
- A plethora of PC add-ons

When most people think of upgrading their PCs, they think of opening the system box and replacing a faulty, worn, or obsolete component with a shiny new one . . .and perhaps uttering strange and colorful murmurings as they work (they didn't have this book!). Upgrading the PC itself is only half the upgrading equation (as you'll see later in this chapter), but it's an important part.

Knowing how to update older components is important if you want to keep getting the most out of your PC. In this chapter you'll see how some typical systems have bogged down over time—and how their owners diagnosed and performed the appropriate upgrade. When a particular section seems to describe your case, simply turn to the chapter dedicated to that upgrade.

But first, I've a promise to keep. Anyone who still doubts that they can perform an upgrade themselves will feel better after reading the section below. (The Joe Confidents in the group can skip it.)

The First Step: Conquering Your Doubts

This may be painful to hear, but some PC users light up at the thought of tearing out old components and snapping, sliding, or screwing in new ones. For the rest of us, fear of upgrading stems from a variety of reasons— or *un*reasons, to be precise (since there are few *real* reasons not to upgrade a PC). Let's tackle the most common objections one by one, and in doing so, banish forever the cobwebs of anguish and doubt.

You're Gonna Laugh at Me, But What's Upgrading?

To the newer user, and even some old hands, the U-word sounds vague and ominous. What exactly *is* upgrading, and how can you tell if or when your PC needs it? For the purposes of this book, upgrading your computer means two things:

☞ First, a typical upgrade might be a simple replacement of a slow, worn, or broken part inside your PC with a newer, more powerful one. For example, you might remove the older, slower, low-capacity memory chips from your motherboard's RAM slots, and insert faster, higher-capacity chips in their place. And you might add a few more to boost the amount of RAM available, while you're at it.

☞ The second way to upgrade is to add a completely new component to your setup. A good example is buying and setting up a desktop scanner, so you can scan and use graphics from outside sources.

How Do I Know It's Time to Upgrade?

In the end, both types of upgrades beef up a PC so it can perform tasks better. That answers the other Big Question: How can I tell when it's time to upgrade? When your computer system is not meeting your goals, running the software you want to run, or otherwise balking at the types of tasks you want it to perform, it's time to upgrade it.

I'll Fry My Hair Worse Than a Home Perm . . .

Sure, they're precision-engineered electronic devices, but PCs aren't as delicate as they seem. The careful advice in each chapter of this book will build your confidence level. Besides, people don't get electrical shocks when they're careful to unplug everything— at both ends—before touching anything but the cord.

I Don't Know My PC Well Enough . . .

Most people don't buy a car planning to become an automotive mechanic. And most folks don't buy a PC with the aim of becoming a computer engineer. But you don't need to work at Joe's Garage to know when your car needs new tires or a better stereo, right? Well, you don't need a degree in computer science to upgrade your PC either. Just think about your needs, see where your PC's not meeting those needs, and compare the user scenarios throughout this book with your own situation.

My Buddy Says This Hunk of Junk's Not Worth Upgrading!

This may be true (gasp). Some of the earliest PCs will never be sleek 486s, no matter how many new goodies you stick inside. If you have any doubts, turn to Chapter 19.

SPEAK LIKE A GEEK

PCs are *modular*, a fancy word that means they're designed so that many parts can be removed and new ones inserted. In fact, some hardy souls have been known to build their own PCs out of parts they buy at computer stores or through the mail. (Do *not* try this at home.) As long as you're calm and patient—and *grounded*, if you're opening the system box—and you follow the advice in this book, you'll be safe (and so will your PC).

SPEAK LIKE A GEEK

You don't have to read a New Age self-help book to *ground* yourself. Humans shuffle around in a constant flow of static electricity. Grounding means discharging that static electricity by tapping on bare metal, wearing a grounding wrist strap, or just hanging onto your PC's chassis. Since static electricity is harmful to your chips and components, ground yourself frequently when upgrading.

> ### By the Way . . .
> You hardly ever hear of someone replacing a worn part with the same exact part. That goes against the nature of personal computing—which, at its heart, is geared towards a dizzying, incessant flow of newer, brighter, faster, more powerful products. Now, you don't *have* to buy into the techno-lust mentality (just as you don't have to drive around town with a license plate holder that reads: "I'd Rather Be Shopping at Nordstrom"). But, hey, as long as you have the system box open, replace the clunker with the latest part. Your ol' PC deserves it. And you'll enjoy its new pizzazz.

I Need Something . . . But What?

It seems like only yesterday the UPS guy practically banged down your door, groaning under the weight of the parcels in his arms. You felt a tinge of excitement in your esophagus even as you signed on line #4 for your new PC. After lugging the mondo boxes upstairs and setting everything up, you wondered why you'd waited this long to take the personal computer plunge.

At first, your new PC seemed almost custom-designed. You found software that solved each new task, and your hardware ran the software well. But slowly, almost imperceptibly, your PC started failing you— bogging down—especially once you upgraded to that hot new Windows operating environment. You caught yourself looking at other systems (the first stolen glimpses leading to open, longing gazes). You may have found yourself in one or more of the following scenarios.

Out of Memory!

One day Debbie chanced upon Chris spell-checking a document. "How'd you do that from within your word processor?" she demanded. "I always get a weird "Out of Memory" message, so I have to quit my word processor before loading the spell-checker."

Chris smiled. "It's really easy," he said. "You just need more memory."

Just about everybody's heard "more memory," either from computing friends or from the computing screen. In fact, adding more memory ranks near the top of commonly performed computer upgrades.

Many popular programs (like Microsoft Windows) require a computer with *at least* 2 megabytes (MB) of Random Access Memory (RAM). When your PC runs software, RAM gives the microprocessor a place to store instructions and data it's not using at the moment. Because today's software is large and unwieldy, today's computers need correspondingly more RAM space. Extra RAM can boost your computer's performance in other ways too, such as speeding up hard disk access (since the hard disk dumps stored data onto RAM first, where it's gobbled up by the microprocessor).

Basically, adding memory means just that: buying little black "chips" of memory and plugging them into special sockets inside your computer, just like dropping a slice of bread into the toaster. Well, almost. But just as that thick slice of French bread won't fit in your cool Salvation Army toaster, not all memory chips work in all computers. For some systems, the best way to go is to add an expansion card with slots for memory chips. Then there's always memory caching and other stuff—confusing for you, but great for your PC. Chapter 20 will help you find your way through the memory upgrade maze.

Not Enough Room to Install That Neat New Program

"The magazine review said this is the best word processor ever written. The reviewer said he even found 'inchoate' in the thesaurus," Jeff called out to his wife as he inserted Disk 7 and obeyed the installation program's prompt. Bing! Jeff looked at the error message on his monitor:

If your PC balks when you try to run new programs, check the software's box (or manual) to see how much RAM it needs to run right. Then boot up your PC and count its memory (instructions in Chapter 28).

Disk Full _ Unable to complete operations.

Ten years ago, ten copies of a word processor fit onto one floppy disk. Today's crop of powerhouses come with a powerful crop of disks that proffer thesauruses, grammar checkers, and even graphics modules. Word for Windows, for example, can consume 15 megabytes of hard disk space. Why, the Windows operating environment takes up 15MB for itself! Suddenly that 40MB hard drive looks peanut-sized.

Today's hard drives find more than one way to dispel that bogged-down feeling. Besides holding tons more data, they access it faster—diminishing the traditional lag of these highly mechanical (read: slow) components. New hard drives sport more intelligent controllers, too, so they work better with today's software. Caching disk controller products offer yet another way to speed data access. Peruse Chapter 21 to find out how to choose a new hard disk with confidence.

Other Common System Upgrades

Some other upgrade signals come in loud and clear.

- ☞ If your ability to take work home is thwarted by the fact that the office PC's packing a 3 1/2-inch floppy drive while yours is a 5 1/4-inch relic, time to upgrade! See Chapter 21.

- ☞ If your new CAD program demands a math coprocessor and you haven't quite gotten around to installing one, time to upgrade! See Chapter 22.

- ☞ Links 386 Pro, Windows 3.1 in Enhanced Mode, and the OS/2 operating system require a 386 or better microprocessor. To use these programs, so do you. Time to upgrade! See Chapter 22.

What If the Problem Is External?

Your PC itself is doing fine. You've a speedy microprocessor, a decent bank of memory chips, and your hard disk seems to be gulping down everything you throw on it. Yet somehow your computer isn't up to the job. Chances are, it's not your PC that's lagging—it's the devices (or lack of devices) that you have attached to it.

The Hottest New Game Comes on a CD-ROM

The minute Barry opened the cool golf game's shrinkwrap, he despised his old computer's low-density floppy drives. The game came on high-density disks! Barry wouldn't soon forget the three-week wait for replacement disks. But the worst part was standing around the water cooler with all the guys at work who were bragging about their pars and birdies.

When Barry bought his new PC, he made darn sure to get both 3 1/2-inch and 5 1/4-inch high-density floppy drives, figuring he'd be set for life. Until he ordered his latest multimedia game, that is—the one with spoken dialogue, video clips, and complete musical scores. It came in the mail: on one of those funky new CD-ROM discs!

CD-ROM discs hold more data than floppies; they're just made that way. That's why it doesn't take a genius to figure out that if software keeps getting bigger, CD-ROMs, not floppies, will await you inside those shrinkwrapped boxes. Already, some programs come in special CD-ROM versions that hold more pictures or sounds (true space hogs) than the standard version.

You install a CD-ROM drive in one of two ways, depending on whether you buy an external unit or one that fits into one of your PC's disk drive bays. For tips on when to buy a CD-ROM drive (they're not just for gamers), which one to buy, and how to buy it—as well as how to install it—turn to Chapter 24.

Software That Talks (with a Sound Card)

"My computer has a speaker," Jennifer told the technical support person over the phone. "So I figured the software would just use that speaker to talk through. What's a 'sound card'?"

Jennifer forgot to examine the software's box before buying to make sure her hardware could run the software. She thought the sound part was a neat perk; when she heard it required a separate component, she decided it wasn't worth shelling out the $150 bucks just to hear words.

Hector, a non-native speaker of English, bought the same dictionary software. He shelled out the money for a sound card, though, since hearing standard American pronunciation would help him master his new language. He settled on a card with a built-in amplifier. Then he hooked up some garage-sale speakers to his new setup. The voice sounded great! Later that evening, some friends brought over the latest adventure game. After hearing the trolls roar and the witch cackle in full stereo, Hector couldn't believe he'd waited so long for a sound card.

Sound cards add the audio dimension of multimedia to your PC—for not very much money. Serious gamers wouldn't be without sound, but it's not just for games; you can find plenty of productivity software jumping on the sound bandwagon. Currently, Windows users can plant recorded speech into their spreadsheets (to explain the basis for cell 31, for example) or add comments to their word processing documents.

Sluggish Windows

"Windows is great," Jack thought to himself as he drummed his fingers along the desk. "With so many programs on the screen at the same time, I can cut the map right out of the paint program and stick it on the party flyer." He drummed his fingers a little faster. "If only those programs would hurry up and appear on the screen."

The wacky world of the Microsoft Windows operating environment can inspire a burst of creativity. But only after a burst of curses about how slow the PC seems. Graphics can deflate the sails of the best PCs, and Windows puts a strain on the fastest computer. Luckily, upgrades like math coprocessors—or even graphics accelerator cards that contain processors—can help. These "Windows-tailored" expansion cards can make the wind blow, carrying that creative cargo across the room and into your document. We talked about Windows accelerator video cards in Chapter 13, remember? To learn about coprocessors, turn to Chapter 22.

Backing Up's a Pain!

Harriet enjoyed commanding MS-DOS to show her how much space was left on her hard disk. She felt more than a little proud to know that her PC was the first in the company to be fitted with one of those new, high-capacity hard drives. She must have needed it, too, for all 340 megabytes filled up soon enough.

The one drawback was backing up her work. Even with special back-up software, that huge drive took forever! Her wrist was wearing out from all the floppy swapping. Harriet knew she was courting disaster, but she decided to turn her back on backing up for a couple of months.

No, Harriet's hard drive didn't crash. Fortunately she saw an ad for a tape-backup unit before that happened. Her PC had plenty of drive bays left, so she ordered an internal unit and set to work installing it herself. The manual actually seemed to be written in English! Thanks to the Windows Launcher, she could install the unit's software from within Windows—and everything worked by clicking on icons. Harriet loved the "Scheduler" option that let her arrange for an automatic, "no-brainer" backup each midnight.

Tape backup drives present an affordable, automated solution to an age-old problem: how to restore a PC's programs and data after a drive crashes or a system halts. Business users in particular should consider this upgrade. If backing up's got your back up against a wall, turn to Chapter 21.

Who Says You Can't Take It with You?

No one would argue that buying a laptop counts as enhancing your computing setup. Yet who has time to keep up with all the confusing jargon? Turn to Chapter 25 for the low-down on mobile computing. Maybe you road-warrior types need a portable printer or want to fax on the fly.

The Least You Need to Know

Fearing computer upgrades is common. It's even okay—as long as you get over it quickly so you can upgrade and enjoy your PC! Upgrading is okay, too. Moreover, it was *meant to be*. To keep up with the advancing software world, you can't avoid buying new equipment for your PC.

☞ Upgrading means two things: replacing old PC components with new ones, and adding completely new peripherals and equipment to your PC setup.

☞ Be aware of these "time to upgrade" signals for upgrading your PCs insides: you have worn, broken, or obsolete parts; your hard disk is full and you don't want to delete any of the files; you want to run a new program that requires more RAM than your PC has.

☞ Many advanced games and multimedia applications come on CD-ROM discs. You might benefit by adding a CD-ROM drive to your system.

☞ A sound card will give your PC the ability to play music and even talk.

☞ When you combine a sound card with a speedy CD-ROM, you've got multimedia!

☞ Tape backup units save time and diskettes when it's time to back up your hard drive.

Chapter 19
What Are My Choices?

In This Chapter

- ☛ When *not* to upgrade
- ☛ Low-cost upgrade tricks
- ☛ Anticipating future upgrades
- ☛ Buying a "Windows workstation"

Upgrading your PC is almost always a good thing. Yet, even in the supremely logical world of computers, there are few absolutes. Depending on your current system and your software's needs, you may be better off chucking your old setup altogether and going with newer technology.

Before you dump it in the trash can, however, try boosting your PC's performance with a few of the software and hardware tricks you'll find here. If you do opt for a new system, or if you don't yet own a PC, be sure to read about upgradable PCs and the recommendations for "Windows workstations" in the last part of this chapter.

When *Not* to Upgrade

Sometimes upgrading just isn't worthwhile. Buying a new PC is the best solution when:

☞ Replacing the old, slowpoke components would cost more than buying an entirely new system. Note that prices for entry-level systems are lower than you'd think. Look for 386DX systems that include a faster hard disk, plenty of expansion slots, a new monitor/video card combo, and even a mouse, for under $900. (For comparison's sake, simply adding a new hard drive runs about $300, and you still haven't added in all the other parts.)

If you were with us back in Chapter 6, you'll know that *286* and *386* are nicknames for the 80286 and 80386 microprocessor chips in PCs. A *386SX* is a less-expensive, slightly less powerful variant of the 80386. You need at least a 386SX to get the most from Microsoft Windows and many other multitasking programs. While we're at it, remember a *386DX* is just another name for a full-strength 386.

☞ You own a no-name or lesser-known brand of 286 computer, but need the multitasking capabilities of a 386SX or better. You'll have a hard time upgrading your microprocessor, since most of the companies who make chip upgrades target their products for a specific line of high-end PCs. For example, Kingston Technology's SX/Now! 286-to-386SX system upgrade *may* work with a lesser-known brand of computer, but the product is guaranteed to be compatible only with certain high-end brands (Compaq and IBM, specifically). The same thing is true of Intel's Snap-In upgrade products, which target True-Blue IBMs.

☞ You want to beef up your XT with an advanced hard disk, a large, fast video card, or another 16-bit (or better) expansion card. The most advanced hard drive controllers were designed to make use of the 80286 chip or higher. (Most of the other, newer devices also shun the XT's older, slower 8-bit bus.) To use some of the newer add-ons, you'll have to upgrade your motherboard, too.

You can see that upgrading isn't the cure-all for every PC malady. Even upgrading a 286 chip to a 386SX leaves you stuck with slower RAM chips, a pokey hard drive, and possibly an outdated video standard. In contrast, an actual, shiny 386 system contains all these updated components, and offers you more for your money.

You're Trying to Talk Me Out of This?

Upgrading is still a viable solution for many PC bottlenecks. Especially when you have a firm grasp of the improvement you want to see in your PC, you know what's possible and what's not, and you're willing to take things step by step. After all, purchasing a component here and there is much easier than plunking down the plastic for the killer, sticker-shocking new system. And that 286 would positively scream with a new 386 motherboard inside.

Besides, many of the newest PCs target hardware-hungry Microsoft Windows and other graphical software. Well, many folks are not the least bit interested in running Windows or its spinoffs. They speed along in fast, command-line-ready DOS software. But maybe they want to speed along a bit faster, by taking the upgrade route.

Low-Cost Upgrade Tricks

There's a zillion ways to put off major hardware purchases. These software (and minor hardware) tricks won't put off the upgrade forever—sooner or later, you'll find yourself outgrowing them and on your way to the computer store.

Upgrading Your System Software

Maybe you're running an ancient version of the MS-DOS operating system. Or perhaps you've longed to try Microsoft Windows 3.1, the hotshot graphical user interface (GUI) on everyone's lips. Each has ways to enhance the way your PC handles everyday chores. Teamed together, these two programs can make your computing sessions easier and more fun.

If you have a 386 or 486, DOS version 5.0 or 6.0 can give you more memory—even if you don't buy the actual chips. See, your first 640KB of memory is the most important because that's the coveted section all the DOS programs try to play in. DOS version 5.0 took the bold step of loading all its DOS system files into a different part of your memory. That leaves more of the 640KB memory for your programs. If you're not using DOS 5.0 or 6.0, it's time to check it out.

If you want to benefit from extra RAM by running several programs at once, you might check out Windows. Windows can download a file from an on-line service in the background, for instance, while you're writing a letter in the foreground. Don't get carried away, though. Windows needs a lot of memory (2 megabytes or more) to function effectively.

Don't have a lot of memory, and still want a graphical user interface? Then check out GeoWorks. It runs on an XT (Windows needs a 286 or higher), and doesn't need as much memory as Windows. It brings a GUI to a bare-bones machine.

Extra Memory and What You Can Do with It

After new system software, your second upgrade act should be to add more memory to your PC's motherboard, or to a RAM expansion card. You'll need to install a software *memory manager*, and then the extra on-board RAM can be used in a variety of ways to enhance your system (this approach can even work with an old XT or other 8088 system):

- ☛ **RAM disks**   The fastest hard drive may not be a disk at all. Check out the section called "Faster Storage with Good Old DOS" later in this chapter to see how to put your spare RAM to work as a disk drive.

- ☛ **Print spoolers**   You can free up the CPU to do other work while it's waiting for the slow printer by installing software known as a *print spooler*. It works by setting aside a portion of your PC's spare RAM. There the print job waits, feeding itself to the printer a chunk at a time.

- ☛ **Disk caches**   Writing your work to disk can take up a lot of the CPU's time and energy. A disk cache writes to disk in the background, freeing up the CPU for other work. The cache uses spare memory as a storage space, and monitors the disk carefully, watching to see what info it needs. If any needed data is already in the storage space, it can be read from there instead, speeding up disk accesses immensely. In many cases, a good software cache can perform as well as expensive hardware disk cache controllers can.

Integrated Memory Helpers

Some software programs, such as PC-Kwik's Power Pak, provide several memory helpers: a disk cache, a RAM disk, a print spooler, and a keyboard/screen accelerator, among others. The benefit to an integrated utility like this is that the various modules share memory with each other—and with DOS programs and Windows when they need it. You still have to buy a memory manager program. Plus, some users will miss out on the sense of achievement they'd get by setting up fixes like RAM disks themselves. Then again, for $75, you could use the time you saved playing with RAM disks to pay some attention to your lonely family members. . . .

Hard Disk "Doubling"

Compression software can squeeze data down to about half its size, essentially doubling the size of your hard disk. These products present an excellent value: They average $100, compared with $300 or so for a new 100MB hard drive. If you get MS-DOS 6.0, its DoubleSpace utility compresses your hard disk files and new files you store on the drive, essentially doubling your storage space.

Another compression product, Stac Electronics' Stacker, stores files on a single Stacker file, which foolhardy DOS sees as a hard disk. Stacker works with both DOS and Windows. The "stacked" disk has a slightly slower access rate than a regular hard disk.

Be sure to back up your entire hard drive before installing any upgrade—especially a compression product.

The Optimized Disk

Nothing bogs down a computing session faster than seeking information on disk, especially if the disk is *fragmented* (patches of data have been lost over time).

DOS stores data anywhere it can find a place, and as you repeatedly write to or erase the disk, it becomes peppered with data vacancies (or *fragmented* in disk parlance). Before you sprint down to the computer store, let some of these software solutions sprint over your hard disk.

☛ DOS's CHKDSK will look for file allocation and directory listing errors. (In DOS 6.2, the command to use is SCANDISK instead of CHKDSK.)

☛ Norton's Disk Doctor will do a test read of every sector, identifying surface errors that might corrupt your data.

☛ PC-Kwik's Power Disk rates as the speediest disk defragmenter. PC Tools (Compress) and Norton Utilities (Speed Disk) are other reliable defragmenting programs.

☛ Gibson Research's SpinWrite will do an in-depth analysis/test of the disk's surface; it can also hasten data transfer by modifying your hard disk controller's *interleave* (which affects the number of times the disk must revolve before an entire disk track can be scanned).

OS/2 users can't benefit from standard defragmenting utilities. OS/2 uses a method different from DOS to store data on a disk. This method, called High Performance File System (HPFS), actually minimizes disk fragmentation as it works, so you don't need to optimize as often. A company called GammaTech makes a utility package for OS/2 that includes disk management modules.

Back Up with Good Old DOS

It's a bit slow, but it's sure, and it's already part of MS-DOS: the BACKUP utility in DOS versions prior to 6.0 and MSBACKUP in DOS version 6 and above. Before you experience a hard drive failure or begin an upgrade, sit down with a stack of floppies and the DOS manual turned to the backup utility page. You don't even need to format the floppies first. If your hard drive should fail, you can use DOS's RESTORE command (DOS version prior to 6.0) or the restore portion of the MSBACKUP utility (6.0 or later) to restore the files you've backed up. These utilities will even prompt you to insert the floppies in the right order. Not as fast or sexy as a dedicated tape-backup unit, or even commercial backup software—but, hey, the price is right.

Faster Storage Using Good Old DOS

Faster than a speeding hard disk! It's a RAM drive, a way to use part of your PC's memory as a pretend, or *virtual*, hard disk. A RAM disk is faster than a real hard disk because the information held in the RAM disk is already in memory—bypassing the (comparatively) time-consuming process engaged in by the traditional hard disk as it finds, fetches, and stores data into RAM for the microprocessor's use.

How do people use a RAM drive? Many PC gurus copy a program they're working in over to a RAM drive they create. Other experts recommend storing certain types of programs that involve unusually heavy disk access in a RAM drive (for example, a word processor's spell checker, Windows' temporary files, or a programming language's program library). Using a RAM drive in these ways can considerably speed up the way the software works.

There's nothing new or strange about using spare RAM in this way. In fact, good old DOS already contains a special program, RAMDRIVE.SYS, that lets you create the RAM drive. To create a "practice" RAM drive for yourself, consult your DOS manual's index, under RAMDRIVE.SYS, or turn to Chapter 16.

No discussion of RAM drives would be complete without these cautionary notes:

☞ Any files you're working in *must be saved often to your actual hard disk.* That's because the information on the RAM disk exists only in the volatile RAM memory that disappears when your PC's power is shut off.

☞ When you create the RAM drive, it appears on your PC as a new drive letter. If your normal hard disk letter is C:, the RAM drive will appear as D:. Since RAM drive D: disappears the minute the PC powers down, gurus working with a program installed on the RAM drive know to save their work to real disk C:, instead.

Sound *Sans* Sound Card

Sound files with a .WAV extension come bundled in Microsoft Windows version 3.1. If you want to hear the sounds, but don't have a sound card, a Windows 3.1 sound driver called SPEAK.EXE can help. Locate the file through users groups or shareware distributors or via CompuServe, among other electronic bulletin board systems (BBSs). (It's also available on the disk that comes with *The Windows HyperGuide,* published by Alpha Books.)

Software Fonts

Windows users will enjoy upgrading their printer's capabilities by adding TrueType fonts. Several vendors sell them, including Microsoft itself. TrueType fonts are scalable, meaning you can size them to your specifications. They work with any printer that works with Windows.

Adding a Switch Box

This last item isn't exactly a software fix, but it presents an inexpensive and easy way to load your PC with even more neat serial devices. For well under $25, you can add something called a *switch box* to a single serial port (COM1:). The box sports several "slots" where you can plug in as many devices as you want. Be sure to connect only those devices you wouldn't run simultaneously, since only one at a time can occupy the COM1: interrupt space. If you take this route, keep plenty of wire twisty-ties handy to organize all the cables.

Anticipating Future Upgrades

If you opt for buying a new system, don't get stuck this time around! Scan the following sections to learn about upgradable PCs. Here, too, you can find out about the type of system Windows needs (demands). If you don't yet own a PC, take a look at some of the upgradables on the shelves.

Upgradable PCs

Several PC makers have come out with systems designed in advance to hedge against computer obsolescence. Here are a few examples.

Acer's ChipUp system lets you upgrade the microprocessor by snapping a new chip into a vacant socket on the motherboard. The old microprocessor stays in place, and the two chips work together (so you can't recoup part of your original investment by selling the old microprocessor).

Amkly Systems make an extremely modular system. The new chip is on a proprietary card that fits into a chip card slot on the expansion board. Nearby, a second microprocessor-dedicated fan cools it. Unique to Amkly is the Power-Drive Pack that holds four drives and a 200-watt power supply, and lifts out at the snap of a lever. Inside, the design allows for drive connectors and cables to nest in a thoughtfully designed recess, safe from hasty lid removals. The PC's BIOS can be upgraded through software, an unusual feature known as *flash ROM* (a recessed button must first be pushed, to prevent unauthorized access to your ROM). Flash ROM makes it easy to tell your PC there's been an upgrade.

Dell Computer makes an upgradable line similar to Amkly's. Want to upgrade to a faster chip? Then pull out the little card with the old chip, and slip in the new card with the new chip! Easy action, and you can still sell the old chip. The smart system instantly knows there's been a new processor added, right at bootup. Plus, the motherboard contains two serial ports, a parallel port, and a Super VGA port, leaving all six slots free for anything you want to plug in there. Fun. The other advantage to Dell's system is that it comes from a reputable, widely-established company that will probably still be around when it's time to buy your upgraded processor card.

If you're in the market for a new (or a first) PC, be sure to compare some upgradables. And keep these buying tips in mind.

- ☞ If the chip is on a proprietary expansion card, will the manufacturer be around in a few years to sell you a new one?

- ☞ Several years from now, will you pay more for an upgraded processor than for a comparable, new system?

- ☞ Can you sell the old microprocessor (or microprocessor expansion card)?

- ☞ How difficult is it to install the upgrade card/chip? Do you have to tear everything else out of your system before you can upgrade?

Buying a "Windows Workstation"

Lately the PC outlets seem filled with systems that claim to be *Windows workstations*. When you decide to succumb to the Windows Syndrome (More, More, More), make sure the PC's claims are founded in fact, or you could end up with just a plain, average (but well-marketed) PC. If the Windows workstation is upgradable, you could be tied to a single supplier for future upgrades.

SPEAK LIKE A GEEK

What is a *Windows workstation*, anyway? In spite of all the hype, it's very simple. A Windows workstation is any computer that's capable of running Microsoft Windows. In most cases, the systems marketed as such have extra features that make Windows run better, such as a graphics accelerator card, a large monitor, and/or a fast microprocessor.

At the time of this writing, PC pundits recommend Windows systems as nothing less than a 386/33 with at least a 120MB hard disk and 4MB of RAM, a Windows accelerator video card, and an SVGA monitor (preferably larger than the standard 14-inch model). That's the minimum model. The preferred system: 486/33, 300MB HD, 8MB RAM, and a 15-inch or larger monitor to squeeze lots of Windows onto your screen.

The Least You Need to Know

It almost always makes sense to bolster your flagging PC with new hardware, but there may be a software solution you can try before you buy costly new goodies. If you and your PC decide to part company, check out some of the smart new upgradables.

- When considering upgrading, decide what bottlenecks exist in your current system—insufficient memory, insufficient hard disk space, monitor too small, etc.

- Evaluate the cost to replace the worst "offenders." Would such an upgrade be cost effective when compared to buying a new system?

- Many system bottlenecks can be remedied with software fixes such as disk compression software and disk cache programs.

- If you want a PC capable of running Microsoft Windows, consider a 486/33 with a large hard disk (200 MB) and at least 4 MB of RAM.

Chapter 20
Memory Upgrading

In This Chapter

- ☛ How much memory is enough?
- ☛ Counting your RAM
- ☛ Buying additional RAM
- ☛ RAM-cram software solutions

It was a dark and stormy night. Maxine bent her head against the blustery gale and trudged onward through the wet streets. "Just half a block more," she urged, trying to lift her own spirits, just as the wind had lifted the tattered umbrella out of her grasp only moments before.

A lone light reflected in the slick pavement ahead. As she neared the shabby storefront, the hand-lettered sign on the door grew clearer: *RAM-O-RAMA—Open 24 Hours.*

Her heart lifted in joy. "More RAM," she cried out, heedless of the spectacle she was creating. "More RAM, please!"

What's the Big Deal with RAM?

RAM stands for *Random Access Memory*, and it's the microprocessor's holding tank for all the flotsam and debris it digs through while working in your software and performing Important Calculations. When it finds the time, the bustling microprocessor comes back to RAM and retrieves whatever data looks interesting.

Thanks to RAM, the microprocessor is able to temporarily offload its jottings, easing its load and working faster. Once the microprocessor is finished, you save its work to disk and shut off your PC, and all the data in RAM disappears forever. But while the CPU's working in a program, the more RAM, the better off you and your PC are. As long as your software can take advantage of it.

How Much RAM's Enough?

As you may remember from Chapter 8, the first PC held only 64 *kilobytes* of RAM (abbreviated *KB* or simply *K*). Today, a few PCs come with at least 640KB RAM. Since most computers have more, they count their RAM capacity in *megabytes* (written *MB* or *M*).

A megabyte of RAM equals about a million bytes, or 1,024K. The fastest PCs on the market, the 486 and the Pentium, generally come with 4 to 16MB of RAM, but these sleek bunnies can access up to 4 gigabytes (4 billion bytes) of memory. If that's not enough to give you the willies, some pundits think we'll be looking at trillions of bytes (*terabytes*) before too long.

Before you can decide how much RAM you'll need, look at your software's box, or read reviews of that software to learn how much RAM it needs to run well.

Everybody Craves RAM

If PC users have one thing in common, it's that they all want more RAM. Well, current software, huge as it is, wants more RAM even more. Here's why:

- RAM helps Windows users run the larger GUI programs—several of them at once, if their PCs have enough memory. Windows runs faster, in part, because it doesn't have to scurry over to the comparatively slow hard disk every time it wants some information—some of it is already in RAM.

- DOS users, too, can use the task-switching abilities under certain user interfaces. Those users with 386 or higher PCs can run the newer, high-powered applications with the memory these programs demand. And even those users who have only 1MB can load all their device drivers and memory-resident programs in an out-of-the-way memory area called *high memory*.

- Even OS/2 aficionados can benefit from extra memory. In fact, folks who want to run the OS/2 operating system shouldn't scrimp one bit on RAM. Even though IBM states that 4MB will do as a minimum amount, 6MB is more realistic—and 8MB is a better estimate. RAM is cheap, so be safe. Figure on 8MB to start for OS/2 itself, and for each DOS or Windows application you want to run concurrently, add 1MB.

SPEAK LIKE A GEEK

High memory, upper memory, and extended memory are all areas of RAM beyond the conventional 640KB that the computer uses directly. For more information about how a PC uses memory, pick up *The 10 Minute Guide to Memory Management* by Jennifer Flynn.

How Can I Count My PC's RAM?

Count how much RAM's already on board your PC by watching the screen carefully at boot-up. The ROM-BIOS performs a memory self-test, where it throws a rapid succession of numbers onto the PC's screen. The final numbers you see represent the amount of RAM it counted.

If your PC does not display a RAM count on boot up, use the DOS MEM command to determine your computer's RAM. At the DOS prompt, type **MEM** and press the **Enter** key. DOS will respond with several lines of numbers. You're interested in the Total System Memory line. That's how much RAM your PC has installed.

What Kind of Chips Should I Buy?

The hardest part of upgrading your RAM just may be figuring what multiples of which size chips to buy. The most commonly-seen RAM chips are DRAMs, and these come in three styles.

DIPs

SIPs

SIMMs

RAM comes in several types of packaging.

- ☞ **DIPs**   This stands for *Dual In-line Package*. It's a boxy, rectangular fellow with eight metal legs on either long side that you plug into a special socket. (These are considered older, and may be getting harder to find. If your motherboard requires DIPs, consider upgrading to full capacity when you do find them.)

☛ **SIMMs**   It stands for *Single In-line Memory Modules*. This type of memory comes on a long strip, with several (usually three or nine) DIP chips fitted onto it. You press it into a special slot on the motherboard.

☛ **SIPs**   This stands for *Single In-line Package* and resembles the SIMM except for the fact that it connects to the motherboard with little pins on the edge of the "card" instead of an expansion-card-like connector.

Now that you know the three types, look at your system's manuals to determine which type you need.

Unfortunately, it's not as simple as just selecting from among three packaging styles; each one comes in a variety of capacities and speeds.

Study your system manual carefully for RAM requirements before you spend your money. Some motherboards require all chips to be the same capacity. Others let you mix and match under certain carefully regulated conditions. Most encourage you to use the same speed for all chips.

☛ **Capacity**   Chips come in capacities ranging from 16KB up to the more common 256KB and 1MB sizes. Chips that hold 4MB are increasingly popular on newer systems. Consult your motherboard's manual to see what capacities your system accepts.

☛ **Speed**   RAM speed, measured in *nanoseconds* (*ns*), ranges from 50ns to 120ns for SIMMs. In this instance, the *lower* the number, the faster the chip's speed. (It's possible to mix speeds, but it's not a good idea. Mixing speeds can sometimes cause memory errors that are very hard to troubleshoot.)

Memory Cards

When your motherboard runs out of RAM room, consider buying a *memory expansion card*. You buy RAM chips and stick them on the card, and then stick the card into one of your expansion slots. Some brands of memory cards actually take the guesswork out of buying RAM chips. For example,

Intel's Above Board memory board lets you mix SIMMS of various capacities and speeds, as long as they're slapped down on the board in pairs.

It's a good idea to fill up your motherboard's RAM slots before taking this route. Before you buy a memory expansion card, make sure the card is compatible with your motherboard design, BIOS, and microprocessor.

Software Solutions

Whatever amount of memory you have, you'll see great improvement with the addition of a memory-management program. Two such programs, Qualitas' 386MAX and Quarterdeck's QEMM, analyze your PC's available memory and put it to use in the most efficient way.

Programs like these also can hunt down and remap memory that's assigned to unused video and BIOS modes. In addition, memory managers seek out memory-resident programs and device drivers (programs that would otherwise compete for the same scant 640KB of memory turf), and load them into vacant corners of high memory.

With a memory-management system in place, you can increase the amount of conventional RAM available to your programs by stuffing drivers and system programs into other RAM that normally sits idle. You can also set up extended or expanded memory for use by any of your application programs that are written to take advantage of it.

DOS 6 comes with the basic memory-management tools to do all these things, but DOS 6's system is not quite as efficient as these third-party products (386MAX and QEMM). The third-party products are also much easier to set up than DOS's memory-management system.

If you're serious about wringing every last kilobyte of value out of your system's RAM, consider 386MAX or QEMM. If you're a laid-back type that doesn't care about "maximum performance" as long as the system functions, stick with DOS's memory management.

By the Way . . .

When early PC users became fed up with the PC's inherent 640KB memory barrier, a few companies banded together and invented the first RAM expansion card. They called it *expanded memory* and devised a standard to go with it called the *Expanded Memory Specification,* or *EMS.* (Since Lotus, Intel, and Microsoft were the companies who invented it, you'll see this written as LIM EMS, as well.)

When the 286 generation of PCs arrived on the scene, they contained sockets for RAM right on the motherboard. Revolutionary concept! The 286's ability to house *extended memory* has carried through to the 386, and currently to the 486 (which has some newer, fancier memory managing abilities of its own).

Okay. So far so good. Card, *expanded*; chips on motherboard, *extended.* Got it.

Here comes the strange part. Wait, don't go. See, DOS programs don't recognize extended memory. When it's running EMS-compatible programs, DOS has to fool itself into thinking it's using expanded memory, instead. Windows, OS/2, Unix and a few other operating systems understand extended memory, but they can do so only after invoking a special *enhanced mode.* (That's why Windows 3.x was such a big to-do.)

The important thing to remember about extended and expanded memory is that your software must *recognize* one of these before you see any benefit from having it. Otherwise you'll end up with some very expensive (but mostly idle) RAM disks and print spoolers.

The Least You Need to Know

The first upgrade you should make is to your PC's memory, especially if you want to enjoy fully the wonders of today's software.

- ☞ Find out how much RAM your computer has using the DOS MEM command.

- ☞ Consult your motherboard's manual to see what type of RAM chips your system accepts.

- ☞ Adding a memory manager to your PC will help you take advantage of existing RAM.

- ☞ If the RAM upgrade path is too steep right now, other software might perform the needed tasks with less RAM.

Chapter 21
More Storage!

In This Chapter

- ☛ Upgrading your hard drive
- ☛ Getting more capacity and speed
- ☛ Learning about hard drive controllers
- ☛ Hard Cards: a hard disk on a card
- ☛ Adding another floppy drive
- ☛ Tape drives and other types of storage

Your hard disk feels better when it has a little breathing room. In fact, a cramped hard disk can cause data loss and all sorts of problems. You don't want that, now do you?

Luckily, it's fairly easy to add a hard disk. In fact, there are all sorts of storage devices you can add to your computer with a minimum of fuss—devices that can breathe a breath of spring into your tired old PC. This chapter gives the whole scoop.

Slap Another Hard Drive in There!

Hardly anyone has to be talked into a bigger hard drive. After all, who would turn down the chance for more closet space? Well, your computer can always use more space, too. Besides holding more data, the new crop of hard drives is smarter. And although they're one of the pricier PC components, the hard drive's price, per megabyte of storage, has fallen steadily through the years.

But "bigger" is not the only consideration when shopping for a hard disk. Many features affect a particular model's desirability. When shopping for a new drive, compare *all* of the features you'll learn about in these next few sections. Some of this may seem familiar if you read Chapter 11; that's okay. This is a full-service book, and we wouldn't want you to have to flip back there just now.

A good rule of thumb for estimating your hard disk needs is to add up the size (in MB) of the programs you use, and double that total to figure in your data. Then double *that* figure to allow for growth (and that neat new graphics program you've been eyeing). Another method, perhaps not as precise, is to take the biggest drive you can afford and squeak past it one notch for good measure.

Formatted Capacity

As with most PC storage options, a hard drive's capacity is measured in *megabytes* (or *MB*). A disk must be readied for use through a process known as *formatting*. Most are sold preformatted, although their capacity may still be advertised at the unformatted rate. Ask. If you buy an unformatted drive, ask what the drive's capacity will be *after* formatting.

Speed

Hard drive speeds are measured in *milliseconds* (*ms*) of average data access time, and range from around 13ms (fast) to more than 25ms (snail-mode). You also need to look at the drive's *data transfer rate*, ranging from around 700KB per second (fast) to 500KB per second (slow). Obviously, look for the fastest drive you can afford.

MTBF

This melodious acronym stands for *Mean Time Between Failures*, measured in the number of hours a drive should rack up before it fails. If a drive has an MTBF of 25,000, the manufacturer is betting on it to keep chugging away for 25,000 hours before it dies. If you look at it in terms how many years the drive should last consider that 20,000 hours is equal to 500 forty-hour weeks or more than 9.6 years. Look for an MTBF of 20,000 or more, but the hard drive makers set these numbers, so be cautious.

Casing Size

Drives come in *full-height* and *half-height* formats (to fit full-height and half-height drive bays) and several sizes, all the way down to 1.3-inch models. Today's PCs favor the smaller-format, half-height bays. Assess the number and sizes of drive bays inside your PC's case before you shop.

Controllers

A hard drive uses a *controller* to direct data access. The controller technology determines the drive's type. Some controllers come built into the drive; others come on expansion cards you put inside your PC. A hard disk controller commonly contains a floppy drive controller too. The dealer will help you select the right controller for your new hard drive.

TECHNO NERD TEACHES

If you're buying a second hard drive, make sure it's compatible with your existing controller card. You'll need a second cable as well. Consult your computer's manual to determine your hard drive type.

A *cache controller* reduces the (often slow) data transfer process by storing often used data in a *memory buffer*. If data there needs to be accessed once again, the cache sends it to the CPU, leaving the slower hard disk access out of the loop.

Hard disk cache controllers are expensive ($500 to $2,000), and work well only in applications that need to check out your hard disk frequently. Be sure to evaluate a software cache solution before you decide on this option.

The term *drive type* can mean two different things. It refers not only to the *basic type of drive*, as discussed in this section, but also to a *type number*, such as 32 or 48. The drive type number, usually written on the casing, is important when you are setting up the drive, as you will learn later in this chapter.

Drive Type

Drive type is closely related to the controller, since the drive type you purchase will determine the controller you need. Here's a summary of the popular drive types:

- ☞ *IDE* stands for Intelligent Drive Electronics, and represents another way of stretching the AT expansion bus: the controller sits right on the drive itself. The drive is mostly self-controlled, offloading the traditional CPU tasks of low-level disk control functions.

- ☞ *ESDI*, or Enhanced Small Device Interface, is a high-end, high-capacity drive controller. ESDI offers high speed and high capacity on a card.

- ☞ *SCSI* is Small Computer System Interface, and connects everything from CD-ROMs to tape drives and hard disks. The SCSI controller is more commonly called a *host adapter*, and once inside your PC's expansion bus, one card can control up to seven drives or other devices (actually, it's eight; the PC itself counts as one). Be sure to read the SCSI section in Chapter 8 to learn more.

Hard Cards

If you're running out of hard disk space, you don't necessarily have to buy a full-fledged new hard disk. A more convenient solution exists: *hard cards*. A hard card is just that: a hard disk on an expansion card. Hard cards come very close to hard disks in speed and performance. Plus, you don't have to worry about matching the proper controller (if it's not part of the drive) with the proper hard disk. If you need an easy solution and don't mind paying the higher price, a hard card may be for you. Be sure to compare this option when you're shopping.

Adding Another Floppy Drive

Maybe you want to avoid the hassle of swapping low-capacity floppies all day long, or perhaps you just want to become compatible with your laptop's 3 1/2-inch drive. As disks hold more and become smaller, sooner or later you'll be upgrading your floppy drive.

TECHNO NERD TEACHES

You don't need a techno-nerd to tell you to buy the fastest, highest-capacity hard disk you can afford. Generally, a reputable firm's fast IDE drive should serve most users well. Those shopping for very large-capacity drives would do well to investigate the merits of ESDI and SCSI drives. And, for those of you installing a second drive, be sure to buy one that matches the first drive's controller card. Some of the older, ST-506 cards get pretty fussy about compatibility with other drives, so you'd do well to choose a second drive that's exactly the same as the one in there now.

You've got four (count 'em) basic choices when adding a floppy drive to your system:

- ☞ A 5 1/4-inch low-density drive, with 360KB capacity. These are nearly extinct; don't bother.

- ☞ A 3 1/2-inch low-density drive, with 720KB capacity. These are pretty limited too; avoid these unless it's being given to you for free.

☛ A 5 1/4-inch high-density drive, with 1.2MB capacity. These beauties can read both high-density and low-density 5 1/4-inch diskettes.

☛ A 3 1/2-inch high-density drive, with 1.4MB capacity. These are fast becoming the drive of choice for most users; they can read both high-density and low-density 3 1/2-inch diskettes.

Floppy drives are mounted on drive bays in the system unit, and are connected to the controller card, which in turn is connected to the motherboard. Whatever model you buy, you'll need a drive unit, a controller card, and a cable. (You may be able to use the controller card that's already controlling your existing floppy drives, but don't take this for granted.) For more details on installation, turn to Chapter 29.

It's possible to buy external floppy drives, which connect to the computer via a port (see Chapter 9). Avoid these, though, unless you are completely out of drive bays in your computer's case.

Two, Two, Two Drives in One!

For years, people have been forced to stick two disk drives in their PCs, a 3 1/2-inch and a 5 1/4-inch model. A sleek dual-diskette drive by TEAC offers both sizes in one half-height unit (check out the figure on the following page). This solution saves on space and on the hassle of connecting cables and controllers, since both drives work off the same power and controller connections. Buy one of these and you can remove the old single-sized drive and have room for a CD-ROM. Now *that's* an upgrade!

Tape Drives to the Rescue!

It bears repeating: you must back up your data regularly, because you never know when a hard disk will suddenly refuse to work, or when you will suddenly do something stupid like reformat a valuable disk. I know, I know . . . backing up is boring. It takes dozens (sometimes hundreds) of diskettes, and several hours of mindlessly plugging disks into the floppy drive.

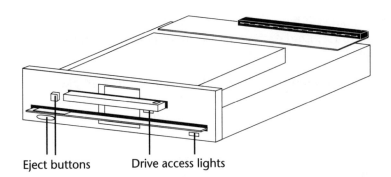

Eject buttons   Drive access lights

A dual-diskette drive crams two drives into the space of one.

But never fear! A tape drive is just what you need to rescue you from the backup nightmare. Actually, tape drives are also a great solution for those who need to archive important but "dusty" data.

Data security is another popular reason to back up with tape—copy the data onto the tape, and then lock the tape away someplace secure. Imagine yourself backing up and lugging home a clumsy pile of floppies each night. Hardly! Now picture yourself with a single tape cartridge shoved into your coat pocket. If the office building burns down in the night, next day you have your client list or billings, all the same. Tape backup systems provide an easy way to copy huge, unwieldy files—and mail them across the country, too! (To be on the safe side, mark these parcels MAGNETIC MEDIA—DO NOT X-RAY.).

Many other backup solutions vie for your backup buck, but the most inexpensive, upgradable solution is still tape. Here are some tape-unit buying hints.

☛ Before you buy, consider which files you'll back up daily, and which ones need backing up less frequently. Figure the capacity you need based on the maximum amount of data you'll back up in one session. Ideally, you'll want your unit to hold at least one hard disk partition's work, and preferably the contents of your entire hard disk. But it really depends on you and your backup needs.

☞ Remember, data on tape is *sequentially accessed*, and can be more difficult to find than data on a randomly-accessed medium like a floppy disk.

☞ Try out different brands before you buy, if possible, to make sure you like the software. Make sure you get automated backups, macros, batch files, and the ability to run under Windows or other operating systems you use.

☞ What's the true data capacity of the unit? Some brands advertise a capacity that's for compressed data only.

☞ Check for compatibility in recording formats: you'll want a unit that follows recording standards. Also, make sure the vendor will be around in a few years to supply your next level of storage capacity; switching brands can mean risking data-conversion hassles.

Other Interesting (and Useful!) Drives

If a tape unit and a floppy drive are just not enough for you, you'll be happy to know that there are some interesting new technologies emerging to help with your data storage needs. As luck would have it, I'm here to tell you about a few.

Flopticals

Just pronouncing it makes you want to turn around and look for Allen Funt behind the candid camera. (Those storage people have such a great sense of humor!) Floptical drives fit into the standard 3 1/2-inch drive bay. The drives can read from and write to standard 720KB and 1.44MB diskettes, as well as special floptical disks holding more than 20MB of data. They're faster than standard floppy drives—a floptical's average access time is around 120 milliseconds (ms). Capacity and performance come at a price: The drives run about $500, while the disks go for $22 each.

Bernoulli Drives

In a hybrid twist on hard disk technology (a combo hard disk and floppy), *Bernoulli drives* hover over the read/write head. Unlike a hard disk, the Bernoulli's high-density disks are removable. They cost about $800 and hold about 90MB of data, and their average access time is 28ms. They have an advantage over tape because their data is randomly accessible. The drive looks like another hard drive to your PC, so you can access whatever files you want just by listing a directory and pulling a file.

Magneto-Optical Drives

If you can picture a compact disc that you can actually write to as well as read from, you can picture a magneto-optical drive. Slow and expensive, current magneto-optical drives run about $2,000 and take 47ms to access data—sluggish when compared to a typical hard drive's 22ms. The bottom line is to wait for this technology to mature some.

The Least You Need to Know

How does the old saying go—"You can never be too rich, too thin, or have too big a hard drive?" Expanding your disk storage is an easy and dramatic way to upgrade your PC. And with prices for storage so low, there's never been a better time. Or, if you're feeling adventurous, spring for a tape drive or one of the new, cutting-edge technology drives such as a floptical or magneto-optical.

- ☛ Before buying a new or additional hard drive, make sure you know what type of hard drive controller your computer has. The manuals that came with your computer should give you the specifics you need.

- ☛ Most hard drive controllers can support two hard drives. If you are adding a second drive, you might not need a second controller.

- ☛ Fast hard drive access times are 20 milliseconds and below. If your computer seems slow, it may be that an old hard drive is slowing things down.

continues

continued

☞ Disk caching programs can help speed up your hard drive's access time, at a much lower cost than buying a new hard drive.

☞ There are many differences between hard drive installation and formatting procedures and those for floppy disks. Read the installation instructions carefully before installing a new drive.

☞ Most new PCs come with two floppy drives, a 5 1/4" high density and a 3 1/2" high density; therefore, floppy drive upgrades on a new computer are not very common.

☞ If you have an older computer with a low-density floppy drive (360KB diskettes), strongly consider adding a new high-density floppy drive (a 5 1/4" 1.2 MB, or a 3 1/2" 1.44 MB) Most, if not all, software now comes on high-density diskettes.

☞ Tape represents the most economical way to back up; however, its relatively inconvenient data access might make one of the other solutions a better buy.

Chapter 22
Updating the CPU and the Motherboard

In This Chapter

- ☛ Upgrading the CPU
- ☛ Adding a math Coprocessor
- ☛ A complete overhaul: A new motherboard
- ☛ Replacing ROM BIOS

It may seem like a drastic measure, but dramatic performance gains are yours if you dare. All you have to do to get them is be willing to fondle and poke mega-hundred dollar chips—or to remove every component in your system box and replace each one, in order, on top of a new motherboard. Piece of cake! Ready?

The Great CPU Upgrade

In general, applications that require a fast CPU also require a fast system bus, video subsystem, and hard disk. That's why it's difficult to find a single chip you can swap out on your motherboard to give you a brand-new CPU type. Each motherboard is usually designed to hold one type of CPU and one only. There are ways around this, though, as you'll learn shortly.

By the Way . . .

Some 486 systems are sold as "Pentium-ready," which means you can upgrade them to Pentium chips with a minimum of fuss (the exact procedure varies depending on the brand).

If you have a PC that advertises itself to be upgradable by switching to a different chip, it'll probably work. To be on the safe side, have a professional do the installation. That way, if it doesn't work, it's someone else's problem to figure out why.

The Hard-Core Benefits

Of course, an upgrade is no good if it doesn't affect your computer's bottom-line performance. Each level of microprocessor can help out in different ways. Check out Table 22.1 to see what specific gains you'll see from that gleaming new chip.

Table 22.1   Microprocessor Upgrade Paths

From	To	Leads to These Performance Upgrade(s):
286	386SX	Better memory management, and multitasking under Windows or Desqview.
386SX	386DX	Full-fledged 32-bit data paths will double the data transfer, and do it faster.
386DX	486SX	Internal 8KB cache keeps often used data at the fore; provides higher performance.
486SX	486	Math coprocessor onboard; higher clock speeds available (top-dog status).
486	486DX2	Under ideal conditions, doubles internal clock speed (e.g., a 25MHz chip to 50MHz speeds).

A few vendors sell a chip-replacement module that boosts a 286's performance to that of a 386SX. This is accomplished by removing your 286 chip with a special chip-removal tool (included in most product packages), and inserting a circuit board that replaces the 286 chip. Software's included that updates your system files. Intel makes a product called SnapIn 386, but they claim it will only work with True Blue IBM PCs. It's costly, and your software only runs 1.5 to 2 times faster. Kingston Technologies makes a similar product, and although it's been used successfully with clones, the company only guarantees and supports installations in Compaqs, IBMs, and some other high-end brands. Other brands of processor upgrade modules undoubtedly exist, but you should research performance gains vs. cost.

Owners of 486 systems who want to upgrade can buy special Overdrive chips that accelerate the chip's internal instruction processing to twice the system board's clock speed. You can remove your 486DX/25 from its socket and insert a 486DX2/25, for example, to gain 50MHz performance rates under limited conditions.

Accelerator boards offer similar advantages as the overdrive chips. They combine faster processor chips and system memory on an expansion card. This is not the best way to upgrade your chip, because you'll only see full performance benefits if you have an MCA or EISA expansion bus, which allows the board a better connection with the rest of the system. (It's improbable that many people are upgrading EISAs, which are relatively recent PCs.)

Coprocessors: Helping Shoulder the Math Load

A *math coprocessor* is a chip that speeds the CPU's ability to do a certain type of mathematical work involving fractions called *floating-point operations*. The math coprocessor adds about 70 extra numeric functions that tackle the math stuff, boosting performance for these specific operations by up to 500 percent.

Numeric operations aren't limited to financial calculations and math. If you do vector-oriented graphics, design (or use) many fonts, or design and test structures using *computer-aided design* (*CAD*), you'll see improvements in speed when you add a math coprocessor. Of course, the applications you'd think would benefit from a math coprocessor, do: namely, spread-sheets, statistical analysis programs, and databases.

Installing a coprocessor is easy—it just snaps into place. See Chapter 29 for a bit more specific info. Keep these things in mind when adding a math coprocessor to your system:

☛ Your software must be able to work with the math coprocessor in order for it to do any good.

☛ For each microprocessor there's a corresponding math coprocessor, as shown in the table below.

Table 22.2   Processor—Math Coprocessor Pairings

Microprocessor	Math Coprocessor
486DX	Already built into 486DX
486SX*	487SX*
386SX/33MHz	387DX-33
386SX/25	387DX-25
386DX/20	387DX-20
386DX/16	387DX-16
386SX/20	387SX-20
386SX/16	387SX-16
286	80287 XL
8088 or 8086 10MHz	8087-1
8088 or 8086 8MHz	8087-2
8088 or 8086 4MHz	8087-3

People found that adding the cost of a math coprocessor to the cost of the 486SX system totaled more than buying a full-fledged 486DX PC in the first place. So the 487SX qualified as one of chip-maker Intel Corp.'s biggest marketing disasters of all time. Intel is currently urging users to fill the vacant 487SX slot on their motherboards with an Overdrive chip instead.

Are You My Mother(board)?

A new motherboard can provide you with the framework of a new PC. It gives you an expanded system bus width and the extra RAM sockets, not to mention the new motherboard's capacity for a coprocessor and other add-ons. Best of all, most computer gurus consider adding a new motherboard just a simple "open the case, unplug everything, take out the old, put in the new, plug everything in again and close up the case" (breathe here) operation. (Sorry, these guys *don't* make house calls!)

Every motherboard upgrade isn't guaranteed to go as smoothly as this. Keep in mind the following factors when shopping:

- ☞ **Size** Before you buy, make sure the motherboard will fit inside your system box.

- ☞ **Microprocessor** Verify that you're getting the chip you want on the new motherboard.

- ☞ **Documentation** You'll need a thorough, well-written manual for the new motherboard to learn what RAM chip configurations you can use, as well as the location of ROM chips, DIP switches, and other essentials.

Replacing your own motherboard is a rather lengthy, sometimes scary production, but it's certainly do-able. See Chapter 29 for some specific help.

Sometimes you must upgrade your PC before you can perform the more essential upgrades to your system. Keep reading to see when you should update your ROM BIOS chip(s).

Replacing Your ROM BIOS

The PC is very impressionable. And it's the ROM BIOS, housed in one or more chips on the motherboard, that stamps its own personality on the PC. The *ROM* part stands for *Read-Only Memory*, a permanent set of instructions etched onto the ROM chip. Part of these instructions are the PC's *BIOS* (which stands for *Basic Input-Output System*). In a lightning-fast series of system checks and verifications, the BIOS *initializes* the PC at boot-up, and assists the CPU in other ways.

Personal computer hardware advances rapidly (as you know all too well, since that's the reason you need to upgrade)! But the ROM BIOS (unlike other forms of memory) can't be written to. Yet a PC's ROM BIOS is in charge of checking on many of the hardware components at initialization; it can't afford to be outdated, or it won't be able to recognize and work with many of the new controllers and other gizmos. What to do? Don't despair. If your ROM has fallen behind the times, you can upgrade it. It's a pretty straightforward chip-swap, but see Chapter 29 for the fine points before you try it, and get a techie friend to help.

The Least You Need to Know

Although these upgrades are a little more trouble than most, nothing changes the nature of your PC more effectively than a new microprocessor, math chip, motherboard, or ROM chipset. Since the new components are costly and fragile, you'll need to proceed carefully, with full documentation (and a techie friend) at hand.

- ☞ Before upgrading your CPU, find out what class of CPU your PC has now.

- ☞ Check your software documentation to see if it requires (or would benefit from) a math coprocessor.

- ☞ Overdrive chips pump up the velocity on your 486 system without actually changing the microprocessor.

- ☞ If you're planning to upgrade your PC's motherboard, be sure the new one will fit into the computer case.

- ☞ Upgrading ROM BIOS chips is not for the timid. If you plan to undertake this operation, bribe a technically-inclined friend to help with the tricky parts.

Chapter 23
More Ports, Please!

In This Chapter

- ☞ Adding a game port to your PC
- ☞ Determining your port needs
- ☞ Adding a SCSI (scuzzy) host adapter

Olga searched frantically for her PC's manual. She was sure she'd never before seen that strange word: *SCSI*. Darn! She couldn't find a word about it, yet the CD-ROM drive that Mom gave her for her birthday needed something called a SCSI interface.

Olga needn't panic. Adding ports to a PC is one of the most common (and easiest) upgrades. (Getting everything to work with the more temperamental SCSI adapter is another story, but one that's told here, too.)

Adding New Ports to a PC

You can give your PC new life (well, room for more serial and parallel devices, anyway) by purchasing a serial or parallel *port card*. Or you can opt for a multifunction card, which holds an assortment of new ports— typically two serial and one parallel, plus a game port for a joystick. Although the upgrade itself involves little more than inserting another expansion card into one of your PC's free slots, you'll need to keep the following in mind:

- ☞ **Will the card fit?** Expansion cards come tall, short, fat, and thin. Before you buy a new card, make sure you know the dimensions of your PC's case. Warning: you may have to rearrange the other cards inside the system box to make the newcomer nice and comfy. (Think of it as *practice!*)

- ☞ **The ports and devices must match.** The type of port card you add to your PC depends on the type of new device you want to hook up. You'll need a serial port for a serial modem, a parallel port for a parallel printer, etc. A multifunction card offers both types, so you don't have to worry so much.

- ☞ **Switches, jumpers, and bears, oh my!** Expansion cards sport tiny switches and things called jumpers that you may be called upon to manipulate in some way. The manual will tell you how to set them to achieve various configurations on your PC and new port.

Switches are nice and familiar. You've seen light switches before, so imagine the smallest possible light switch—on and off. That's it! Jumpers can be likened to bridges that sit atop pilings, only the pilings are tiny pins. The jumpers can connect two pins horizontally, or you can move the jumper to connect the pins vertically instead.

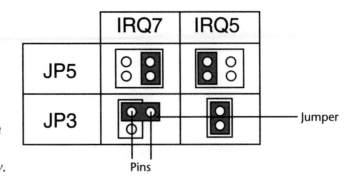

Jumpers connect pins in various layouts, which gives your PC versatility.

☛ **Contention**   Some motherboards can't handle conflict and just send everyone to bed without any supper. Since ports, cards, and devices all clamor for the PC's attention, if any two clamor in the same spot, the PC throws up its hands in disgust (not a pretty sight!). Think carefully about the devices you already have and about the new ones you're adding. Be sure to set jumpers and DIP switches carefully, and use the chart at the end of this chapter to determine vacant playground turf. (If you added another serial port and now you have no vacant areas, that's contention. You'll need to set switches on the new serial port to let the newcomer know its turn is next.)

☛ **Connectors**   Place your new card carefully on the motherboard, taking into account any connector cables that may need extra room.

Game Ports

The original game port was designed for the anemic first IBM PC/XT, not the powerhouses of today. Since the dark suits at IBM never bothered to update the specs on something as un-businesslike as a game port, the joystick makers took up the slack themselves. If you're having trouble with your joystick on a high-speed computer, look for the replacement game cards by joystick makers like Advanced Gravis and Kraft. These hopped-up models have a special knob right on the card that lets you match the card's data rate with your computer's speed.

SCSI Time

Question: When is a port more than a port? When it's a SCSI port. SCSI is short for *Small Computer System Interface*. Like a PC's other ports, a SCSI port links external devices like printers or CD-ROM drives to the expansion bus. That's where the similarity ends.

Whether it's called an *expansion bus* or just plain *bus,* it's the same: the system of expansion slots on a PC's motherboard where you can add neat goodies.

The ultra-fast SCSI *host adapter* offers a connection between your PC and as many as seven other SCSI devices (the PC/host adapter together count as one device). These link to each other in a "daisy-chain" fashion, and are able to run simultaneously. A SCSI is more like a bus itself, effectively multiplying the number of expansion slots in your PC. As increasing numbers of SCSI drives, printers, and other devices appear, SCSI provides an optimal solution for those upgraders who own small-footprint PCs that proffer few expansion slots.

The Downside to SCSI

Sound great? All is not roses with SCSI. Until very recently, SCSI standards were askew, resulting in a motley crop of device drivers and interface cards. A new specification, SCSI-2 (Son of SCSI?), is breaking through the fracas, and soon a universally recognized SCSI-2 command set will reign triumphant.

Until SCSI-2 implements truth, justice, and the SCSI way, however, existing hosts and devices continue to run amok. SCSI's non-standard nature shouldn't concern you if you only need to connect a single device. It's when you try to link more than a couple that all hell breaks loose.

Write down each step you take while installing your SCSI adapter and devices. That way, if you encounter any problems, you can unravel the SCSI chaos thread by thread.

The Lazy Path to SCSI

Some PC gurus recommend avoiding the whole SCSI mess by purchasing a separate SCSI host adapter for each SCSI device you buy. No way! Who needs the extra expense? And who wants to give up all his or her spare expansion slots to house all those host adapter cards? Besides, contention and conflicts are frequent enough with PCs without adding fuel to the fire.

Unfortunately, right now there's no easy path to SCSI. Take it slow and be methodical. And write down everything you do.

Buying a SCSI Host Adapter

One of the best ways to avoid problems is to consider your SCSI purchase wisely. These guidelines can help you make sense of it all.

☞ **Speed** Look for a 16-bit SCSI host adapter to enable faster data transfer between device and motherboard.

☞ **Compatibility** Before you buy, find out as much as you can about the SCSI adapter's compatibility with other brands of SCSI devices. (Save your research notes. You may need them later as ammunition against over-optimistic vendors.)

☞ **Cache ability** Determine how you'll use your SCSI adapter. If you often need to access the same database off a hard disk, or off a slower device (like a CD-ROM drive), you may benefit from a more expensive SCSI adapter equipped with a data cache. Note that caching only works well with often accessed data.

A *data cache* holds often used info so your CPU can fetch it more quickly by avoiding the usual rooting around on the disk for it. Some extra-smart caches even predict what your CPU needs next!

☞ **Full device addressing** Make sure the SCSI adapter actually can host seven SCSI devices—if you think you'll make use of the additional expansion room (you will). Remember: the PC and host adapter together count as one device. Some of the addresses may be disabled by the manufacturer, so check on this.

☞ **Cables** Since SCSI devices connect in a daisy-chain arrangement, you'll need plenty of cables. Count on at least one 25-pin to 36-pin cable to run from the adapter to the first device. As your daisy chain grows, you'll need to remember to buy additional cables, plus internal connectors for internal SCSI devices. Be sure to count the pins on the devices as well as those on the cables.

Ports in a Storm

The CPU endeavors to teach some manners to the rowdy devices clamoring for its attention. It does this by assigning each one something called an *interrupt.* Interrupts let the device catch the PC's attention (by "asking nicely," you could say) to make the PC do its bidding. Pressing the "Y" on your keyboard, for example, sends an *interrupt request* (or *IRQ*) to your PC. The PC stops what it is doing and slaps a Y up on the monitor. Each card or port has its own unique interrupt, expressed in a number. Although two devices can share an interrupt, only one can be in use at a time—when they're behaving nicely.

Sometimes a PC experiences *interrupt conflicts*—mainly when two devices break the rules and go for the same interrupt, confusing the poor PC. The installation process should tell your PC how to assign your new port an interrupt. If you get an interrupt conflict anyway, you'll need to know how to assign an interrupt manually. (Don't worry, you don't have to slap the device and risk imprisonment for device-abuse.) Set the interrupt by moving jumpers or switches on the new card. If you have an AT, you can use any vacant interrupt between 3 and 15. Those of you upgrading your XTs can use interrupts 2 through 7, if they're free.

To find out which interrupts are free, use a diagnostic utility program. Popular diagnostic software includes The Norton Utilities and Quarterdeck's Manifest. As an alternative (since system components are usually assigned standard interrupts), you could use the table below to narrow down your free interrupts by a process of elimination. Table 23.1 shows the AT (286 and above) and XT standard interrupt assignments.

Table 23.1   Standard PC Interrupts

Interrupt Number	AT-Standard Device Assigned:
3	Serial Port #2 (COM2:)
4	Serial Port #1 (COM1:)
5	Printer Port #2 (LPT2:)
6	Floppy controller
7	Printer Port #1 (LPT1:)
9	Math coprocessor
14	Hard drive controller

Interrupt Number	XT-Standard Device Assigned:
2	XT-math coprocessor
5	XT hard disk

The Least You Need to Know

Adding more ports to your PC can quickly enhance your computer's capability to communicate with devices such as printers, CD-ROM drives, joysticks, scanners, and hard drives. Consider the following reminders when adding ports to your PC.

☛ PCs typically come with one parallel and two serial ports.

☛ If you have a game or other piece of software that requires a joystick, you'll need a game port. Many new PCs come fully equipped with a game port, so don't buy an add-on until you've checked your system's existing setup.

☛ A SCSI interface (or host adapter) provides a way to connect several devices to your PC, and you only need to add one SCSI interface card. Scanners, CD-ROM drives, and hard drives are but a few SCSI devices available.

☛ Each port in your PC needs to have its own interrupt (IRQ) assigned to it. Read the port's installation instructions carefully to learn how to choose a unique interrupt for each port you add.

**There is nothing on this page.
Stop looking at it.**

Chapter 24
The Multimedia Workstation

In This Chapter

- ☞ What the heck is multimedia?
- ☞ Lights, sound, action: The ingredients of multimedia
- ☞ The root of multimedia: CD-ROM
- ☞ Multimedia upgrade kits

"I'll use this new Multimedia upgrade to create business presentations," Jerry told himself as he plopped down his credit card at the Computer Superstore. "Of course, the kids can learn math and spelling with one of the educational CDs that came bundled with the package."

He came home, pushed his wholesome intentions to the back of his mind, pushed the compact disc into the front of his PC, and started pushing buttons on his joystick, scooting his Nova 9 spacecraft over the planet's craggy surface, keeping a wary eye out for Gir Draxon's lethal drones.

What's Multimedia?

A *medium* is a way of conveying information. *Multimedia* means combining media—sound and video, for instance. An ordinary television set could be called "multimedia." In fact, while the computer industry tries to label multimedia as a "serious business tool," most consumers recognize multimedia for what it is: entertainment, just like television.

But it's expensive entertainment, unfortunately. Computers were designed to store numbers and words, not rollicking sounds and splashy video. That's where the upgrade comes in: enabling your PC to handle music and pictures.

It's relatively easy for a computer to play sounds and video. Sound cards pop inside a computer, hook up to a pair of speakers or a home stereo, and play back music and sound effects. And most of today's high-quality video cards and monitors can already play back "television-like" movies.

Multimedia Checklist

Unfortunately, the MPC standard keeps changing as computers become more powerful. Basically, here's what your machine will need in order to qualify as an "official" multimedia PC:

- ☞ A 386 or more powerful microprocessor.
- ☞ The Microsoft Windows operating environment, plus Windows-compatible software.
- ☞ A 100MB hard drive.
- ☞ A Super VGA monitor.
- ☞ A joystick (game) port.
- ☞ A CD-ROM drive.
- ☞ A sound card that has digital sound and an onboard synthesizer.
- ☞ A pair of speakers.
- ☞ An inexpensive microphone (optional, but invaluable for embedding "Get to work" sound bites in your e-mail memos).

Know Your Ingredients

Some companies sell "Multimedia-ready" PCs, straight out of the box. Or, you can upgrade your PC to multimedia standards in two ways: by buying a multimedia upgrade package, or by buying all the parts separately and installing them yourself. Either way, here's what to look for in the individual components.

Sound Cards

Sound cards are expansion cards that enable your PC to blare sounds; that part's obvious. But the key is understanding the two kinds of sounds: digital and synthesized. The two types may sound similar, but they're very different.

Digital sound consists of sound waves that have been recorded on a PC. A recorded scream, for instance, or the sound of a cello quartet at the symphony hall last night, would be digital sound. The sound card records by turning sound waves into numbers; it plays digital sound by converting the numbers back into sound waves.

Synthesized sounds, on the other hand, originate from the sound card itself, a modern version of the "Moog" synthesizers of the '60s. One of the first sound cards, called AdLib, set a standard for synthesized sound that's still followed by most software today.

AdLib holds the synthesized-sound market, and a card called the SoundBlaster has the handle on the digital sound market. To run the most DOS software, make sure your sound card is compatible with both AdLib and SoundBlaster. This rule of thumb is slowly changing, however, as more multimedia applications run under Windows. As long as your card contains drivers for Windows 3.1, you're safe.

By the Way . . .

Most sound cards come with a small amplifier built-in. You'll have to supply the speakers, however. For the best sound, run a cable from the "out" jack on the sound card to an "in" line on your home stereo system. Then you can really *hear* Gir Draxon scramble to avoid those laser blasts!

What Can I Expect to Pay for PC Sound?

Look to spend anywhere from $100 to $300 on a sound card. It all depends on the quality your application requires. (See? Software calls *all* the shots when it comes to PCs!) For professional, music-industry quality, count on spending more than $1,000. If you're interested in this level of PC sound enhancement, however, you'd be wise to visit user groups where other PC/music enthusiasts gather. (If you're investing in this level of music hardware/software, you're facing a huge cash outlay—so seek the opinions of experts on current products.)

Video Cards, Monitors, and PC TV

Most Super VGA cards installed in computers can already handle the demands for multimedia video. And most VGA or better monitors can show off all the neat new things multimedia can do. However, a new computer toy has arrived: PC TV! That's right: a television on a card.

By plugging a card into one of your computer's internal slots, you can see a television screen on your monitor. Some cards fill the monitor with a TV picture; others reduce the TV picture to a small window. When placed in the corner of the screen, the "TV window" lets you watch the stock market reports, for example, while updating a spreadsheet. (Or watch soap operas while you're at work!)

Images from the screen can be captured to disk for later use. A Candice Bergen close-up from a "Murphy Brown" episode can turn up as Windows wallpaper; add a sound card, and you can hear a perpetually obnoxious laugh track as well!

The main drawback to these "TV cards" comes with their price tag. Shooting skyward at more than $500, they're several times more expensive than a real (desktop) TV. It all comes down to what your application requires; if you need to screen full-motion video, this is the upgrade you'll need. Other, more advanced expansion boards increase your PC's capability to alter and output video images.

CD-ROM Multimedia Quarterback

One problem comes with storing all those sounds and pictures: they take an enormous amount of space. A floppy disk can barely hold ten seconds of speech. So, a new component has entered the scene: the *CD-ROM drive*.

CD-ROM drives work much like the compact disc players in your home stereo. Just like the CD drive in your stereo, these CDs can only be played. You can't write information to them with your computer. You pop in a CD, and your computer can grab the sounds and pictures from it. CDs can hold much more information than an average hard disk (and way more than any floppy)—making these laser-etched frisbees a natural for multimedia fun.

Internal and External Drives

CD-ROM drives come in two flavors, internal and external. The internal ones fit into the front of your computer, just like a floppy disk. When you push a button, a tray pops out. Drop the compact disc into the tray, push the tray back in, and you're on your way. External CD-ROM players come in a separate box that sits next to your PC; a cable connects to your PC's back end. Both varieties work with your PC by means of an expansion card that sits in one of your PC's slots.

SPEAK LIKE A GEEK

To software aficionados, "compact disc" may look like a misspelling. The "c" in "disc" is a holdover from the CD's origins in the music industry; *disc* meant "record" long before there were floppy *disks* for PCs.

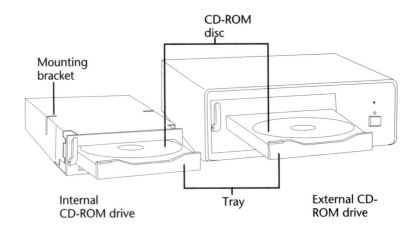

CD-ROM disc

Mounting bracket

Internal CD-ROM drive

Tray

External CD-ROM drive

Compact disc (CD-ROM) drives come as internal or external units.

When multimedia hit the market a few years ago, a group of manufacturers were ready. They'd already learned something from the VHS/Beta VCR wars a decade earlier. They de-cided to create a standard for multimedia early on. They dubbed the new standard *MPC*, a wildly creative acronym meaning Multimedia PC.

How Fast is Fast

When shopping for a CD-ROM drive, look for two numbers to tell how fast the drive is; average access time and data transfer rate. The average access time tells how fast the drive can find the data you're looking for and the data transfer rate tells how fast the drive can get the data into your PC.

CD-ROM drives are getting faster and faster as the technology matures. You'll see speed designations such as double-spin and triple-spin, or 2X and 3X respectively. These designations are touting faster average access times— two times the normal, or three times the normal, but who's to say what's normal. To sort it all out, fall back on the numbers. Look for a drive with an average access time of at least 300 milliseconds and a data transfer rate of at least 350 kilobytes per second.

Audio-Files for Audiophiles!

Most CD-ROM drives come with an *audio port*, usually called an *earphone jack*. That means you can listen to your favorite compact discs while you work! Unfortunately, you can't listen to an audio CD and access your CD-ROM drive at the same time. In fact, that's why you need a sound card in addition to a CD-ROM drive. The compact disc merely drops information into your computer. The sound card and video card then handle the chores of converting that information into sounds or pictures.

What Does CD-ROM Cost?

Depending on their features, CD-ROM drives currently cost from about $300 to more than $1,000. Depending on your application, you can get away with a slower, cheaper drive for less, especially if you need to access mostly no-frills, text-based data from one of the many databases that come on CD-ROM discs. If you need to play killer sound and animations, though, prepare to dig deep in your pockets. (Yeah, I know—all the fun stuff seems to throw the ol' credit card balance off kilter.)

If you buy a double- or triple-spin CD-ROM drive, make sure the software you're using will make use of the additional speed. Some multimedia software on the market can't keep up with the fast drives. Check with the publisher of your software for drive compat-ibility and ask if your software will have to be updated to take advantage of these drives.

Multimedia Upgrade Kits

Some companies sell kits designed to upgrade your PC automatically for multimedia fun. CompuAdd and Media Vision both sell a bundled kit containing a sound card and CD-ROM drive. When you buy a bundled upgrade kit, you'll not only get a "matched set" of equipment that works well together, but you'll get some extras: compact discs containing games and reference works, and software letting you connect the sound card to a synthesizer/keyboard to write songs or play back special Musical Instrument Digital Interface (MIDI) music files.

The disadvantages of buying a bundle? Well, you don't get to choose your own sound card and CD-ROM drive, meaning you usually won't get the most state-of-the-art package.

Media Vision sells a complete multimedia kit containing everything: a CD-ROM drive, a sound card, and speakers bundled into a

Too loud! When buying CD-ROM drives or sound cards, make sure it's easy to change their volume. The volume knob is on the back of some sound cards, hindering your attempts to turn down the sound when a game's sound track belts out a hideous scream. Some CD-ROM drives have a volume knob on the front. Look for a sound card with which the volume is con-trollable by the software: that way you can just punch a button on your keyboard to turn the sound up or down.

separate case that resembles a boom box. By setting the case near your computer, you can upgrade without the inconvenience of taking apart your computer and dropping in individual components.

Roamin' and a-ROMmin'!

Need to take your sound on the road? Then look for Media Vision's AudioPort. About the size of a pack of cigarettes, it plugs into your laptop's printer port. A small built-in speaker then plays back the sound and music data stored on the laptop's hard disk. The sound won't be as loud or flashy as an Ozzy Osbourne concert, but it's loud enough for small boardroom presentations. (Or for boring airplane flights, until the flight attendant asks you to turn it down!)

The Least You Need to Know

Readying your PC for the multimedia boom that's been "just around the corner" for years now is possible, but it requires several upgrades. Store these bits of digital wisdom in your noodle:

- ☛ For a full multimedia setup you'll need a sound card, a CD-ROM drive, and an SVGA card; you'll want at least a VGA monitor, as well.

- ☛ Make sure the multimedia software you want to run will support the sound card you're planning to purchase. Cards from AdLib and SoundBlaster are compatible with most software.

- ☛ The backbone of any multimedia setup is the CD-ROM drive. A CD-ROM drive with fast access times (300 ms or less) is important for smooth-running multimedia software.

- ☛ Many companies offer complete multimedia upgrade kits that include a sound card, CD-ROM drive, and sample software.

- ☛ Numerous multimedia applications are available, from talking encyclopedias to futuristic games complete with video-like animation and sound.

Chapter 25
Taking It on the Road

In This Chapter

- Portable computing
- Laptops, notebooks, and palmtops
- Examining the features of portable PCs

By now, you're The PC Upgrade-Meister. But wait. There's something else. One last, ultimate computer upgrade, to satisfy the Wanderlust that lies deep within us all: going mobile.

A laptop computer is a completely different animal, and almost everything about it works differently. Keep that in mind while shopping, and you'll end up with a system that can really move!

Decide What You'll Use It For

Whatever size portable you settle on, be sure to decide beforehand what you intend to do with it. After that, your decision will fall into place quicker than dust on a monitor.

Portable computers use different parts, and offer a new lexicon of jargon and terms to decipher. Other than that, the process of buying a laptop isn't all that different from buying a desktop model.

- ☞ First, decide what tasks you'll want your portable to perform.

- ☞ Second, track down the software that performs the job.

- ☞ Third, check out that software's minimum requirements.

- ☞ Fourth, find the lightest portable with the most suitable screen and keyboard that can handle that software.

- ☞ Fifth, buy the portable that meets your needs from the dealer who offers the best price, warranty, and service plan.

Laptops aren't even called laptops anymore! The smallest ones measure little more than a Big Mac; they are called *organizers*. Some of the slightly larger *palmtops* run DOS-compatible software; just don't trip over the teeny keyboard. Then there's *sub-notebooks*, bigger than palmtops, but smaller and lighter than their *notebook* ancestors. When a laptop's not really fit for a lap, it's called a *luggable*.

Fill Your Needs (Not Your Luggage)

Take a sheet of paper and jot down all the tasks you want your mobile unit to perform. Word processing? On-the-road faxes? Spreadsheets and other math-oriented work? Graphics? All of these tasks make different demands on a portable computer. Take an extra moment with your task list. The tasks you deem most important will carry a lot of weight (especially when your new computer's dangling from your shoulder at the airport).

For instance, do you need a floppy drive? They're indispensable on a desktop model, but unless you work with numerous files between several computers, dispense with it for your portable. When you need to move your road-gathered information to a desktop computer, you can connect the two machines with a serial cable and null-modem adapter, and zip the files back and forth. Admittedly, it's a little awkward, but so's a heavy laptop—and a floppy drive definitely adds weight.

How often do you work with numbers? If spreadsheets or other number-heavy applications feature prominently on your career path, figure that in when testing the portable's keyboard. On some models, the number keys are buried under other keys—accessible only after a session of finger "Twister."

Function Drains Power (Yours and the Battery's)

If you won't be using a feature very often, don't buy it. The key here is weight. Six pounds may not seem like much at the computer store, but try this: Rest the computer on your shoulder for two minutes. Now, imagine how your shoulder-bone zone will feel after two hours of the same pressure, especially when a shoulder strap has been digging into your tender flesh.

Every feature you add to a laptop not only adds weight, but increases the drain on its batteries, as well. Now you're beginning to understand the golden rule for buying the perfect laptop: Keeping it small and light not only makes it easier to carry around, but easier for your batteries to hold out during those transcontinental Solitaire sessions!

What Model's Best for Me?

Palmtop to luggable—and every model in-between—each has its pluses and minuses, depending on the most important factors: you and your needs.

Where Did I Put That Address? Get an Organizer!

If phone numbers and to-do lists threaten to bury you in sticky notes, perhaps you don't need a laptop at all. The pocket calculators of the '70s have turned into the pocket computers of the '90s. Today's pocket-sized "organizers" can perform dozens of computing features. Sharp's "Wizard" series of personal organizers will not only keep track of your appointments and phone numbers, but also can connect to modems to check your "electronic mail" while on the road. They can even use special software "cards" to do everything from designing draperies to managing stock portfolios.

What *can't* these "organizers" do? They can't handle large files. And the keyboards and displays are too small for serious word processing. But for tracking travel expenses and keeping a long battery life, they can't be beat for convenience.

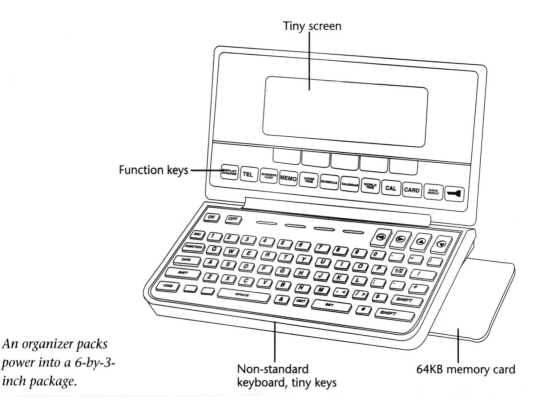

Tiny screen

Function keys

An organizer packs power into a 6-by-3-inch package.

Non-standard keyboard, tiny keys

64KB memory card

Palm Power

A DOS user to the death? You may be satisfied with a palmtop computer, like Atari's Portfolio, or Hewlett-Packard's HP95 series. Memory management's the key here: RAM not only provides program working space but serves the purpose of a hard disk as well, thanks to the "saving" grace of a small internal battery.

Optional credit-card sized software modules slip in and out of these palmtops, expanding on their preinstalled database, spreadsheet, and word-processor modules. You can add an optional external card reader unit to your desktop's expansion bus for seamless data transfer between computers. Another optional card expands the Portfolio's 128KB storage/ memory capacity to 4MB.

If you need to run large-scale programs, however, or require a full-scale (touch type-able) keyboard or display, count on dishing out another thousand for a "real" notebook computer.

Sub-Notebooks

Bigger than a palmtop, sporting more memory—and even the occasional hard drive—are the sub-notebook models, relative newcomers to the portable scene. Count on better keyboards and displays on these light-weight (under 3 pounds) computers; they're still not quite on a par with notebook or desktop models, however.

I Need a Notebook

Power user? Take a look at these. Measuring up to a typical school note-book in size, these portables can be tossed into a briefcase. Barely tipping the scale at 7 pounds, most come with a VGA screen, 386-class (or better) processor, generous hard drive, 3 1/2-inch floppy drive, and full-sized keyboard.

Couldn't One Computer Suit All My Needs?

One of the many drawbacks to portables (dismal displays, cursable cursor keys) is the hassle of transferring files between your desktop and mobile computer. One strategy on the horizon just may solve all these problems at once: the desktop expansion station, or *docking station*.

Your notebook's fine for road use, but once you get home, you'd rather be on your full-sized monitor at your full-sized keyboard. With a docking station, simply slide the notebook into an expansion base, press firmly, and you have access to the regular amenities—as well as ports, power supplies, and a large, fast, desktop-level hard drive. Pop the levers and grab the notebook when it's time to hit the road.

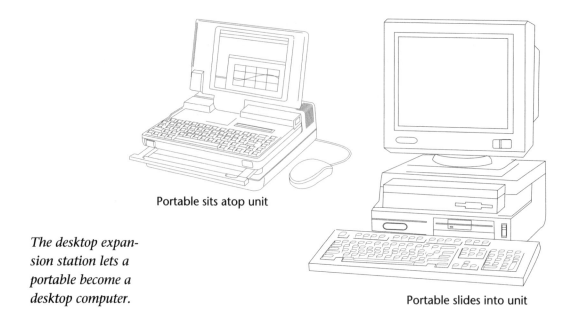

Portable sits atop unit

The desktop expansion station lets a portable become a desktop computer.

Portable slides into unit

You'll pay a price for this versatility. Since they're new, expect to pay in the $3,000–$5,000 range for the notebook-and-base unit. Tack on some more for the external monitor and keyboard that make life easier. As more manufacturers catch on to the expansion station concept, expect prices to drop. This just may be the one-computer answer . . .the ultimate upgrade.

Look Carefully at These, No Matter What Model You Buy

Some features must be scrutinized extra closely on portables. These include keyboards, displays, disk drives, battery/power management, and RAM/ROM cards.

Keyboards

A portable computer's keyboard may look the same as the one on your desktop, but look closely. The same keys will probably be there, but in different locations. Look for the term *full travel*, which means that the keys can be depressed just as far as on your desktop computer's comfortable keyboard.

You may find a *trackball* lurking among the keys. You move the ball with your thumb, and the pointer scuttles across the screen. This portable version of mousing is fun, and it's essential for applications like desktop publishing or spreadsheets.

Displays

Laptop displays are based on *liquid crystal display* technology, similar to digital watches. These screens often improve upon desktop CRTs in matters like screen flicker or distortion. Look for screens with Supertwist, where ultra-flexible molecules catch the light better. Make sure the screen tilts easily and offers a range of viewing angles. Although the newer active-matrix screens offer crisper displays and better color, they won't be "cheap" for some time.

Look for the cursor keys to be arranged in an "inverted T." This makes it easy to tell which key does what, even if you aren't looking at the keyboard. Avoid special function keys, too (for example, some layouts have you hold down a special key and press the Up cursor key to mimic the "PgUp" key found on regular keyboards).

Color Portables

You can expect great things from today's color portables. For one, expect to pay a high price for a color portable, thanks to the trade restrictions on the superior thin-film transistor (TFT) active-matrix displays. (Passive-matrix displays cost less, but don't offer the bright, rich hues or stunning contrast of the active-matrix models.) On the bright side, pricing is always driven by supply and demand, so count on TFT display prices to fall as computer store shelves fill with these models.

Color impacts a unit's weight, video performance, battery life, and display quality, so watch how quickly the screen redraws, and how long it'll keep up. *Before* you buy, ask yourself if you honestly like the way it looks (you'll be looking at it a long time). Ask questions about power management and hard disk speed/capacity, in addition to CPU power, memory, and other performance concerns. Finally, sit down and see how it feels.

Floppy Drives and Hard Drives

You'll want a hard drive, preferably one equipped with the latest energy-saving features. Do think twice about springing for a floppy drive. They add weight, cost more, and drain precious battery resources. If the portable will be your sole computer, however, you should add a floppy drive so you can load software into the PC.

Batteries

As laptops grow more feature-laden, battery life diminishes. Look for power-saving features like Intel's SL line of chips, designed to save power by cutting off juice to parts not being used. "Auto Resume" mode lets you turn your portable off, and when you turn it back on, you find yourself right where you left off in your software. Ask whether the battery recharges, and how long it takes.

Also, be sure you get an AC adapter for use in hotel rooms or at home, to save on your batteries. Ask if surge protection's available for the adapter, as well.

RAM/ROM Cards

Mentioned in the section on palmtops, these credit-card software "disks" can be read from and (in the case of RAM cards) written to: a tiny battery keeps track of your data. No moving parts are involved, meaning less wear and tear and longer battery life.

The Least You Need to Know

A portable computer expands your horizons so intensely, it just may be the ultimate upgrade. Although the procedure for buying a portable is the same as for buying a PC, the actual components differ in many ways from their desktop brethren. Be extra selective when putting together the best portable for your money, since you'll "wear" every feature.

☞ Carefully consider the conditions in which you'll use a laptop.

☞ If you'll need to transfer files between your portable and a desktop PC, make sure the portable has a floppy drive, or cables for a direct transfer. Don't forget the file transfer software.

☞ When considering a color notebook PC, avoid passive-matrix displays. They're hard to read and don't offer the stunning contrast of active-matrix displays. Active-matrix displays cost more, but they're the only real color solution.

Oh, look! Here's another blank page!

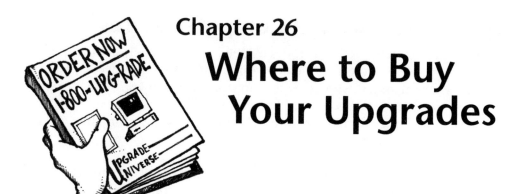

Chapter 26

Where to Buy Your Upgrades

In This Chapter

- Shopping computer stores for upgrades
- Mail order upgrade options
- Used components—an inexpensive option
- Warrantees, service, and reputations

A lot of people buy their PC upgrades through the mail. Yet some folks still feel shaky about mail-order computer stuff. These wary types prefer to shop in person. After all, it's one thing to return a mail-order sweater because the sleeves are too long—but a delicate hard drive? A 90-pound monitor?

Besides, even if you use magazines and catalogs to research a buy, nothing beats a visit to a computer store for that "hands-on" evaluation. But what's the best type of store to visit? Or, if you muster enough courage to pick up the phone, how do you know if you can trust the mail-order company?

Perhaps you'll buy your upgrades from the same place you bought your PC. Or maybe you seek a different level of service and support this time around. Well, there are almost as many ways to buy upgrades as there are upgrades to buy. And each outlet comes with pros and cons.

Upgrading Through Computer Stores

How can you tell whether a store's reliable? First, discreetly ask the staff people you meet how long they've worked there. High turnover's a bad sign. Store managers who know how to treat their staff know how to treat their customers. Is the sales staff knowledgeable and courteous? That's a great start. If they're crabby before you even make a buy, think how it will be when you're trying to return your purchase.

Here are some less obvious tips to help you size up a computer store or mail-order vendor. If a dealer can answer the questions below to your satisfaction, and the prices and selection please you, buy your PC's new upgrade from him or her.

What Type of Store Is the Best?

It seems like everyone's getting into selling computers these days. Each store below differs slightly in levels of selection, support, or discounting.

- ☞ Local clone sellers generally stock the best-selling, most popular components. Expect the staffers to be highly knowledgeable. They'll help you select (and possibly even install) your upgrade, especially if they have experience.

- ☞ National retail chains with names like Computerland and COMP USA target the corporate buyer. Prices vary on upgrade items. Selection may be limited to well-known, high-recognition brands, or high-ticket items only, like monitors. Official support should be excellent here, possibly *without* the personal touch a local clone seller can offer.

- ☞ Computer Superstores stock a huge, ever-changing variety of components. Once you manage to flag down one of the sales-people, he is helpful, even if he seems a bit harried. Free classes are often part of the deal. Don't forget to negotiate on price, installation, or warranty (or all three!).

- ☞ Membership warehouse stores offer sizable discounts on name brands. Possible tradeoffs include limited selection on upgrade components. Some stores offer tech centers, where staffers can be highly knowledgeable. However, if a warehouse store doesn't feature a specially trained staff, don't expect the salesperson to be super-familiar with late-breaking product developments. Ask about support and service policies. If your components need repair, they may have to endure being shipped back to the manufacturer. (This is hard on you and the component.)

Each Mail-Order Outlet Is Different, Too

A bewildering array of mail-order companies offer their own set of pros and cons. Here are some pointers on this intimidating-but-economical way to shop.

By the Way . . .

Most of the large mail-order vendors run electronic bulletin board systems (BBSs). Here, customers who have modems can call and obtain utility programs to improve their PCs. In addition, these BBSs offer tech support and give users a place to exchange information.

There's one drawback. Although users share electronic mail about problems and hassles with the vendor's equipment, there's a chance that the vendor may censor the more derogatory messages. (After all, it's the vendor's BBS, and complaints aren't good for business.)

There's a way to hear more objective reports from past customers, but you'll need a temporary account, or guest account, on an on-line service like CompuServe. Just log onto the vendor's *forum* (or discussion area) by typing **Find**, a space, and the name of the vendor.

Even though the vendor sponsors these discussion groups, users here freely discuss issues, swap hints and tips, and download the same programs and fixes that are available on the vendor's own BBS. Plus you won't have to make a toll-call. (America Online, Delphi, and GEnie are some of the other on-line services that carry vendor forums.)

Sometimes top executives are available for "conference calls," where they discuss users' questions. And you can *flame* (leave crabby e-mail for) the company president if his company's not responding to other complaint channels!

General Mail-Order Marketers

They have names like PCs Compleat and USA Flex, and sell an enormous variety of PCs, monitors, hard disks—even floppy disks and software—from a huge range of manufacturers. They're found in the backs of PC magazines, where their ads take up several closely printed pages (read the fine print first!). Some charge shipping, which you should never have to pay.

Watch your step! Before you buy from general mail-order marketers, try to get feedback from past customers. Try attending a meeting of a user group or a computer club at a local university. *PC/Computing* magazine features a monthly "Phantom Shopper" column, where the writer calls anonymously and orders stuff—and reports his findings on competence, honesty, support, and reliability. Most libraries carry *PC/Computing*, and you'd be smart to spend an afternoon in one, going over back issues and searching out write-ups on the mail-order marketer company you're considering.

Direct PC Sellers

With names like Dell and Gateway, these direct marketers sell only their own brands. These PCs and components can cost slightly more than no-name clones. Direct PC sellers compete heavily for customers by outdoing each other in service and warranty policies. Look here for affordable and speedy on-site service contracts. Toll-free support goes without saying (but ask anyway!). And these vendors sponsor in-house BBSs where users can download useful programs and documentation, chat with other users, and keep up with product news. Many of these vendors offer upgradable PCs.

Component-Specific Vendors

They concentrate on one thing only: memory, motherboards, hard drives, or some other specific product. Theoretically, this level of focus lets the *component-specific vendors* develop expertise in their product. Call and check this out for yourself. Because these vendors move a large volume of merchandise, their prices (and selection) should be great.

Used Components

Computer swap-meets and users' groups are good places to find used components. Brokerage firms that deal in used PCs may have items you need, as well. Try the American Computer Exchange, 800/786-0717; the Boston Computer Exchange, 800/262-6399; the Computer Exchange Northwest, 206/820-1181; or the Western Computer Exchange, 505/265-1330. As with buying any used equipment, *caveat emptor*. Try to get whatever documentation, manuals, etc. are available.

Help with Installing the Stuff You Buy

Have you ever noticed how some people can't *stand* to ask for directions? Even if they're hopelessly lost and two hours late—no sir, they just can't bring themselves to pull over into one of the zillion gas stations on every corner and ask the way. Well, if you're one of those people, you probably will laugh out loud at the next suggestion, which is: Ask the dealer if he or she provides installation pointers, just in case you need a hand.

For people who welcome friendly assistance when they need it, make sure your dealer will oblige. (Obviously, mail-order upgraders will have to speak slowly, go step-by-step, and be extremely precise when obtaining help over the phone!)

Threading Your Way Through Warranty and Service Lingo

In the section above on how to check out a dealer, you saw some brief items about warranty and service policies. That's important stuff, so here it is again, expanded.

First, Reputation

Attend a user-group meeting, and ask members about their mail-order experiences. Is there any recurring theme in the horror stories (a particular dealer's name, perhaps)? Call the mail-order vendors that interest you, and ask how long they've been in business. Try asking for customer references (don't be disappointed if you don't get any, though).

Service and Repair

Have the dealer send you a brochure that lists his sales and support policies in writing. Don't buy unless you get a 30-day, money-back guarantee. Many dealers charge a "restocking" fee for returned merchandise. Ask about this. If they press it, don't bother with this dealer; you should never agree to a restocking fee.

Make sure the mail-order company has on-site repair facilities. You don't want your PC enduring any more shipping than is absolutely necessary. And insist on reasonable turnaround time on repairs. The dealer should pay all repair-related shipping costs. If you decide to return the item within the 30-day guarantee period and call the dealer to obtain authorization, the dealer should also pay shipping costs on returns. After all, dealers want your repeat business, and good referrals build a customer base.

Warranties

Examine the dealer's warranty policy. If they fail at all, electronic systems will do so within the first 30 days. Negotiate a one-year, parts-and-labor warranty. While you're at it, ask for a two-year, parts-and-labor warranty. (Don't be disappointed if the dealer settles on a two-year, parts *or* labor warranty, however—it's tough to get a full warranty extended to two years.)

Who will honor the warranty? If you're buying from an outlet that stocks only its own brands, that base is covered. Otherwise, make sure it's the dealer—not the manufacturer—who backs the warranty with service.

It's hard enough to keep track of all your upgrades without keeping track of manufacturers' phone numbers, addresses, shipping records, and technical support on each component.

Support

Look for toll-free technical support during expanded hours and preferably some evenings or weekends. If English is not your best language, make sure the company has representatives whom you can understand.

Shipping

Ask how soon they'll ship the item. Nail down a firm ship date, and don't let them debit your credit card before the merchandise ships. Ask about policy on a package lost in shipment. Most vendors ship UPS ground. Make sure you get the dealer to pay for a *ground tracking number* (75 cents extra, and worth lots more). A company doesn't have to pay for a returned item to be shipped outside of the 30-day guarantee period.

Credit Cards Count!

Pay for your upgrade with a credit card, if possible. You may choose to pay off your purchase when your bill comes, yet you get the consumer protection many cards provide. (Be sure to check with your bank card company to verify what protection you're entitled to, before you make a huge purchase.) For example, if you don't receive the item as shipped, you can request your money back from the bank within 120 days.

Some mail-order houses tack on an extra fee for credit card purchases, 3 to 7 percent. Don't pay it! Instead, report it immediately to your credit card company—you may not have to pay the surcharge. Also, verify that the vendor charges your account only after the system is actually shipped. Determine in advance how billing takes place, so there won't be any surprises.

The Least You Need to Know

An alarming variety of dealers and mail-order companies vie for your upgrade dollar. Relax, take your time, and remember that nobody's doing you a favor by selling you a component.

- ☛ Whether you're buying from a computer store or mail-order house, your upgrade components should be covered by at least a 90-day parts-and-labor warranty.

- ☛ Buying used computer components is a cost-effective way to upgrade your system, but do your homework to make sure the parts can be relied on and the seller will accept returns of faulty parts.

- ☛ Pay for your upgrades with a credit card. The consumer protection plans of most cards will help protect you from unethical sellers. Be sure to check your card's protection policy before you make any purchases.

Part V
Getting Down to Business

Just a few more short chapters, and you'll be a computer-buying guru—pretty exciting, huh? It's time to tie up some loose ends here, and talk about the practical side of PC ownership. In this part, you'll learn all about keeping your PC from hurting you (ergonomics) and minimizing its environmental impact. (Yes, even PCs are killing the Earth. Wouldn't you know it?) There is also a healthy chunk of advice about setting up a PC and installing all those upgrade parts you ordered.

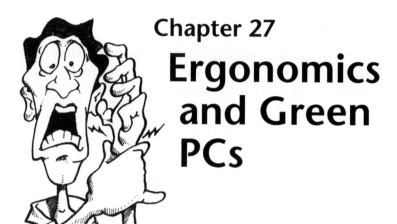

Chapter 27
Ergonomics and Green PCs

In This Chapter

- ☞ Using your PC—pain free
- ☞ Protecting your wrists, eyes, and back
- ☞ PCs and the environment
- ☞ Buying a power-conscious PC
- ☞ Proper battery disposal

Using a computer can be hard on you, especially when you spend lots of time at the office cranking out reports for your boss, or in the den playing reflex enhancing games. Proper setup of your computer environment and a few accessories can keep your office work from becoming a literal pain, and the space aliens you're shooting at from seeming like they're really shooting back.

The proliferation of computers in every home, office, and truck stop is also taking its toll on the environment. The millions of PCs out there consume large amounts of power and the processes used to create some of the PCs' components give off ozone-damaging pollutants. If you have both feet planted firmly in the 90s, you can help save the planet (and a few dollars off your electric bill) by buying an energy-conscious PC.

Can Your PC Hurt You?

Painful wrists, eye strain, and back pains. All of these nasty sounding problems are the result of poor ergonomics. Just what is ergonomics? Aside from being one of the buzzwords of the computer industry, *ergonomics* is a fancy term for the study of how you physically use your computer. For example, how high is your chair? At what angle do you hold your wrists when typing? Is your monitor angled up or down, or faced straight ahead? All of these positions determine how comfortable you'll be using your computer over time.

While it sounds like the awful subject in school that dwelled on supply and demand, *ergonomics* is the science of designing machines (like office furniture, cars, computers, and desk chairs) so they are easy and healthful for people to use.

Lighting

Make sure any window light that falls on the screen can be shielded with curtains or blinds. There should be a light source at right angles to the monitor, and any lamps should be adjustable, as well as dimmable. Viewing angle is crucial to head and neck comfort—and your vision stamina. Try for a 60-degree viewing angle, if possible.

Chair

The chair you sit in at your computer is one of the most important pieces of furniture when it comes to your computing comfort. Your chair should be as comfortable as a car seat. The engineers in Detroit (or Japan, Germany, or Italy) have geeked away hours making sure you're comfortable on long drives in your Lexus. Likewise, your computer chair should provide you the support and flexibility for long stints at the computer.

Look for an adjustable chair with a 5-prong base for security. The seat should swivel and sport at least a 1-inch padding on the bottom. Some users speak highly of tilting seats that angle slightly forward and relieve pressure on the back and thighs (once you get used to the feeling that you're sliding off it).

You should be able to rest your arms on adjustable padded arm rests. They take pressure off your neck and shoulders. The chair should also have back support, both lower (lumbar) and upper, and have a height adjustment. Your feet should rest firmly on the floor— otherwise your back will take the heat. If you can't adjust the height of your chair, get a foot rest or similar contraption to raise your feet.

To sum it all up, the ideal chair is adjustable in almost every direction. But like the car seat that slices, dices, and purees in 87 directions, an office chair loaded with features will cost you. If you will be in this computing thing for the long haul, invest in a good chair; its features will not become outdated nearly as fast as your PC's features.

Desk

Likewise, the desk height should complement the chair. Depending on your height, the desk should be 24 inches to 30 inches high for optimum arm comfort. If you want to buy a special desk for your computer there is an entire industry that creates and sells computer furniture. Fork over the bucks and you can get specialized computer hutches that are configured for each part of the PC system—special drawers for the keyboard, slots and holes for power cords and printer paper, adjustable shelves for software, and on and on. Along with all the bells and whistles, these desks can typically be adjusted to suit your needs.

Wrist Protection

When you're done adjusting your chair and have warned your family and friends of the dangers of readjusting "your" chair, move on to your keyboard. Make sure the keyboard's angled with a slightly upward tilt.

Ideally, your keyboard should be level with your elbows. There are keyboard drawers and shelves that fit under your desk, allowing you to adjust your typing height. You can and should adjust the angle of the keyboard, with the back end raised slightly.

If you prefer to rest your palms on the desk while typing, give them a little padding by adding wrist supports. There are dozens of these available, some made of the same foam that mouse pads use, others a bit more high tech. Choose something within your budget; there are many available, and they all accomplish the padding part of your ergonomic needs.

Eye Strain

Moving from the keyboard to the monitor, we'll look at what you can do to ease your eyes while working hour after hour. Eyestrain is a common complaint of computer users. With side effects like headaches, red eyes, and vision degradation, it's worth your while to look into your setup.

Improper lighting and glare reduces the monitor's contrast, making it difficult to see the letters and images on the screen. If you have to squint to read the screen, or if you shift your head from side to side to avoid glare on your screen, adjust the lighting in the room to eliminate the glare.

You might also try blocking out overhead light around the monitor. There are three-sided shields that hood your monitor, preventing overhead glare. Also, it's a good idea not to position your monitor in front of a window. The light from the window competes with your monitor for your attention, causing eyestrain and headaches.

If you can't position the PC to avoid the glare, you might try a glare filter. A glare filter is the same size as the face of your monitor, and is like a window shade you can see through. Unlike the shiny surface of your monitor, the glare filter does not reflect light, which reduces the glare.

Once you've tackled the glaring problems, make sure your monitor is slightly tilted back (some experts suggest that a 15 degree tilt is optimal). Don't get out your protractor, just adjust the monitor so you're looking down at the screen slightly. Most monitors have stands that allow you to adjust the angle or swivel from side to side. If you don't have an adjustable monitor stand, a few books will do nicely.

You Deserve a Break Today

Better yet, you deserve a break every hour. This is perhaps the most cost effective way to keep computing comfortably for hours. Take a break, get up and stretch, walk the dog. Even if it's only for 30 seconds, breaking up a repetitive routine goes a long way to keeping you comfortable.

If you can't remember to take breaks, there is software that can help. User Friendly Exercises from PM Ware reminds you to take breaks and leads you through a series of exercises. A product called Vision Aerobics takes the battle against eye fatigue one step further by exercising your eyes with arcade style games. Tell that to your boss.

Green PCs: Can Your PC Hurt the Environment?

Now that you and your PC are treating each other with respect, the next step is to make your PC treat the environment with respect. Back in Chapter 9, you looked at power supplies and you were told to make sure the one in your PC is big enough to handle additional boards. Well that still holds, but big power supplies are also a drain on your electric bill. However, there's a new breed of "green" PCs available that use less power, and therefore, have smaller power supplies.

Sleepy Power Supplies and the Fed

Even the fed (federal government) has jumped into the 90s by issuing a set of guidelines for computers and energy efficiency. The *Energy Star* guidelines issued by the federal government give computer manufacturers a set of standards for making energy efficient computers and accessories.

In addition to using less power, some new computers have a sleep mode that they fall into if they are not being used. The sleep mode further reduces the amount of power the computer uses.

By the Way . . .

Laptop and notebook computers have had sleep modes for years. Because they run off batteries, these computers need to conserve as much juice as possible. Only recently did the sleepy concept move to desktop computers.

Keep in mind that these PCs need special BIOS chips to tell the PC when to go to sleep and turn down the juice on the power supply. The PC manufacturers have taken care of the new BIOS, but this means you can't buy an energy conscious power supply and pop it into your old PC.

The power-conscious sleep mode is also showing up in other power-hungry components, such as monitors and laser printers. If you're interested in saving on your electric bill, shop around for these new accessories.

Laptop Batteries

If you opted for a laptop or notebook computer, don't think you're exempt from all the green PC stuff. Unless you're using a really, really long extension cord, your laptop is running off a battery. It's that battery that can hurt the environment if you dispose of it improperly.

Even though batteries for portable computers are rechargeable, they don't last forever. With typical usage, a laptop battery will last two years, but under heavy usage it'll need to be replaced in as soon as one year.

When your battery has had it and won't keep a charge very long, don't just toss it in the trash. Laptop and notebook computer batteries are made of industrial-sounding materials like alkaline manganese, nickel-cadmium (nicad), lithium, and lead acid. With names like that, you can bet that these chemicals can leak into the ground and contaminate drinking water, or release harmful fumes if incinerated.

Some states have passed laws requiring that batteries be recycled. You or your company could be charged and fined if batteries are not disposed of properly or recycled. Look into your local laws and find a place to take your batteries. Many grocery stores and drug stores offer receptacles for used batteries.

The Least You Need to Know

The computer is a marvelous tool for doing all kinds of things, but it can also cause you and the environment all kinds of problems. If you're not ready for this 90s kind of stuff, skip these reminders, otherwise, remind yourself:

- ☞ Keep yourself comfortable and free from aches and pains by adjusting your chair, keyboard, and monitor.

- ☞ Reduce the glare on your monitor by reducing overhead light.

- ☞ Take frequent breaks while using your computer. Splitting up repetitive routines can be good for you and your body.

- ☞ "Green" PCs use power supplies that require less energy to keep the PC running. They also have sleep modes that further reduce electricity usage.

- ☞ Laptop batteries can be hazardous to the environment if improperly disposed of. Do the right thing.

**There's nothing to see here.
Move along, move along...**

Chapter 28

Set Up, Turn On, and Kick Back

In This Chapter

☞ Setting up a computer

☞ Finding a place to set up

☞ Checking your PC's components

With boxes scattered all around him, Bob Bungle has begun the task of unpacking and setting up the equipment he purchased.

"There's too much of this packing stuff," Bob grumbled as he sliced the top off each cardboard box with his trusty Exacto-knife and fished out parts. Bob removed all the styrofoam packing from around each piece, broke each one into garbage-can-sized pieces, and tossed them in the trash. "We can give these boxes to Cousin Ronald, who's moving next month," Bob said to no one in particular.

His wife Penny stood back, concerned. "Bob, shouldn't we be saving the packing materials in case there's something wrong with it and we have to send it back?" Penny gingerly examined the discarded packing material, finding the instruction manual wedged into one of the pieces. "And shouldn't we make sure all the pieces are here?"

Setting Up Your New PC

Bringing a new PC into the home or office can be one of the most exciting events you'll experience—partly because, unlike other major purchases like a car or a refrigerator, there's practically no limit to what a PC can do. But play it safe—avoid Bob Bungle's mistakes by following these guidelines.

☛ When your boxes arrive, open the boxes carefully. Don't mutilate the box; you may need to use it to ship the equipment back to the manufacturer someday.

☛ Carefully unpack each component and compare the parts you received to the packing list. If anything is missing (and you're sure it's not embedded in the packing material somewhere), call the seller immediately.

☛ Don't throw away the packing material! Save each little bit of styrofoam to cushion the ride for that someday when you need to move the computer.

Take a Look Inside

Once you've freed your PC from its fetters, open up the case to make sure you got what you paid for. Removing a PC's case is quite easy—they all vary but they've improved quite a bit over the old-style cases you had to practically pry off.

If you already fired it up in that first rush of glorious enthusiasm, turn it off before attempting to look inside; shut off peripherals first and then switch off the system box. Then make sure they're all unplugged. Don't let any screws get lost in the carpet, either.

Peek at the add-in boards to make sure they fit without crowding. Make sure the hard disk brand, printed on the drive, is the one you specified. Look at the memory chips to see that they're the right speed and in the right amount. Shoot a glance over at the microprocessor, just to make sure it's the one advertised in your system. Count the expansion slots left over after configuring your system with the video card. Look at that, too—make sure it's the high-end, color-extravaganza card you paid for, complete with any video memory chips you added onto it. And finally, glance at the FCC certification sticker. It should wear a scarlet "B."

When you're done admiring it, replace the cover and tighten it down with the screws.

Think Before You Choose a Location

A good location for a PC is both convenient and out-of-the-way. It seems like a contradiction, but think about it: the PC must be somewhere where the whole family can use it, but not where anyone will bump into it or trip over it. A special room set aside for computing, of course, is ideal, but a corner of the family room or den can be just as good.

When choosing a PC location, think of comfort too. You already got quite a big dose of "comfort advice" in the ergonomics discussion last chapter, so turn back there if you have any questions.

Making the Right Connections

If you're not lucky enough to have some expert available to help set up your PC, you'll have to tough it out alone. Arrange the pieces the way you want them.

It's best to lure one of the computer store techs over with a bag of Oreos to set up your system for you and show you how to start and exit each of the applications you'll be using.

- ☞ For a desktop model, the monitor normally sits atop the PC's case, with the keyboard sitting in front of the case and the mouse to one side.

- ☞ For a tower case, the same thing except the case goes on the floor and the monitor and everything else goes on the table.

- ☞ With a "mini-tower", you can put the case either on the floor or the table—it's your choice.

Next, connect each component to the PC case. If you don't have the right cables, start a shopping list. Draw a picture of the ports on each device that the cable should plug into, and show a salesperson in the computer store what you want.

Each component must also be plugged into an electrical source. It's best to plug them all into a power strip. Most PC components have detachable power cords, which means you have to plug one end into the component and the other end into the electrical outlet.

Turning It On

This one seems like a no-brainer—just flip the power switches. If you've done something wrong (like forgetting to plug in the keyboard) the PC will tell you. Unless, of course, you have also forgotten to plug in the monitor.

When you see a program run (like Windows) or a DOS prompt appear (like C> or C:\>) or a request for the date and time, you know that everything is okay. If you see an error message or nothing at all, turn everything off and follow these guidelines:

- ☞ Make sure all plugs are plugged in securely.

- ☞ Inspect each component for physical damage, such as dents or burn marks.

- ☞ Open up the case, and make sure each interface card is seated firmly in an expansion slot. Wiggle each one to check for looseness.

Now, replace the case and turn everything on again. Does it work? If so, you're all set. If not, call the technical support number that came with your PC.

Gleaning Info from a Techie Friend

Do you know anyone who knows a lot about PCs? If so, invite him or her over for dinner. Have him/her show you how to find two essential files: AUTOEXEC.BAT and CONFIG.SYS. While you're at it, print out their contents—you might have to read this information over the phone to a software or hardware support staffer someday. Each time these files are changed, as with the addition of a new mouse or another device, for example, print out a new copy and keep it handy. Print out a copy of your system setup information, as well.

The Least You Need to Know

Despite the effort it took to buy the best PC for your needs, this is only the beginning. What lies ahead is the fun part: using and becoming productive on your new PC! But before you move on, double-check your PC's setup and consider these reminders:

- ☞ Choose a convenient location in which to set up your PC.

- ☞ Check your PC's insides to be sure you got what you paid for.

- ☞ Save the boxes and packing that your PC came in, in case you need to send it out for repair.

- ☞ Plug everything in, connect the cables, and fire it up!

- ☞ If it doesn't work, turn it all off and make sure the cables and interface cards are all securely in place.

Special Bonus: virtual text page.
(There's virtually no text on it.)

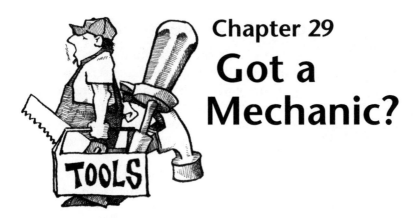

Chapter 29
Got a Mechanic?

In This Chapter

- ☛ The tools of the trade
- ☛ Ground rules before you start
- ☛ Adding memory, expansion cards, disk drives
- ☛ Accessing your PC's setup program
- ☛ Adding a new hard drive

Ready for some fun? Here's the chapter that has you tapping on metal and wielding screwdrivers, pressing down parts and testing everything out.

Have a great time playing mechanic. Remember to take your time, be patient, be awake, and be in a well-lighted room. And (while you're being a Do-Bee) *do* read this entire chapter before you touch anything.

Tools to Have Ready

There are tools you *think* you need (witness the numerous kitchen cabinets that serve as appliance graveyards), and then there are the tools you can't live without. The following tools fall into the second category. These tools will see you through almost any upgrade.

- Non-magnetic Phillips screwdrivers, small and standard sizes.

- Non-magnetic regular screwdriver, also called flathead, in a standard size.

- Pliers, standard type, standard size.

- Leadless mechanical pencil, or substitute a bent paper clip (for setting DIP switches).

- Notepad and pencil.

Never use a tool that's magnetic near your PC; magnetic fields can zap data for good! Check by seeing if your tool will pick up a screw; if it does, eschew that tool!

General Practices Before Any Upgrade

Clear off a desk, clean your room—do whatever makes you feel prepared for a project. Then perform these upgrade preliminaries. One more thing: Before performing any upgrade, *make sure you can always go back*. These safeguards will help you keep your peace of mind:

- Print out a list of all the directories/ subdirectories on your hard disk.

- Keep your PC's setup information handy on a floppy disk. Copy all CONFIG.SYS and AUTOEXEC.BAT files to that disk, as well.

- If you're adding a drive, know what type of drives you have. Each drive type is designated by a number that appears on the drive's external case and in its manual. This will be in your PC's setup program as well. (Details about this later in the chapter.)

The following are general steps to follow whenever you are working on your PC. You'll learn some specifics later in this chapter.

1. Exit any programs you're running.

2. Back up any data (you already did that the night before, right?).

3. Turn off your computer.

4. Turn off all peripherals connected to it.

5. Unplug your computer—at both ends, if you're really feeling nervous.

6. Unplug any peripherals—from the computer and from the power supply.

7. Clear off a large workspace.

8. Place all tools, a pad of paper, and a pencil near the work area.

9. Place your computer, its manuals, and any other extras that came with it, near the work area.

10. Remove the computer's casing, generally by unscrewing the outside screws with a Phillips screwdriver and sliding off the case, pulling it toward you. (The Dell and Amkly upgradable computers come apart with nice easy thumbscrews.)

11. Without touching anything, study the inside of the computer. Make a mental picture of what's there.

12. Perform the upgrade, as discussed in the appropriate section later in this chapter.

13. Before closing the PC's case, check the work area and count all the tools, making sure no tools or screws get left inside the system box.

14. Test the PC to ensure that the upgrade "took."

That's the basic procedure; you'll learn some specifics in the remainder of this chapter. Here are a few pointers that apply in all situations:

☛ Ground yourself before handling card or chips.

TECHNO NERD TEACHES

It's important to "ground" yourself frequently during the upgrading process to prevent static electricity from harming your components. To do this, tap the computer's power supply; this will discharge any static electricity.

☞ Handle cards and chips only by their edges. Avoid touching the card edge that goes into the slot and those little legs on the chips.

☞ When installing a new device, read the accompanying manual, no matter how difficult it is to decipher.

☞ Be firm yet kind when pushing cards, chips, or other components into a slot. If it doesn't fit, don't force it!

Dealing with Device Drivers

Many of the add-ons you can buy for your computer come with software disks that contain something called a *device driver* (in addition to other files and programs). A file on your PC's root directory called CONFIG.SYS tells your PC what hardware you want it to load up and get working. The mysterious file name stands for *configure system*, and does just about that. Adding a device driver is no more difficult than telling CONFIG.SYS where to find a file that controls that device.

We'll use a mouse in the example that follows, so if you have a different device (a CD-ROM drive or a scanner, for example), just substitute that in your mind when you read "mouse."

Some mouse software comes with an installation program that will create the directory for you; refer to your mouse documentation before going any further, because the steps here might not apply to your situation.

1. Make a subdirectory for the mouse software. A good place might be a MOUSE subdirectory under the SYSTEM directory: **C:\SYSTEM\MOUSE**, for example.

2. Copy the mouse's software into the mouse subdirectory.

3. Start a text editor program (your word processor will do, or DOS's EDIT program), and load the CONFIG.SYS file from your root directory.

4. Add a new line in your CONFIG.SYS file that reads:
device=c:\system\mouse\mouse.sys.
(If your directory name or device name is different, use the appropriate names.)

5. Save the altered CONFIG.SYS file and exit the program. If you're using a word processor, make sure you save it as an *ASCII* or *plain text* file. Generally, you'll need to use the word processor's "Save As" command to save a file as plain text. Consult your user's manual or on-line help for more about ASCII text files.

> **TECHNO NERD TEACHES**
> Occasionally, a device's driver file will have a .COM extension instead of .SYS. If this is the case, you would add the line to your AUTOEXEC.BAT file instead of CONFIG.SYS. For example, for a .COM mouse driver, you might add **C:\SYSTEM\MOUSE\ MOUSE.COM** to your AUTOEXEC.BAT file.

6. Reboot your computer to load the device driver, and then test the device to make sure it works.

DOS 5 and DOS 6 let you "load" device drivers into high memory and conserve RAM for other uses. A typical command under this version of DOS would read: **devicehigh=c:\system\mouse\mouse.sys**. Consult your DOS manual for more ways to have fun with DOS 5.

Accessing Your PC's Setup Program

Many of the upgrade instructions in this book mention something about your PC's *setup program*. A setup program provides a way for you to tell a special type of PC hardware memory—the *CMOS memory*—what hardware changes you've made. You access it, change the settings, and then reboot your PC.

Although this all sounds unfamiliar (and perhaps a little scary), changing your setup basically means following a menu-driven program. In fact, the only difficult part about it is that each PC's manufacturer has found a different way for you to access the setup program. Otherwise, I could spell it out for you here. So find your PC's manual and look up your setup program. You might try accessing it just for practice. (Mine comes on-screen if I press **Ctrl+Alt+Esc** simultaneously after booting up. How about yours?)

Installing an Interface Card

Many upgrades require you to install an *interface card*, a.k.a an *expansion card*. These instructions will get you through just about any card.

1. Follow the preliminary steps and guidelines earlier in the chapter (the first set of numbered steps).

2. Without touching anything, look at your PC's expansion bus. How many 8-bit slots do you see? How many 16-bit slots? Do you see any 32-bit slots? Be sure not to use up one of your larger slots on a small card. Make a sketch on your notepad of the slots that remain, and the size of each. This will come in handy for future upgrades.

3. Now, ground yourself. Do this by smartly tapping the unpainted side of the PC's metal framework or the power supply. Now that you're grounded, don't move your feet. And even though you're grounded, don't touch any parts on the motherboard, upgrade component, disk drives, power supply, etc., unnecessarily.

4. With feet still, unwrap the expansion card from its protective packaging. Holding the card by its edges, examine it for any gross defects. Then put the card down gently on the work area.

5. Find the most suitable slot inside your PC. That is, find a slot that has the right size slot for the metal edge of the card to fit into. Choosing a slot that's too big wastes the slot's capabilities; if you choose a too-small slot, the card won't work.

6. Look at the back "wall" of the PC. There you'll see a row of metal brackets, covering the "hole" at the back end of each unused expansion slot. Find the metal bracket that aligns with the slot you've chosen.

7. Carefully, so you don't drop the screw onto the motherboard (very tricky to find again and pick up), remove the screw holding the metal bracket in place.

8. Put down your screwdriver and place the screw and bracket to the side of the work area where they won't be lost.

9. Ground yourself again. Pick up the expansion card, hold it over the selected slot with the bracketed end facing the back "wall" of the PC, metal feet facing down.

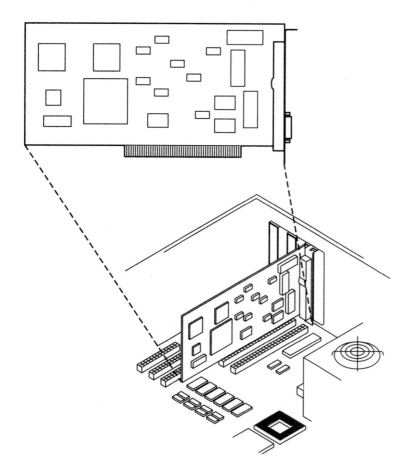

Placing an expansion card into a motherboard expansion slot.

10. Position the card's metal "feet" into the selected slot. Gently rock the card back and forth, pushing gently until the card eases itself into the slot.

11. Screw the old bracket's screw into the expansion card's bracket. Save the old bracket in case you ever remove the card and want to cover the hole again.

12. Reconnect the PC's power cord, keyboard, and monitor and power up your PC to test to see if the new card is working right. If you're satisfied the upgrade "took," close everything up and hook up all the cables again.

13. Run any setup software that came with the expansion card. (You might want to review the section on software drivers, later in this chapter.)

Adding Memory

There's really nothing to adding memory, and it's probably the most popular upgrade among PC users. Read your motherboard manual to see the configurations of memory chips it'll accept. Then buy memory chips in the appropriate size, speed, and configuration for your system. Memory comes in several different shapes, depending on the model of PC.

1. Open your computer's case, paying attention to the general guidelines given earlier in this chapter (the first set of numbered steps).

2. Locate the memory bank on the motherboard or on the memory card.

3. If there are old chips in the sockets you need to use, pop out the old chips carefully, lifting them straight out of their slots with your fingers. For example, if your computer uses SIMMs (small circuit boards), it would look like this:

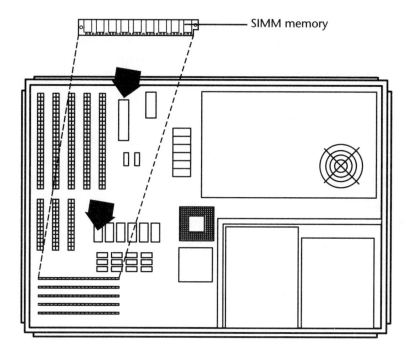

SIMM memory

*Many PCs use
memory that comes
on small circuit
boards called SIMMs.*

4. Hold the new memory over the appropriate socket.

5. Guide the memory into the socket, snap it into place, and make sure it's firmly seated.

6. If your motherboard manual indicates that it's necessary, change the settings of the DIP switches (locate them first, using your motherboard manual's diagram) to account for the new memory.

SPEAK LIKE A GEEK

A *DIP switch* is a tiny on/off switch on a circuit card that controls a specific system setting. For example, some motherboards use DIP switch settings to tell the system how much RAM it should expect to find.

7. Before you replace the PC's case, turn it on and see if the upgrade "took"; watch for the memory check to appear on-screen. Then turn off the PC, hook everything back up, and run the CMOS program (next step).

8. Run your PC's setup program so your CMOS will take official note of your new RAM. (PCs differ greatly in how they invoke this setup program. There's more guidance later in this chapter.)

Installing a Coprocessor

To install a coprocessor, you need to turn off your PC and all peripherals, unplug everything, remove the lid, tap the unpainted metal framework to ground yourself, and locate the vacant coprocessor socket. Whew!

Carefully take the chip in hand, oriented with the chip's notched corner to the notch on its destined socket, and press it gently into place. Now press a little more firmly. Voilà!

You'll want to tell your PC (whatever model you own) about the new intruder. You do this by setting the proper DIP switches (on an XT), or running the setup program (on an AT) to see if the AT has recognized the math coprocessor automatically. You might have to reconfigure your software, too, to get it to work with the new chip.

Replacing ROM Chips

ROM chips are available by mail order, or some local dealers may stock them. The important thing is to get written instructions for both the ROM chips *and* your motherboard before you start. Motherboards vary, so you'll need to dig up (and have handy) the manual for yours to learn where the ROM chips are housed, and how many you'll need. The new ROM chips should come with documentation, as well as telephone technical support (preferably toll-free).

Do not attempt to install ROM chips without clear, illustrated documentation. Have I warned you enough? The reason you need illustrated, clearly written documentation before you change ROM chips is to *make sure you don't insert them backward.* Otherwise you will fry the chips and your motherboard; quite possibly, your whole house will explode (well, okay, maybe not, but it wouldn't hurt to be *that careful*).

To replace a chip on the motherboard, you should have a chip-pulling tool for removing the old one. Sure, you can pry a chip out with a sharp object, but why take chances when you're dealing with a machine that cost hundreds (probably thousands) of dollars?

Replacing the Motherboard

After you've purchased the new motherboard, you'll want to exercise every precaution to ensure that it goes from the package to your system without being stepped on, fried by static electricity, bent, folded, stapled or mutilated. Here are some tips:

It used to be that a PC was stuck with the ROM chips it came with—unless these were physically removed and new ones stuck in their place. After all, ROM stands for read-only memory, which means you can't write new instructions to it, right? Right—sort of. A fairly recent technology called *flash ROM* enables ROM updates through software that effectively erase and reprogram the ROM chips. Alas, only those people who have flash ROM chips already installed on their motherboards can upgrade their ROM in this way.

☞ If you need a large, clear working surface for most upgrades, you'll need the largest, clearest working surface for this one, since *everything*—every component and every RAM chip in the system box—will need to come out and hang around on your desk or table.

☞ You'll need to turn off the computer and all components, unplug everything and take everything out of the system box (as you know, the motherboard's underneath the other parts). Before you remove components it's a good idea to connect masking tape labels to the connectors and cables, labeling the position of each. And don't worry about residual electrical charges; this isn't your old audio tape deck.

☞ It wouldn't hurt to grab some large sheets of butcher paper and draw a nearly-scale template of the motherboard's layout. As you remove labeled components, plop them down on their approximate locations on the template. This ensures a (relatively) care-free reassembly.

☞ As you remove screws from the old board, keep them in a small cup on your working surface. Slide out the old motherboard, then slide the new one into the space and reconnect the cables.

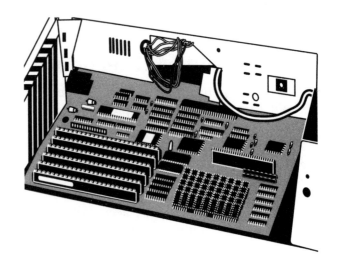

Once all the connectors have been removed, the motherboard slides easily out of its frame.

☞ *Be careful how you plug in the power supply.* I cannot overstress this point. It is possible to plug in the power connectors to the motherboard *backward*. Doing so will damage your entire new motherboard (and possibly damage you). The power supply shoots power to the motherboard via a single long connector, or two multi-wire connectors. Before you disconnect the connector(s), examine them carefully. You must reinstall them properly, and not try to jam them on backward.

These tips give you a place to start, but don't rely on them as instructions; use the documentation that comes with the new motherboard as your guide, referring to the original system documentation as needed.

Removing and Installing Disk Drives

Whether you're installing a floppy or hard disk drive, you'll follow the basic steps below. You'll want to retain some of your old data from the old drive, so be sure to back it up before you begin the upgrade. If you have a spare device bay, you may find it easier to install a new drive without removing the old one.

If you've upgraded your XT's motherboard to a 386 or better, determine your power supply's wattage. If it's the old XT's 135-watt model, you'll need to upgrade to a 200-watt power supply or your new motherboard won't be supported. Also, some XT power supply connectors will not fit the new 386 motherboards, so a new power supply might be in order anyway.

1. Follow the preliminary steps from earlier in the chapter. Remember to ground yourself.

2. If you are removing a hard drive, identify the one you're going to remove.

3. Remove the old drive's screws, which are found along the mounting rails. Put the screws to the side of the work area.

4. Ease the old drive forward.

5. Disconnect all cables. When you disconnect a cable, tug on its connector, *not on the cable itself.* Keep all connectors evenly aligned to avoid bending any connector pins.

6. Continue easing the drive out of the bay, and remove it. Set the old drive aside in the work area.

You can't open the drive's case, so don't *even* think about it.

7. Remove the mounting rails from the old drive.

8. Attach the mounting rails to the new drive.

9. Ease the new drive into place.

10. Make sure both connectors are correctly oriented and aligned. Then attach the cables.

11. Tighten all screws with a screwdriver.

12. Replace the computer's casing and reconnect all the cables.

13. Turn on the PC, and run its CMOS setup program to tell the PC about the new drive's type.

These same directions work for floppy drives too.

Preparing a Hard Disk for Use

Just physically installing a new hard drive is only half the upgrade process. In order to be able to work with software, including your disk operating system (probably MS-DOS), you need to perform the following:

- ☞ A low-level format
- ☞ A disk partitioning
- ☞ A high-level format

Performing a Low-Level Format

A disk must be *low-level formatted* to define tracks and sectors on it, grooves for your data, so to speak. Most disks you buy (particularly IDE-types) come with the low-level format already done. If you're not sure your drive has been low-level formatted, DOS comes with a utility called FDISK that can help you check. Consult your DOS manual for directions on how to use FDISK.

If you run FDISK and it doesn't recognize the new hard drive, you need to perform a low-level format. The new disk comes with a floppy disk that contains the low-level formatting utility and a small program called HDSETUP or something very similar. Run this program according to the on-screen (or manual's) instructions to perform your low-level format.

A few cards expect you to conduct the low-level format using DEBUG, a powerful program that comes with DOS. Proceed carefully, in this case, for you will be altering the hardware instructions on the hard drive controller's ROM chip. It's best to phone the place where you bought your hard disk, and either get them to low-level format it for you, or at least walk you through DEBUG on the phone.

Use FDISK to Partition Your Drive

Next you need to *partition* your hard drive. Think of partitioning as laying down one or more filing cabinets on your drive. DOS or another operating system will only feel at home on the new drive when it knows what filing cabinet area it will "live" in.

Insert a floppy disk that contains a backup of your MS-DOS files and utilities, and type the DOS command FDISK at the DOS prompt. (If you're adding a second drive, you won't need to run it from a floppy, but can run DOS from your hard disk prompt, as usual.)

You'll see a menu of choices; answer the questions according to how you want your disk set up. At this time, you can choose to partition the hard disk into one, two, or more *logical drives* ("C:" and "D:" for example), just by telling FDISK to do so. (But even if you want just one primary DOS partition on drive C: you'll still need to run FDISK.)

A High-Level Format

The hardware part's over, but you can't get crankin' on your new disk until your PC gives it an official Howdy! That's done through a process known as a *high-level format*. You will use software to perform this format: your computer's setup utility (usually a part of your PC's BIOS/CMOS, so it doesn't go away with your old hard disk), and MS-DOS's FORMAT and FDISK commands.

TECHNO NERD TEACHES

A *logical drive* is different from the virtual, or RAM, drive you read about earlier in this chapter. The physical hard disk drive you buy is a certain size, say 100MB. Let's call this real drive *the* real drive. After running FDISK from a floppy, you'll choose one or more drive areas where you can store data. Each separate drive area you set up on your real hard drive is called a logical drive. For instance, you could take your real hard drive's 100MB and divide it into a logical drive (or primary DOS partition, C:) of 50MB, and a logical drive (or secondary DOS partition, D:) of 50MB. Or you could keep it as one big drive, and then you'd have one primary DOS partition (your logical drive C:) of 100MB.

You're about to perform the scariest DOS command: FORMAT C:\. (And FORMAT D:\, if you've used FDISK to create a logical disk D:.)

You're familiar with FORMAT from readying floppy disks for use. Well, you also know that formatting a disk erases all the data on it. Erasing a floppy's not the end of the world (especially if you follow a sensible backup procedure). But erasing all the data on your hard disk? Shiver. Good thing there's no data on the new hard drive yet.

The *drive type*—the one expressed as a number—is very important. If you specify the wrong drive type, you could have big trouble, either right away (your new drive won't work) or later (a year later your hard disk may choke for no apparent reason). The drive type is listed on a label on the new drive; double-check it before you enter the number in the setup program.

Telling the PC What It Has

When you try to access the new drive, a DOS prompt will say **Cannot Access Drive C**, or something similar. Press the appropriate function key (or insert the proper floppy) to start your PC's setup utility, which you may remember from earlier in the chapter. (All models differ; you're on your own here, so consult your PC's manual.)

Your setup screen will pop up, listing your PC's hardware specifications. (Some PC's can "autosense" whatever new hardware you stick inside, so the new info's already there, as on my Dell 450DE PC.) Make sure the specs for your new hard drive match those on the screen. If they don't match, consult your hard drive's manual, and then type in the drive's new number and whatever other information setup asks you for.

By the Way . . .

Most people are content with just having one "logical" hard drive, typically **C:**. However, many experienced users find that dividing their hard disk into two or more logical partitions helps to keep their files organized, and makes them look "cool" in front of their friends. You could, for example, keep your system files and utilities on your **C:** disk and store Windows, programs, and games on **D:**.

But partitioning a disk isn't done just for aesthetics. Earlier versions of DOS couldn't handle a hard disk formatted to more than 32MB. Bigger drives had to be partitioned into C, D, and even E to fool DOS. The current DOS version (5.0) can handle any partition size, but old habits linger. . . .

Installing a SCSI Host Adapter

Remember the SCSI host adapter from Chapter 26? As with the other installations in this chapter, being *very* methodical helps here. Good luck!

May I See Some ID?

First, you'll need to assign each SCSI device a unique ID number. Simply push special buttons on an external device's rear, or flick switches on an internal device. Remember to tell your device driver software which number you've given the device. The host adapter will be (usually) device number 0. Although your adapter is quite willing to let any device take any number, some hardware manufacturers rigidly require that a device be granted a predetermined ID. Whatever you do, look up everything in advance and write down the numbers you assign to devices. And don't assign two devices the same ID number, or your SCSI chain will fail.

The Terminator

A SCSI device connects to the adapter, another device connects to the first, and so on. You'll need to decide what device will bring up the rear (if you're linking more than one), and single out this device by flipping its switches, jacks, or plugs in a ritual ominously known as *termination*. This prevents SCSI signals from bouncing off the end device and back into the cable. (Check your devices to make sure you don't need to disable pre-set termination, as well.) Just to complicate matters, if you install an internal SCSI device (a floppy drive, for example), this end of the chain will have to be "terminated" too, since the host adapter (which comes "terminated") is no longer considered to be at the end of the chain.

Connect the Devices

Link the devices firmly. Then power up the devices and reboot your PC. You'll want to install any drivers and other software for each device. After that, try out your new SCSI peripheral(s) with some software. What fun!

If at First You Don't Succeed . . .

If you've connected a single device, everything should work great. In the case of problems connecting multiple devices, first make sure you didn't assign two devices the same ID number. If that checks out, check for loose cable connections, or rearrange the cables altogether. You may have to select a different device as the end (terminated) unit. If all else fails, take each device and test it out alone with the host adapter and driver software. You may need to make a call to the host adapter vendor, to get assurance that his adapter brand is truly compatible with the device's brand.

The Least You Need to Know

Installing new parts in a PC is not rocket science, but it can be tedious. Follow the guidelines in this chapter and the instructions in the parts manuals; but if you're impatient, at least remember these rules:

☞ Ground yourself before working with any computer components. Those little static sparks that jump off your finger are deadly to computer chips.

☞ If doesn't fit, don't force it.

☞ Read the manual, whether you like it or not. Do it!

☞ Keep the boxes the parts came in. If anything should go wrong, and you need to ship a component back to the dealer or manufacturer, use its original case (and, if possible, the custom-fit padding) to pack it.

☞ Make friends with a computer wizard. He'll be able to help when things go wrong (and most of them really aren't bad people anyway).

**There's nothing to see here.
Move along, move along...**

Glossary

Speak Like a Geek: The Complete Archive

While tracking down the best PC or upgrade for your money, you're sure to spend hours in deep discussions with computer store clerks and mail-order sales representatives. Sidestep the jargon they're bound to toss out by turning to the listings in these pages.

132-column carriage   Extra-wide dot-matrix printer feature.

24-pin printer   High-end dot-matrix printer; prints true near-letter quality output.

286   Nickname for an 80286-powered PC, or the chip that bosses one around.

3 1/2-inch disk   Micro floppy disk enclosed in hard plastic case; comes in double- and high-density, fancy words for the simple fact that one holds more than the other (1.4MB versus 720KB).

386   Nickname for 80386 chip; a 386-based PC.

386DX   Full-fledged 80386 chip; a PC powered by one.

386SX   386 chip with part of its 32-bit external bus disabled (to 16-bits) so it's more affordable; a PC driven by one.

486   Nickname for 80486 chip; a 486-based PC.

486DX   Full-fledged 80486 chip; a PC powered by one.

486DX2/50   One of a recent series of chips from Intel Corp. that doubles a PC's processing speed for internal chip tasks; ominously known as The Doubler.

486SX   486 chip with the math coprocessor disabled so it's more affordable; a PC that sports this chip.

5 1/4-inch disk   Floppy disk enclosed in semi-hard plastic coating; comes in two capacities, or densities: 1.2MB and 360KB.

80-column carriage   The carriage-width on a standard-width dot-matrix printer.

80286   Older chip, or PC powered by this chip; the first AT (advanced technology) PC driven by this chip.

80386   The 80386 microprocessor; PC based on this chip.

80486   The 80486 microprocessor; PC bossed around by this chip.

80586   What some people called Intel's Pentium prior to its release.

8080   Honorable ancestor of today's 80x86 microprocessor/PC family.

8086   Early IBM PC-compatible chip; a PC driven by one.

8088   Powered the first true IBM-brand PC; a PC powered by one.

80x86   The microprocessor family of the IBM PC-compatibles.

9-pin printer   Low-cost, low-resolution dot-matrix printer.

add-on board   An expansion board; a new device may come with one; so do upgrades like memory boards or hard disk cards; fits into a spare slot in the expansion bus.

application   Another name for software; suggests more the task or problem to be solved by the software: a word-processing application, for example.

arrow keys   See *cursor movement keys.*

AT-compatible   Said of software or hardware that works with '286-class or later-model PCs; oddly, even though the 80286 was the first AT, 80386 and above computers fall into the AT-clan as well.

back up   To copy data or programs onto floppy disks or storage media, other than the hard drive, for safekeeping.

basic input-output system (BIOS)   A PC's permanent start-up instructions, found on the motherboard's ROM chips.

baud   Used interchangeably (to be picky, wrongly) for bps to measure a modem's transmission speed; actually measures the number of transitions in the modem signal per second; from J.M.E. Baudot, French telegraphy wizard.

BBS   See *Bulletin Board System.*

binary digit   Abbreviated as bit; the smallest unit of data a PC processes; bits are actually switches, either 1s or 0s (on or off) in the binary, or base 2, number system.

BIOS   See *Basic Input/Output System.*

bit   Short for binary digit, the smallest unit of info a PC processes at any one time.

bits per second (bps)   Measures rate of data movement to and from CPU and other components; also measures speed of modem transmissions.

board   1. nickname for expansion board, a way to add new devices to a PC; 2. short for BBS, or Bulletin Board System.

booting up   Starting a PC; powering it up; turning it on.

bootstrapping   The "start-up" process a PC goes through when it's turned on.

bps   See *bits per second.*

buffer A place in memory to store data temporarily, while it's waiting to print, for example.

Bulletin Board System (BBS) A hobbyist's computer running special software and one or more modems; modem enthusiasts enjoy calling BBSs for news, social interaction, and recreation.

bundled Packaged as part of a PC system; can be software, or hardware extras like a mouse.

bus The system architecture, especially the data path and expansion slot design, of the motherboard; circuitry on a PC's motherboard by which data travels to and from the microprocessor.

bus mouse A mouse that connects to a PC through an expansion card.

byte Measure of data quantity: eight bits make a byte; more commonly seen in thousands, kilobyte; millions, megabyte; or even billions, gigabyte.

cache Memory chips that store frequently used data to speed up CPU access and thus, processing time.

card See *expansion card.*

cathode ray tube (CRT) The guts of a monitor (or TV set).

CD-ROM Short for Compact Disc-Read Only Memory; CD-ROM discs store software and are read by CD-ROM drives you attach to your PC; you can't copy data, or "write" to one; this increasingly popular method of software distribution enables big, piggy software to grow even bigger and piggier.

central processing unit (CPU) Primary chip, or microprocessor, inside a PC.

CGA Short for color graphics adapter, an early, crude color display technology; refers to monitor; also refers to adapter card that powers the monitor.

characters per second (cps) Measures a dot-matrix printer's speed.

chip   Nickname for microprocessor; the silicon engine of computing; not necessarily the main chip, or CPU.

Class A rating   FCC approval rating for work-site-only PCs.

Class B rating   FCC approval rating for home PCs, more stringent than Class A; this rating won't cause as much radio interference (and neighbor interference!).

click   To press and release a mouse's button; software often directs you to click on a command to activate it.

clip art   Digitized graphics; used for adding pictures to a document; many software packages come with clip art bundled inside.

clock speed   The basic operating speed of a microprocessor, measured in megahertz (MHz).

clone   A copy; usually refers to an IBM PC-compatible, but video cards, mice, software, or almost any product can be a clone of a more famous, or standard, brand.

clusters   The smallest section of a disk that can be used to store data.

cold boot   To power-on a PC; turn it off and on again after a system crash (hard on the system and to be avoided).

COM   See *communications port.*

communications port   COM, or serial port; named for the communications devices called modems that plug into these. Typically seen as COM1, COM2, and so on.

configuration   A PC's particular hardware set up; sometimes, software set up.

controller   Mechanism on a hard drive that tells it what to do; determines the hard drive's type.

conventional memory   The first 640KB of memory in a PC.

convergence   Perfect alignment of electron gun beam and shadow mask; this video-display nirvana produces a high-quality monitor image.

cps   See *characters per second.*

CPU   See *central processing unit.*

crash   Short for system crash, from hard disk heads *crash*ing onto platters; the PC goes down, and everything comes to a halt until the system is rebooted; can be caused by hardware or by software.

CRT   See *cathode ray tube.*

cursor   The blinking typing point or "hot spot" on-screen.

cursor movement keys   Keys that move the cursor. Most keyboards feature four arrow keys: up, down, left, and right; four other keys, home, pg up, pg dn, and end, move the cursor, too.

daisywheel printer   Impact printer; works by striking hammer on spinning letter wheel.

data   Information used by a PC; also, data files are your work in a software program, as opposed to the program files themselves.

data bus   Circuitry on a PC's motherboard by which data travels to and from the microprocessor.

daughterboard   A small board that is added to a larger board to enhance or extend the performance of the board it is added to.

device   A monitor, keyboard, mouse, or any peripheral that can connect to a PC.

dinosaur   Older PC model no longer sold or supported with software; see *XT.*

DIP switches   Toggle switches found on the motherboard and on expansion cards; they control settings you manipulate by "flipping" the switch.

disc   Fancy word for disk, used with CD-ROM discs.

disk   Data storage medium; see *floppy disk, hard disk.*

disk operating system (DOS)   Software that runs the PC's basic functions; other software is added on top of an operating system; typically abbreviated DOS; often seen as the brand-name MS-DOS, for Microsoft Disk Operating System, the most widely used brand; OS/2 and UNIX are two of many PC-level alternates to MS-DOS.

diskette   Nickname for floppy disk; comes in two sizes, four capacities.

DOS   See *disk operating system.*

dot pitch   Qualitative measure of a monitor; determines picture focus; here, smaller numbers mean better quality.

dot matrix   System of pin arrangement on printhead of dot-matrix printer; this printer family.

dots per inch (dpi)   Measure of resolution on monitors and printer output quality; higher is better.

double-density disk   Sounds like a big deal, but really just a lower capacity floppy; comes in two versions: the 5 1/4-inch version holds 360KB, and the 3 1/2-inch version holds 720KB of data.

double-click   Two rapid, successive mouse clicks.

Doubler   A series of CPUs that can double a PC's processing rate for certain tasks.

download   To bring data into a PC through a modem or serial connection.

downloadable font   Printer lettering style, stored in software form.

downward compatible   Works with older models of like components: a Super VGA monitor is downward compatible with a CGA video card (shiver).

dpi   See *dots per inch.*

draft mode   Quality of printout acceptable for a rough draft.

DRAM   See *dynamic RAM.*

drive bays   Horizontal carriers in the system box for hard and floppy drives.

driver   Small program file that communicates a new device's configuration and set up requirements to the PC's operating system and other software.

DX2/*n*   Recent chip model that doubles PC processing to *n* speed for internal microprocessor functions.

Dynamic RAM (DRAM)   A variety of memory chip.

EGA   Short for enhanced graphics adapter; semi-early color display technology; refers to monitor and to adapter card that powers the monitor.

EISA   Abbreviation for enhanced ISA, an enhanced model of system bus architecture.

emulation   To copy, act like; a hardware device, such as a printer, can emulate a more standard printer brand, for example.

enhanced keyboard   Keyboard with separate arrow keys; function keys along top.

Enter key   On PC's keyboard, works like the carriage return, or to invoke commands in software.

environment   A program that runs on top of DOS to help you avoid direct communication with DOS itself.

ESDI   Fast hard disk controller; found on high-end, large hard drives.

expanded memory   RAM added through an expansion card on 286 PCs and lower or through software on 386 PCs and above; a good thing, because software makes use of all the spare memory it can get its greedy little hands on.

expansion bus   System of expansion slots on a PC's motherboard; individual PCs vary in bus architecture; it's essential to look for an expansion bus that allows for sufficient additions later.

expansion card   An add-on card for a new device like spare memory, a mouse, or a modem, for example; fits into a spare slot in the expansion bus.

expansion slot   Slot on the motherboard's expansion bus where you add expansion cards; PCs average five spare slots—more is better.

extended memory   Usable memory over 640KB.

external data path   Conduit for data from microprocessor to system memory and expansion bus; partially disabled on the 80386SX chip.

file   The work you do on a PC, a program or other data is stored in files on a floppy or hard disk, or on other storage media.

fixed   Nonremovable, as in fixed disk, for hard disk.

flash BIOS   This unusual feature allows the ROM BIOS to be updated, electronically, to reflect hardware upgrades and other changes to a PC's configuration.

floppy   Short for floppy disk, also diskette; removable media that stores data for use on a PC; comes in two sizes, four capacities.

floppy disk drive   Mechanical device inside system box that reads from and writes to floppy disks.

font   Style of lettering, form of type style; used to compare a printer's capability to use different type styles; each bold, italic, or heavy version of a type style is a separate typeface, or font; from the old photo-typesetting days; increasingly, and wrongly, coming to mean type family.

font cartridge   Plug-in printer cartridge that adds new fonts to a printer.

forums   Discussion areas focusing on specific topics on electronic bulletin board systems or commercial on-line services.

freezing up   The PC refuses to work; system crash.

function keys   Keys on PC keyboard not found on a typewriter; perform various operations depending on software in use.

game card   Expansion card containing a special port for a joystick to plug into.

game port   A special port on a game card for attaching a joystick.

GB   See *gigabyte.*

gigabyte   Roughly a billion bytes.

graphical user interface (GUI)   Presents a way of using computers through activating pictures, or icons, that represent commands, programs and files.

graphics   Images, charts, clip art; the programs and peripherals that let you use graphics, as in graphics printer.

graphics card   Expansion card that runs a monitor.

GUI   Pronounced *gooey.* See *graphical user interface.*

hand-held scanner   Device that transforms an image into digital data with which PCs can work.

hard copy   A printout; paper copy you can carry around to show off your documents or other PC labors.

hard disk drive   Mass storage device for a PC to safeguard programs and data.

hardware   Any equipment that can be used in a PC configuration, from the PC itself to peripherals, like a music synthesizer.

Hercules graphics adapter (HGC)   A monochrome graphics standard.

HGC   See *Hercules graphics adapter.*

high-density disk   High-capacity floppy disk; comes in two versions: the 5 1/4-inch version holds 1.2MB and the 3 1/2-inch version holds 1.4MB.

IBM PC-compatible   Works with computers or chips of the IBM PC family; also, a PC that sports a nationally recognized brand-name, like Compaq. See *clone*.

icons   Graphic representations of programs, files, or commands on a PC; seen in GUI software or on Macintosh PCs.

IDE   One type of hard disk controller, common in mid-range, low-cost drives.

impact printer   In these, the print mechanism strikes the print carriage; usually noisier than non-impact variety.

inkjet printer   A nonimpact printer that works by shooting ink blobs through dots.

input device   Any of a group of mechanisms to input information to a PC; keyboard, mouse, joystick, microphone, and so on.

interface card   Serial or parallel board, also multifunction board; usually already bundled inside PCs.

interlaced   A monitor whose electron beams scan alternating lines; older technology; causes flicker that results in eye-fatigue.

internal data path   One of a microprocessor's two data "hoses"; data moves around and is processed within the CPU via this path.

ISA   The original system bus architecture of the AT-model PC; still a viable standard.

joystick   Pointing device used primarily to blow up invading spacecraft and other bad guys; these vary in quality: don't bother unless you get a good one.

K   Abbreviation for kilobyte, approximately one-thousand bytes.

kilobyte   Approximately one-thousand bytes, abbreviated as K, more rarely seen as KB.

laptop   Small, portable PC weighing less than 15 pounds, generally powered by batteries; notebook computers are lighter, smaller laptops.

laser printer   Nonimpact printer that works similarly to a photocopier; this expensive, fast, high-quality printer drove thousands of innocent people to desktop publishing.

letter-quality   High-quality printer output, as opposed to near-letter quality or draft mode.

line printer port (LPT)   Another name for parallel port; more commonly seen abbreviated and numbered, as in LPT1, LPT2, and so on.

local bus   Enhanced expansion bus circuitry that provides direct data exchange between the CPU and expansion cards, speeding operation of that device; not widely supported and limited to video cards, for now.

LPT   See *line printer port*.

Macintosh   The other leading PC family; often shortened to Mac; strangely, its slogan is "The computer for the rest of us," even though the IBM PC-compatible family has a much larger software base and user population.

math coprocessor   An add-on chip that takes some of the load off the microprocessor by performing arithmetic functions and graphics processing; not every motherboard sports a slot for a math coprocessor; the 486DX has one built in.

matrix   An array; often seen describing the arrangement of pins on a dot-matrix printer.

MB   See *megabyte*.

MCA   Abbreviation for micro-channel architecture, IBM's version of an enhanced system bus architecture; see *EISA*, *ISA*.

MDA   Early monochrome monitor/video card standard.

megabyte (M or MB)   Roughly 1 million bytes of data; more often seen as M or MB.

megahertz (MHz)   1 million hertz, or clock cycles per second; measures speed of CPU.

memory   Generally refers to volatile memory, or RAM, where a PC's microprocessor stores data temporarily; ROM, a permanent set of PC housekeeping instructions, is another type of memory.

memory cache   Chips that form a holding zone for frequently used data; speeds up CPU access and thus, processing time.

menu   A list of choices or a range of commands in a software program.

MHz   See *megahertz.*

micro floppy   Official name for 3 1/2-inch disks.

microcomputer   Official name for the entire PC species, including Macs, Amigas, Ataris, and every other PC family.

microprocessor   Official name of the CPU, or main PC chip; the brains behind a PC.

millisecond   One one-thousandth of a second; measures hard disk access speed, for one.

MIPS   Short for millions of instructions per second; speed rating for CPU processing instructions; differs from megahertz, rating a chip's clock speed.

modem   Short for modulator/demodulator (you can see why they came up with a shorter name); scrambles a PC's data to enable transmission over ordinary phone lines, where a modem at the other end unscrambles data to be understandable to that PC.

monitor   PC's video display unit; can be color or monochrome and capable of any of several video standards.

monochrome   Single-color, refers to monitor display; usually amber or green on black.

motherboard   A large, green, printed circuit board carpeting the system box; provides framework for the CPU, expansion bus, memory chips, and all other parts of a PC.

mouse   *Mus musculus*, family *muridae*, order *rodentia*; also, pointing device, more resembling bar soap than creature; comes in serial and bus, optical and mechanical, and corded or cordless species.

mouse pad   Pad used for rolling a mouse over; comes in plain rubbery form for mechanical mice, and optically readable, gridded form for optical mice.

mouse pen   Pointing device shaped like an oversized pen with roller ball on bottom and buttons similar to a mouse's.

MS-DOS   Abbreviation for Microsoft Disk Operating System, the most common operating system seen on IBM PC-compatibles.

multi-frequency monitor   Capable of switching to nearly any video mode.

multi-function card   Expansion card containing multiple ports, usually a parallel and two serial ports, sometimes a game port, too; generally, at least one comes bundled inside a PC system.

multi-scan   Another name for multi-frequency.

multisync   Same thing as multi-frequency.

N-key rollover test   One way to check a keyboard's quality.

near-letter quality (NLQ)   Midrange printout quality; almost letter quality; one standard for measuring printer output.

NLQ   See *near-letter quality*.

non-impact printer   Laser, inkjet, and other printer technologies that don't involve the striking of a printhead or hammer to produce printed output; quieter than impact printers.

non-interlaced monitor   Technology where inner monitor surface is scanned all at once by electron beams instead of in alternating sections as with older, interlaced models; minimizes flicker and eyestrain.

numeric keypad   Dual-function PC keyboard area, located on keyboard's left, housing a matrix of number keys and operands in a layout similar to a calculator's; eases numeric input and arithmetic computing applications; arrow, or cursor movement keys are found here, too.

NumLock   PC keyboard key that toggles the numeric keypad between numeric or arrow key (cursor-movement) mode.

on-line service   Any commercial service accessible via modem; CompuServe, Prodigy, GEnie, and America On-line are a few examples.

operating system   See *disk operating system.*

OS   Short for operating system. See *disk operating system.*

OS/2   Alternate PC operating system to MS-DOS; although in development many years now, it has been slow in catching on.

pages per minute (ppm)   Measure of a laser printer's output speed; for printing multiple copies of the same page, 6 ppm is the average.

palette   Monitor/video card term for the total, maximum numbers of colors possible; only a fraction of the card's palette can be seen at any one time.

parallel interface card   Expansion card that adds parallel ports to a PC.

parallel port   Extension of the PC's expansion bus; enables parallel devices to be connected to the PC; often called printer port.

PC   See *personal computer.*

PC-clone   See *clone.*

PC-compatible   PC from a line of name-brand, nationally distributed PCs, like Dell or Compaq; see *clone.*

peripherals General term for any device outside the actual PC system box: includes monitors, keyboards, pointing devices, music keyboards, and, by extension, the expansion cards needed to run any of these devices.

personal computer (PC) Common name for the microcomputer family of computers; more generally, has come to mean IBM-compatible family of microcomputers, even though Mac- , Amiga- or Atari-brand microcomputers, technically, are also PCs.

pixel Short for picture element; the smallest part of an image on a PC's monitor, likened to a dot; the more pixels a monitor displays going across and down, the tighter the monitor's focus, or resolution is.

pointing device Peripherals that input data into a PC; used in conjunction with a keyboard to enhance precision in navigating through software.

points per inch (ppi) Gauges mouse agility. A higher number means a more sensitive mouse.

portable computer Loose term for any PC that can be carried around; ranges from heavy, 15-pound luggables to tiny palmtop PCs weighing less than a pound.

ports Gateways to your PC's innards so devices can connect to it; see *serial ports*, *SCSI*, and *parallel ports*.

PostScript Page-description language used with sophisticated laser printers.

power strip Extension cord-like device fitted with eight or so sockets; something you forget to buy and have to run out to the store for, once you get your PC home and set up.

power surge Fluctuations in electrical current that can be dastardly to your data.

power supply Metal box inside the system box that supplies power to the PC; sports a fan for cooling purposes.

ppi See *points per inch*.

ppm   See *pages per minute*.

printer   Device that lets you print your work; most commonly attaches to parallel port; enables you to share "hard copy" printouts with others.

printhead   Printer mechanism that strikes ribbon and paper.

processor   Short for microprocessor; also CPU or just chip.

program   1. Short for software program; also application software; the special files full of data and instructions that make your PC do something; 2. To write computer-readable code that makes a PC do what you want.

RAM   See *random access memory*.

RAM cache   See *cache memory*.

random-access memory (RAM)   Volatile memory used as a temporary data storage tank by the microprocessor; disappears into thin air when computer's shut off.

read-only memory (ROM)   A set of permanent instructions that tell a computer how to coordinate its various components and get to work; contains a system's BIOS.

refresh rate   Monitor's vertical electron scan rate; faster scanning ensures less flicker.

removable media   PC file storage media that can be carried around, like a floppy disk or CD-ROM disc, as opposed to a fixed hard disk.

reset button   Button on outside of PC's system box that lets you restart the PC without turning off its power.

resolution   Measure of image quality; determines focus and overall picture sharpness; used to compare video cards and the monitors they control, as well as the output of printers and scanners.

ROM   See *read-only memory*.

RS-232 Port another name for serial port; deriving from an industry standard for typical connectors to the port.

scan rate Two types, vertical and horizontal scan rate, determine the monitor's overall quality; higher rates make for a better picture, less flicker and less eyestrain.

scanner Device for digitizing and inputting graphics into a PC; resulting images can then be incorporated into party flyers, computer art, and other creations.

SCSI (small computer system interface): pronounced scuzzy; nearly always abbreviated as SCSI A high-end interface you can buy and add to a PC's expansion bus; accommodates SCSI devices like high-capacity hard drives or CD-ROM players; faster than the more commonly bundled parallel and serial interfaces under certain conditions.

select To use a mouse or cursor key combination to highlight text or commands in software.

serial interface card Provides a computer with a serial port to which serial devices like modems can be attached; goes in PC's expansion bus.

serial mouse Pointing device that comes with no expansion card; instead it connects to a serial port on the PC.

serial port Connects to the motherboard by means of a serial interface card; provides a place to connect serial printers, mice, and modems, among other serial devices, to your PC; most PCs come bundled with at least two serial ports.

shadow RAM Sounds like a character in a '40s radio serial, but it's really just a feature to speed microprocessor access to the BIOS instructions by loading these into fast RAM at boot-up.

shareware Although not free, this type of software's okay to share with others; a try-before-you-buy marketing concept that depends on the honor system for payment to software's authors.

silicon Material most commonly used in making computer chips.

slot   Short for expansion slot; raised, narrow opening in PC's expansion bus where you plug in expansion cards; can be 8-bits, 16-bits, or 32-bits in width.

small computer system interface   See *SCSI*.

software   Programs to make the computer do an enormous, dazzling variety of tasks. See *program*.

sound card   Peripheral you can buy to add sound capabilities to a PC.

stacked drive   1. disk drive stacked on another in a vertical drive bay configuration; 2. hard drive on which the data's been compressed using one of several commercial compression utilities.

standard keyboard   PC keyboard that improved upon the original IBM PC model but was largely replaced by the enhanced keyboard.

static RAM   A type of memory chip; faster than DRAM chips.

super VGA   Graphics mode that, right now, is quickly becoming the high-end standard; refers both to video card and to monitor models.

surge protection   Precaution against electrical current fluctuations that can harm a PC or at least destroy work in progress that hasn't been backed up to a disk; surge protector units are sold in computer stores.

system box   The hard plastic case enclosing a PC's motherboard, power supply, disk drives, and other components.

telecommute   Work at home enabled by modem that can transfer work to and from the office PC; named for the telephone lines that the data transmits over.

tower   Vertical system box—usually large—with plenty of expansion slots and drive bays and an oversized power supply to cool all the goodies you can pack inside.

trackball   Pointing device housing a mounted ball and adjacent buttons; cursor manipulated by rolling the fingertips across ball and pressing, or clicking, buttons.

tractor-feed paper   Printer paper that features continuous-feed holes along the side edges that accommodate the pins of a tractor-feed paper-advancement mechanism.

turbo mode   The faster of a computer's operating speeds.

typeface   Technical term for lettering; each bold, italic, or heavy version of a type style is a separate typeface, or font; term hails from the old photo-typesetting days.

UNIX   Operating system seen infrequently on PCs; fiercely beloved and defended by users, usually researchers, scientists, and engineers.

upgrade   To boost the power and versatility of a component or an entire PC by adding memory chips, a math coprocessor, a bigger hard disk drive, or other upgrades.

uploading   Sending information from your PC to another PC through a serial device like a modem; see *downloading*.

utilities   Software family designed to beef-up any (sometimes many) of a PC's deficiencies; virus-scanning software is an example of a utility; differs from other software in that it doesn't necessarily aim to accomplish your task but instead tries to make the computer generally more efficient.

vertical scanning frequency   A monitor's refresh rate; higher frequencies reduce annoying flicker.

very-large-scale integration (VLSI)   The engineering technology that has enabled dense circuitry on microprocessors, motherboards, and other computer hardware, and thus faster, more capable components.

VESA   Video-card manufacturer consortium that sets standards for high-end video modes.

VGA   Acronym for video graphics array; high-resolution monitor/video card standard.

video-adapter card   Expansion card essential to operating a PC video display, or monitor.

video display   Another name for monitor, the screen of a PC system.

viruses   Programs written to intentionally destroy the computer or software of another, devised and implemented by maladjusted people.

volatile memory   RAM, which empties itself when its electrical source is cut off (when the PC's turned off or accidentally unplugged, or as the result of a power surge or system crash).

wait state   The time a computer spends between instructions waiting for something to do.

window   Programs run in boxes, or windows, in Microsoft Windows and other GUIs and even in some non-GUI programs like DESQview, an alternative PC operating environment.

Windows   Microsoft Windows, a graphical user environment in which users point at pictures, or icons, instead of typing text to invoke commands.

XT-compatible   Compatible with the original IBM XT computer; this model of computer, or an XT-clone.

zero wait state   A PC with this feature probably sports a RAM cache that reduces the time a computer spends between instructions waiting for something to do.

Index

Symbols

A

E

Q

R

S

T